7th Heaven

Based on the hit TV series created by Brenda Hampton

7th Heaven™

Four Years with the Camden Family

Cathy and Mark Dubowski

HarperEntertainment
An Imprint of HarperCollins*Publishers*

HarperCollins books may be purchased for educational, business, or sales
promotional use. For information please write: Special Markets Department,
HarperCollins Publishers Inc., 10 East 53rd Street, New York, NY 10022.

FIRST EDITION

Designed by Jeannette Jacobs

Library of Congress Cataloging-in-Publication Data has been applied for.

ISBN 0-06-106624-9

00 01 02 03 04 RRD 10 9 8 7 6 5 4 3 2 1

Contents

Welcome to the Family

Millions of television viewers like us have two families. One is our "real" family. The other is our "Camden family," the one we join each week when we tune our sets to *7th Heaven*. We stand by the Camdens as they struggle against themselves and against the world. We share the Camdens' ups and downs. We watch, and we care.

Over the four seasons that *7th Heaven* has aired, we have learned that our real families and our Camden family are much alike. It's reassuring to know that in our triumphs and tragedies as families we are not alone.

The thing that makes our Camden family different from our real family, perhaps, is the way the Camdens manage to cope with modern problems so surely and so well. Life is never easy for the Camdens, but it is always doable. Sometimes it is even rewarding. Oftentimes it can be beautiful.

In this way, Annie, Eric, and their seven children give us hope. They remind us that a family can be a gift unto itself, a source of strength and courage. We look to "Heaven" for answers to the problems we face in our everyday lives.

Created by Brenda Hampton, *7th Heaven* was a surprise hit, which by the end of its first season was the fastest-growing show on TV. It has set viewership records for the WB network in all key demographics. Total viewer count for a single episode has surpassed 10 million. As Marvin Kitman of *Newsday* put it, the Camdens are not "the usual dysfunctional group that came to pass for the norm on TV in the 1990s." They are like a real family.

Over the four seasons that are covered in this book, the show has won praise from the Parents Television Council, Viewers for Quality Television, the Anti-Defamation League, the Film Advisory Board, and the American Mothers' Council, among others. It has also won a Prism Award for addressing issues of drugs and violence.

As it plays out its fifth season on the WB, *7th Heaven* still stands alone. Compared to other shows on the network and cable lineup, it is just as surprising and unique as it was in the beginning. Perhaps even more so.

What makes *7th Heaven* so popular? In an entertainment medium that offers everything from the supernatural to the hip to the outrageous, why do so many of us turn to an "old-fashioned" family drama instead?

Because *7th Heaven* is not just a show about a TV family.

It is a show about our family.

Season 1

We meet the Camdens: Eric, Annie, and their five children, Matt, Mary, Lucy, Simon, and Ruthie. The family lives in a parsonage provided by the church for which Eric is the minister. Romantic ups and downs preoccupy the kids, while Eric and Annie cope with their extended families. Annie's mother passes away early in the season, and Eric's sister arrives with alcohol problems. Mary gets hit by a car. Amid all this chaos, one thing never changes— the love that holds the Camden family together.

Anything You Want

written by Brenda Hampton; directed by Sam Weisman

For a preacher and his wife who have five growing children, life can sometimes be . . . well, the opposite of heaven! But with faith and love, the Camden family manages to make their home "7th Heaven"—even as Grandma Jenny visits to tell Annie and Eric her devastating news.

It's a beautiful Saturday morning, and the Reverend Eric Camden and his wife, Annie, would love to sleep in, but it's not easy to catch a moment alone in a house shared by seven people! One by one the kids—Ruthie, Simon, Lucy, and Mary—barge into their parents' bedroom, needing something. Matt tries to save the day, but it's hopeless.

At the dinner table Simon's in a rush to say grace, with his own special P.S.: "If there really is a God, I know you will find a way to get me that dog I've been wanting."

Meanwhile, fourteen-year-old Mary begs Matt to help her with her basketball, but he says he has other plans. Which reminds Annie . . . Matt is supposed to shoot pool with his father that night. But Matt retorts that he has a date. Trying to include his middle child in the conversation, Eric compliments Lucy on how grown-up she's looking. Lucy bolts from the table, crying, "I'm not a baby anymore!" The rest of the family is totally baffled.

Outside, Mary tells Matt that she's taller than all the guys her age, and then admits that she's never been kissed. She asks Matt to show her how to kiss, but he find the demonstration too awkward. Later, while Simon talks to his mom about getting a dog, Eric goes up to check on Lucy and finds her standing on her head—hoping it will help bring on her first menstrual period. Eric tries to talk to her about "coming of age," but she's too embarrassed and locks herself in the bathroom. So Eric and Annie switch talks: Eric reminds Simon about his history of pet disasters. But Simon promises he'll be more responsible this time. Eric finally agrees . . . sort of. If a dog with no owner wanders into the yard, Simon can keep it.

Upstairs Annie finds Lucy hiding in her bedroom closet. She says all her friends have already started their periods, and she feels like a freak. Annie gently reminds her, "For everything there is a season . . ."

That night at the pool hall, Eric lectures Matt about his smoking and tells him to fork over that part of his allowance that he spends on cigarettes. Matt protests. So Eric suggests he pay for his habit by taking a job driving an elderly woman on her errands.

At church the next morning Eric coincidentally begins his sermon with: "For everything there is a season . . ." Lucy panics—she thinks her dad is about to discuss her period in his sermon! As she runs out of the church, a startled Eric jokes that he guesses his family has heard this sermon before.

That afternoon Mary takes Lucy jogging. When they run into Matt's best friend, Jeff, Lucy drops a tampon Mary gave her; mortified, Lucy runs away. Mary simply scoops it up, then asks Jeff if he would come by later to help her with basketball.

That afternoon Jeff arrives just as Matt is on his way to his job. Matt says he doesn't like the idea of Mary dating his best friend. Mary, of course, resents Matt interfering.

When Matt arrives at his job, he's shocked to see elderly Mrs. Bink open the door wearing an oxygen mask and coughing horribly. As she takes off her mask, she complains that he's late and searches for her cigarettes. Matt can't believe the condition she's in. While out on her errands, she insists that they stop to buy more cigarettes, but Matt refuses to help her ruin her health.

Later Mrs. Bink phones Eric and gleefully reports—without coughing once!—that their little scheme to scare Matt about smoking seems to have worked.

When Annie comes home, Simon hears a bark and races out into the yard. "It's a miracle!" he shouts. "Come look!" They all watch as Simon greets his new dog, which has miraculously appeared in the front yard. Inside, Annie confesses to Eric that she went by the pound. Eric is upset; she should have checked with him first. But Annie couldn't help herself: they were going to put the dog to sleep.

Moments later, Jeff comes by for his basketball date with Mary, but Matt ruins it, warning Jeff not to try anything with his sister.

Later Eric tells Annie that Matt volunteered to drive to the

airport to meet her parents, who are due to arrive soon. Annie thinks Matt's too inexperienced a driver; he's had his license only three months. Eric confesses that Matt has already left. Now it's Annie's turn to be angry that Eric didn't discuss something with her.

When Matt comes home with Annie's parents, after much hugging and kissing, they all sit down to a wonderful meal. As the grown-ups linger over dessert, the kids run out to play. But Annie senses that her mother has something important to tell her. At last Grandma Jenny tells them her news: she has leukemia.

Annie and Eric are stunned by the news. Grandma Jenny explains that while the doctors say treatment might slow the spread of the disease, nothing will cure it. So Grandma Jenny has decided not to undergo the difficult treatments. Instead, she wants to enjoy her last months with her loved ones.

Out on the lawn, the kids have their own secrets to share: As they play with Happy, Matt whispers to Simon that he thinks Happy is going to have puppies. Simon begs him not to tell their dad.

The happy sounds of children playing draw Annie and Eric outside, reminding them that for everything there is a season.

Family Secrets

**written by Brenda Hampton;
directed by Mark Sobel**

Matt's in trouble for staying out
all night with a friend who's
pregnant. But when Eric and Annie
learn her true story, they try to
help her, too. Mary has her first date
with Jeff. Lucy thinks she's blown
her chances with Jimmy Moon.

Season 1: Episode 1

It's not easy to keep a secret in a house with seven people.

Simon is trying to find a good time to tell his parents his secret—that Happy is going to have puppies. Meanwhile, Annie tries to convince her mother to reconsider having treatment for her leukemia. But Grandma Jenny is certain she would rather die a calm death than upset the whole family with the painful difficulties of treatment. After Grandma Jenny and Grandpa C.J. leave, Annie and Eric decide not to tell the kids about her yet. But Matt sees tears in his mother's eyes, and he suspects she's hiding a secret.

Matt has secrets of his own, and they're hard to keep when two of his sisters keep breaking in on his phone calls. When they finally get off the phone, Matt makes a secret date, then asks his mom if he can borrow the car "to go study at the library." When Matt finally sneaks in at 5 A.M., Eric is ready to explode. Matt tries to explain that it was all very innocent: he went to visit a girl named Renee and accidentally fell asleep. Annie and Eric ground him for three weeks.

At school the next day Matt confronts Jeff about dating Mary. Meanwhile, Lucy is in heaven when Jimmy Moon, the boy she has a crush on, actually smiles at her.

Later that day Annie intercepts a call from Renee and invites her to dinner so they can get to know her. When Matt finds out, he wants Annie to cancel, but it's too late. The doorbell rings, and in walks the secret Matt was hiding—a very pregnant Renee. Eric and Annie react with shock. But Renee quickly explains that Matt is not the father, and Eric and Annie sigh with relief. Simon asks if this would be a good time to tell them that Happy is expecting puppies. Eric gazes heavenward, asking for help.

After dinner Eric praises Matt's friendship, but points out that what Renee really needs are her parents and the father of her unborn child. Matt explains that Renee's mother deserted the family years ago, and that neither Renee's father nor her boyfriend want anything to do with her now. Then Mary interrupts: She's just talked to Jeff, who canceled their date, and she's furious at Matt for interfering with her love life. When she storms off, Matt tells Eric he shouldn't let Mary date Jeff, who's two years older than she. Hasn't he learned anything from Renee's story?

Worried, Eric drives across town to speak to Renee's father, a policeman, but the man says he doesn't have a daughter and slams the door in Eric's face. Later Eric keeps calling and leaving messages, but he can't seem to get through.

Over a cup of coffee, Matt finally gets Annie to confess that her mother—Grandma Jenny—has cancer and is going to die. Matt is upset and says they shouldn't tell the younger kids yet.

Later Eric goes by to try to talk to Renee's boyfriend. He meets a younger man who is obviously not well off, and Eric tells him of a job opportunity. Eric is surprised by how little interest the boy seems to be taking in the problem. But after a while a different teenage boy comes by the house. As it turns out, he's Renee's boyfriend. He thanks the reverend for getting his big brother a job and wonders if Eric can help him, too. Eric invites him to Sunday service.

At school Mary and Jeff make an agreement to avoid kissing. At least for a little while. Jimmy Moon asks Lucy if people have been telling her he likes her. She's so nervous, she doesn't know what to say—which Jimmy interprets as rejection. Lucy is upset that she blew her big chance with him.

After clearing up a misunderstanding, Mary finally has her first date with Jeff. Eric has a tough time waiting for his oldest daughter to come home and keeps making up excuses to go downstairs to watch for her. Letting Happy out becomes a great way to cut short Mary and Jeff's good-night kiss on the front porch.

Meanwhile, Simon has a great idea. He wants to open a lemonade stand to earn money to pay for his father's shoes that Happy chewed up. His parents suggest instead that he do something for others—some community service. So Simon decides to give away the lemonade for free, after Sunday school. Maybe that will encourage more people to stay for the Sunday service. But on Sunday, when a lady asks why he's not charging, Simon answers, "I was going to charge plenty so I could get my dad some new shoes, but he wouldn't let me." She insists on paying him double.

During the service Matt introduces the newest member of the choir: Renee, singing a solo about angels. And as her beautiful voice fills the church, Matt enters . . . with Renee's father. Eric smiles, knowing a happy reunion is in store.

In the Blink of an Eye

written by Catherine LePard; directed by Duwayne Dunham

Matt, still grounded, gets in trouble for sneaking in a date while he's supposed to be delivering Meals on Wheels. Lucy has her first date with Jimmy Moon. Mary's angry she can't go to a party. Ruthie moves in with Simon to make room for Grandma and Grandpa, who come for a final visit.

Annie and Eric have a surprise for Simon. "Bunk beds?" Simon exclaims happily. Yes, his parents tell him. But there's a catch. Grandma and Grandpa are coming to visit, and they're going to sleep in Ruthie's room, so Simon has to share his room with Ruthie. "But I sleepwalk!" Simon argues. "I might walk on her one night. It just wouldn't be safe. . . ." Ruthie is delighted and gives her big brother a great big kiss.

Meanwhile, Mary wants to go to a big party with Jeff, but when her parents find out she doesn't know any details about it—like, Will the parents be there? Are the kids older? Will there be alcohol?—they won't let her go. Mary is so mad, she tells Lucy she's going to see if Jeff wants to watch an R-rated movie. "You're not allowed!" Lucy protests. But Mary says, "The point is to avoid looking like a total geek who does everything her parents tell her to do."

In the meantime, Annie's parents call to say they're post-poning their trip. But Annie's worried about her mother's health, and decides to fly out to Arizona to spend a few days with her. At first Lucy is happy, as it means Dad will be busy with Mom's Meals on Wheels duty. And that means no chap-erone for her TV date with Jimmy Moon! But then she learns that Matt, still grounded from staying out all night at Renee's, has had his driving privileges restored so he can take care of Meals on Wheels. Mary tells Lucy that Dad ruined her first date by playing his guitar and singing every country song he knew. Lucy freaks. "This is the most impor-tant night of my life!" she exclaims. She begs Mary to can-cel her date so she can keep Dad out of the living room. When Mary says no, Lucy uses her secret weapon: "I promise to never mention the R-rated movie." Mary's trapped and reluctantly agrees.

While Annie is gone, Eric is getting grief for not doing things "like Mom." He brings in groceries—and leaves Ruthie strapped into her car seat. He makes a casserole for dinner—and it's so awful the kids try to feed it to Happy. But even she turns up her nose.

Meanwhile, Annie arrives at her parents' home in Arizona and finds the house empty. She panics and calls the hospital, fearing the worst. But then her parents breeze in from a flight on a hot-air balloon. Annie can't believe how blasé they seem. Not only that, they're living it up: shopping, eating out, drinking fine wine. When Annie reminds them there's a houseful of people back in Glenoak waiting to see them, they decide to fly back right away—in first class!

When Jimmy shows up for his date with Lucy, Eric is stunned to hear that he's brought "the director's cut of an unreleased French film" to watch on video. When Mary peeks in on them later, she's surprised to see Jimmy putting the moves on Lucy. She hurries to find her father. Together they stand outside the living room and sing a duet of corny songs, and a mortified Lucy races out. Angry at Mary for not keeping Dad away, she blurts out that Mary plans to watch an R-rated movie with Jeff.

That night Matt rushes through his Meals on Wheels duty and sneaks by the restaurant where his latest love interest, Diana, works. Outside, they find a homeless man who wants food, and Matt gives him a couple of dollars. As Matt backs out of his parking space, Diana snuggles up to him and pops open a beer. Startled, Matt declines a sip, but he's so distracted by her romantic overtures that he backs into a parked police car—and Diana spills her beer all over him. The police officer comes out of the restaurant and makes Diana call her parents. Matt insists he wasn't drinking, but the police officer takes a sniff of the beer on Matt's shirt and says, "Well, that's an interesting cologne you're wearing. Step outside." When Eric gets there, Matt's negative test proves that he has no alcohol in his system. But Diana's father arrives and yells at Matt to stay away from his daughter. Eric is mad at Matt for going by the diner in the first place. Matt says none of it would have happened if Eric hadn't asked him to deliver church food. Eric can't believe it. "You are never going to drive my car again!" he exclaims.

Back at the house Annie arrives with Grandma and Grandpa, and their love and attention help soothe all the squabbling. They have a talk with Mary and Lucy and remind them that they're lucky they have each other to confide in. Grandma tells Simon she appreciates his sharing his room with Ruthie so that she and Grandpa can have a room of their own. "It's a sure sign you're growing up," she says. When Matt comes home feeling like an idiot, Grandma reassures him he's just a normal sixteen-year-old kid trying to find his way.

As the evening winds down, everyone goes to bed except for Grandma and Grandpa, who stay up dancing and reminiscing about when Annie was a little girl. Grandma is tired but has had a wonderful day. "I'm so glad Annie came and got us," she says. The two tell each other "I love you," then go to bed.

In the early-morning hours Annie wakes up, sensing a presence in her room. It's as if she felt a kiss on her cheek. Then she thinks she hears a voice say, "I love you, but I have to go." Worried, Annie quietly slips out of bed and hurries down the hall to her mother's room. Her father comes out to tell her the sad news: "She's passed on, Annie. She's gone." Eric comes out to console them as Annie cries in her father's arms, grieving that the life of her wonderful mother is gone "in the blink of an eye."

No Funerals and a Wedding

**written by Molly Newman;
directed by Mark Jean**

Season 1: Episode 3

Annie struggles through her mother's funeral. At least she has her family and friends around her. But when it's over, she's surprised to see a cab show up, and even more stunned when she learns it's for Grandpa. When Annie begs him to stay a few days, he makes excuses—he's got work piling up, fish to feed. "I'll be fine," he tells them, then says he'll be in touch. Annie feels abandoned as she watches her father drive away.

At home, friends gather to chat and eat. Simon asks Annie, "Where exactly did Grandma go when she died?" "To heaven," Annie explains, "a place filled with love." "But I need to know where that is," Simon insists. Annie motions upward: "You know . . . up there." But Simon wants a more specific answer.

Later Eric tries to explain that heaven "isn't a geographical place like Iowa or France. It's more of a spiritual place." But he's interrupted by the sobbing of a young woman named Susan. He tries to console her, thinking she's upset by the funeral. But it's something else. She's certain her husband, Steve, is having an affair. Eric is surprised. He performed their wedding ceremony only seven months before, and they seemed deeply in love. But in Eric's study Steve confesses to the minister that "I'm a tortured man because . . . I'm a bigamist!" Eric's taken aback. Steve explains that he never told Susan he was married before. His divorce was supposed to be completed by his and Susan's wedding day, but it wasn't because the papers didn't come through in time. Now he's afraid that if Susan finds out, she'll

divorce him. "Good news," Eric says. "She can't divorce you. You're not legally married."

Meanwhile, Matt is upset when he learns Mary has decided to cool things off with Jeff because he's "too clingy." But Matt's worried it'll make things weird between him and his longtime pal if Mary breaks up with him. He makes Mary promise not to break it off just yet. She agrees, and when Jeff shows up, Mary ducks out of sight. Matt then gives Jeff tips on how to play hard to get.

Upstairs, Eric finds Lucy crying about Grandma. "It's like there's a party going on and she wasn't invited," she cries. "It's like life going on without her. It's just not fair." Later, after calming down, Lucy runs into Jeff and says she's sorry Mary dumped him. As soon as she sees his face, she realizes he didn't know.

In Eric and Annie's bedroom, Ruthie asks Annie to sing "the Grandma song," the one Grandma first sang when Annie was little and was going away to camp—when suddenly Renee comes to the door: her baby is ready to be born! Matt goes along to help her until her husband, Lou, gets there. Eric tells Annie he thinks it will be the most effective birth-control lesson Matt will ever have.

When Annie confides in Mary how upset she is with her father, Mary reminds her that when she's upset with her own dad, Eric, he makes her tell him what's wrong. Then she always feels better. Realizing this is good advice, Annie calls her father, but gets his answering machine. She leaves a message, telling him she feels as if he's abandoned her. Later she calls again and apologizes—she's just sad and confused, and she really misses her mom. She asks him to call her as soon as possible.

Meanwhile, at the hospital, Renee's husband doesn't show up in time, and Matt winds up coaching Renee through the birth.

When Eric finally gets to spend a few moments with Annie, she's in tears from emotional exhaustion. He tries to comfort her, but, well, he has to rush off to the church. Can he borrow her white dress? And can she meet him at the church in ten minutes?

Ruthie finds Simon sitting on the stairs thinking about heaven. Ruthie says she knows where Grandma is: "I don't know the name of it, but it's where I was before I was born." Simon sighs. He can't picture Grandma there. Ruthie puts her hand over her heart. "Picture Grandma here." Finally Simon seems satisfied.

When Annie reaches the church, she finds Eric performing a wedding—for the second time—for Steven and Susan, who is wearing Annie's dress. Smiling, Annie silently repeats the wedding vows along with them. When Eric and Annie are alone after the wedding, Eric apologizes for letting her down, and adds, "Twenty years later, you still make a beautiful bride." They go home to find the kids eating pie, as they've still got five left over from the funeral reception. Matt comes in and tells them all about the birth of Renee's baby, a girl. She's going to name her new daughter Jenny, after Grandma.

Then Annie goes upstairs to finally sing Ruthie "the Grandma song." Ruthie asks her, "Are you going to pass away, like Grandma?" "Not for a very, very long time," Annie assures her, and promises that "I'll always be there if you need me."

Just then Grandpa walks in and says he wishes he'd lived up to that same promise today. He says he's never been good at handling tragedy, and he ran out because he was afraid he might fall apart. But he never made it to the airport. He went back to the cemetery and sat at Jenny's grave all day. But he decided if he was going to feel terrible and alone, he wanted to do it with someone he loves. Annie smiles. "We can help each other get through this."

Then a sleepy Ruthie asks once again for the song. As one by one the Camdens join in the silly camp song, Annie looks around at the wonderful family that surrounds her, and she knows that everything is going to be all right after all.

The Color of God

written by Brenda Hampton;
directed by
Burt Brinckerhoff

The Camden family is shocked
when the local black church of
their friend the Reverend
Morgan Hamilton is burned to
the ground. When the Hamiltons
move in for a few days, it forces
them all to confront complex
issues of race and prejudice.

Season 1: Episode 4

The Camdens are enjoying Saturday-morning pancakes when Simon and Ruthie hear a news bulletin: Last night Trinity Church, a local black church, was burned to the ground. The pastor, Morgan Hamilton, is a friend of Eric's. The Camdens are deeply concerned and want to help out however they can.

On Sunday Eric invites the Trinity congregation to worship at his church. Reverend Hamilton is invited to speak, and he reminds people that "we cannot fight hate with hate." He asks his listeners to ask themselves, "What are we teaching our children today that will make things better tomorrow?" Eric then invites Reverend Hamilton, his wife, Patricia, and their four children over for dinner. But it's not easy. Everyone is upset about the attack, especially the older Hamilton kids, who seem suspicious of anyone with white skin. When Mary suggests they go play basketball, John resents her suggestion because he thinks she's implying that that's all African Americans do. When Lucy says she's sorry about their father's church, Keesha snaps, "That's the third time you said that." As Eric and Morgan work on dinner, Morgan says he feels a mixture of sadness and anger. He also reveals that they got a note from the arsonist warning of another attack. When Eric finds out the Hamiltons slept at a hotel the night before because the parsonage was damaged, too, he insists that they stay at the Camden home.

Mary finally gets John to play basketball, but John plays rough, and Matt accuses him of taking out his anger on Mary. "You don't know anything about my anger," John says, then storms off.

At dinner Eric announces that the Hamilton children will be staying at the Camden house, while Eric and Morgan stay at the Hamilton house. Over dinner young Nigel Hamilton says a simple but appropriate blessing: "Dear God, please stop the fires."

The next morning, at the Hamilton house for breakfast, Morgan tells Eric he's the worst cook he's ever seen, "but the best friend I ever had." Eric tells him the deacons of his church have voted to donate a percentage of their building fund to help rebuild Reverend Hamilton's church.

Meanwhile, back at the Camden house, the kids get ready for school. Lucy proudly shows off her cornrow braids that Keesha has fixed for her. Then Keesha and John pile into the front seat of the van with Matt. Lucy and Mary explain to Simon about Rosa Parks, the black woman who galvanized the civil rights movement by refusing to sit in the back of the bus.

On the school playground Simon and some friends are playing battle games. When Nigel gets "killed," Simon rushes up and gives him "the latest in antideath vaccines" and proclaims, "He's alive again!" But a kid named Mark says Nigel can't play anymore and calls Simon a "nigger lover." "Forget it," Nigel tells Simon. "You can't fight ignorance with violence." But Simon is upset, and when Mark won't apologize, Simon hits him hard in the stomach.

When Matt comes to pick up Simon and Nigel, he finds Nigel waiting alone. As Mary goes in to find Simon, a security guard hassles John for loitering. When Matt speaks up, the guard demands that he show him his license and registration for the van. Matt can't believe it and tells the guard he's not a real policeman. The guard gets angry and orders them off the property. Matt insists on waiting for Mary, who rushes out to tell them that Simon got suspended and Dad has already picked him up.

At home, Annie and Eric have mixed feelings: they can't help but be proud of Simon for standing up to a bigoted kid, but they still feel that fighting is never the answer. He'll need to be punished.

Outside, John confronts Matt about the incident with the guard. Matt says the guy was a jerk. But John thinks there was more to it, and he also accuses Matt of being scared of him because of the color of his skin. Matt admits that he is afraid of John—but not because he's black. It's his attitude that scares him. John's surprised, but he thinks about what Matt has said.

At dinner Morgan announces that they got a new security system put in at their house and the police have offered a twenty-four-hour patrol, so he thinks it's time they move back into their own home. The Camdens convince them to stay one more night, and Eric suggests they party with a game of Twister. John and Matt exchange a look. "Parents!" Matt says.

After days of avoiding the issues, Patricia and Morgan finally discuss their fears about the fire. Morgan muses that life would be easier if he had a different kind of job. He feels inadequate knowing that he couldn't protect his church and worries that he won't be able to protect his family. But Patricia insists she loves what he does.

Eric tells Morgan that he is welcome to share his pulpit until the church is rebuilt. Morgan thanks him for the offer, and says he is more worried about rebuilding the spirit of his congregation than the building that houses them. He wants to start holding services on the grounds again Sunday morning—and says all they need are a tent and a few folding chairs.

On Sunday morning Eric surprises Reverend Hamilton by showing up with the white congregation of his church. Morgan thanks them for their show of support and friendship. Then he begins his service by repeating his son Nigel's simple prayer: "Please, God, stop the fires."

Saturday

written by Jack LoGiudice; directed by David Semel

The Camdens are upset when Mary tells them not to come watch her basketball game. Ruthie and Simon get lost while Lucy is supposed to be baby-sitting them. Eric worries about his kids after dealing with a teenager who uses drugs.

Season 1: Episode 5

The Camdens are excited about going to see Mary play basketball. So they're stunned when she asks, "Would you mind not coming to my game?" Mary explains that they make her nervous: Dad and Matt yell out instructions; Mom hollers at the refs; Simon and Ruthie are loud; Lucy keeps going to the concession stand and checking out cute boys.

Mary's family is really disappointed—especially Lucy, because she's invited a popular girl named Ashley to come along. To make matters worse, Annie tells Lucy that she and Ashley have to baby-sit while she's at the grocery store.

Upstairs, Ruthie begs Simon to let her play detective. At last he agrees, but he makes her promise to do exactly as he says.

When Matt shows up at Susan Barrett's house for a tutoring job, her father comes to the door. He says he hasn't seen his daughter this excited in ages. Matt protests that he's just her tutor, but when Susan comes down, she winks at her dad and says, "Told you."

At the Camden house, Ashley arrives and promptly insults Lucy's clothes. And when she hears they can't go to the game, she starts to leave. "Wait!" Lucy blurts out. "My parents will be gone, so we can call boys!" This temptation is enough to keep her new friend from leaving, and when Eric and Annie leave, Lucy and Ashley hurry to call Jimmy Moon.

Outside, Simon spots the mailman and decides to pretend he's the bad guy in their detective game. He and Ruthie trail him down the street.

At the store, Eric and Annie spot a boy named Terry Daniels, whom Eric just recently got into a drug rehab program. They see him steal a watch and leave the store. Just as the security guard stops Terry, Eric hurries up and jokes about how easy it is to accidentally walk out with something. The guard recognizes Eric as a minister and doesn't press charges.

At school, Mary tells her friend Cheryl that she told her family not to come. "It's bad luck not to invite your family!" Cheryl tells her. "You're going to ruin this for the whole team!" Mary rushes to phone home, but the line is busy because Lucy is talking to Jimmy, with Ashley secretly listening in on the extension. When Lucy asks him if Steve likes Ashley, he says Steve thought she was a babe—until he talked to her and realized she never shuts up. Now he hates her. Angry and humiliated, Ashley shouts, "Well, tell him I hate him, too!" As she storms out of the house, she tells Lucy, "Your boyfriend's a jerk, and so are you!" Lucy starts to run after her, then realizes something awful . . . Simon and Ruthie are gone! Lucy races out to find them.

When Annie gets home and finds everyone gone, she wonders if they all sneaked off to the game. Meanwhile, Eric tries to talk to Terry, convinced he's back on drugs. Terry tells him to butt out of his life. Later Eric spots him in an alleyway smoking pot and confronts him, but Terry again tells him to leave him alone.

By this time, Simon and Ruthie have followed the mailman to the end of his route. Suddenly they realize . . . they're lost!

At Matt's tutoring session, Susan throws her arms around him, but her father comes in and thinks Matt is the one who's making passes. Matt decides to quit while he's ahead, but Mr. Barrett says, "Nobody quits on me, boy. You're fired!"

Annie goes to the basketball game, but the rest of her family isn't there. She sits down anyway and waves to Mary on the court.

Meanwhile, Eric's friend Sergeant Michaels finds Simon and Ruthie, but when he takes them home, nobody's there. He offers to drive by the school to see if they went to the basketball game.

At the gym, Mary's team is trailing by several points. Outside, as Sergeant Michaels drives up with Simon and Ruthie, they meet Eric, who's looking for Annie. He and the kids go inside and find Annie and Matt cheering for Mary. As the clock ticks down, Mary gets the ball, races down the court, and makes a basket, tying the score. Confident now, she then saves a missed shot by another player and tips the ball through the hoop at the last minute—winning the game. No one cheers more loudly than the Camden family. Mary realizes she's glad they're there.

Back at home, Lucy is worried sick about Simon and Ruthie, until her family comes home and she learns that everyone saw Mary's game except her—which makes her really angry.

Annie is stunned when Eric lets the kids off with no punishment, but Eric feels his kids' problems are small compared to what's happening with Terry. But Annie argues that if they don't stick to their rules, the little problems could turn into bigger problems. Eric goes up to discipline them, but—thinking of Terry Daniels—he instead winds up making them promise not to do drugs. Matt tells him not to worry. He says most kids do drugs so they can belong to a group and fit in, but that's not a problem with the Camden kids. Matt says he's a born loner, Mary has her basketball team, Simon has a strong sense of who he is, and Ruthie . . . she's five. "What about Lucy?" Eric asks. Matt nods. "She's the one you should worry about, because she always feels left out." Considering this advice, Eric finds Lucy and asks her to go out to dinner—just the two of them. She's delighted.

That night, just as Eric and Annie are about to go to bed, the doorbell rings. It's Terry Daniels; his face is dirty and scratched, and he looks beat up. "I guess you were right, I am a loser," he says. Eric replies, "You knocked on my door; you're not a loser." Eric invites him in and explains that the best place to start is by calling his parents.

Halloween

written by Molly Newman;
directed by Nick Havinga

When Lucy meets "Mike the Mutant" and Matt gets a dream date with a beautiful girl, they both learn that you can't judge people by how they look. Eric resolves a thirty-year-old nightmare about a Halloween fight over a coonskin cap. Mary cunningly avoids both the dance and the carnival to indulge in a secret pleasure.

In a darkened room upstairs, Matt tells the younger Camden kids a ghost story about "Mike the Mutant," an ogre who lives in a spooky house "not far from where we are right now," when—Aaaagh! Eric bursts in and scares everybody, including himself. Annie comes in and joins the storytelling, but Eric declines. "Daddy hates Halloween," Lucy says.

The next morning Simon complains because Annie is going to let Ruthie enter the pumpkin-carving contest at tomorrow's church carnival. He's won three times in a row and wants to win again. Annie mentions to Eric that she ran into a woman at the supermarket who was from his hometown. They just moved here, she explains, and her name is "Cindy something." Her husband's name was Howard, no, Henry Bernard. Later Eric goes upstairs and searches through his old fifth-grade yearbook until he finds a picture of Henry Bernard.

At school a friend of Jimmy Moon's, named Sam, says the "Mike the Mutant" story is true. They talk Lucy into going to see his house after school.

At the high school Roxanne—a beautiful blonde Matt has a secret crush on—tells Mary she's dying to go to the school Halloween dance, but she doesn't have a date because no one realizes she's broken up with her boyfriend. Matt leaps at the chance and asks her out. To his surprise, she accepts.

After school Lucy bikes over with Jimmy and his friends to see Mike the Mutant's house. Sam says the guy grows giant mutant vegetables. They get to a small trailer and sneak into the garden. But just as Lucy picks up a big pumpkin, Mike the Mutant appears. Terrified, Lucy runs off with the pumpkin.

At home, Simon is complaining about the lame pumpkins that Annie brought home when Lucy comes in with the most beautiful one he's ever seen. Annie questions her, figures out she "liberated" it from someone's garden, and she insists that Lucy return it and apologize.

Lucy takes the pumpkin back and meets Mike the Mutant. She learns he is actually a shy, gentle man who is afraid of people. She tells him about the pumpkin contest, and he says she can have any pumpkin she wants. She asks him how he got the scar on his face, and he tells her he got shot, but he doesn't remember much about it. When she suggests she might bring her family over, he gets upset and slams the door in her face.

At home Mary searches the upstairs closet for a cape for Simon's Superman costume. "Isn't Halloween over yet?" Eric complains. Then Mary pulls out an old coonskin cap. Eric smiles and explains that he was quite obsessed by Davy Crockett when he was a kid.

That night Eric dreams about something that happened when he was a child. At school, the children got to pick out Halloween costumes. Eric wanted the Davy Crockett costume so bad! When his friend Henry Bernard grabbed it away from the other kids, Eric got angry and hit Henry. As the teacher pulled them apart, Henry tearfully explained, "I got it for you, Eric. I wasn't going to keep it." Eric bolts awake from his dream, still filled with shame.

At school the next day, Roxanne tells Matt she's borrowed costumes from the drama department for them: Roxanne and Cyrano de Bergerac. "The guy with the big nose?" Matt asks. Roxanne convinces him by telling him how Roxanne fell deeply and completely in love with Cyrano despite how he looked.

As Eric works on a Halloween banner, Lucy mentions Mike. Eric tells her that Mike used to be an artist who built abstract sculptures out of scrap metal. To make ends meet, he took a job pumping gas at night. A couple of guys came in to rob the place, Mike tried to stop them, and they shot him. Lucy can't believe how mean the kids are to him. Eric replies that "lots of times we make decisions about people based on appearances, rather than taking the time to find out the truth."

Meanwhile, Annie tries to console Ruthie because her dinosaur costume is hot and uncomfortable. Just then Matt enters in his Cyrano costume—all lace and plumes, plus a big hat and a huge, ridiculous, ugly nose. "I look like an idiot," Matt moans. Annie looks from Matt to Ruthie and realizes that both problems seem unsolvable. "Maybe nobody will know who you are," Annie suggests.

Out in the backyard, Simon brings Lucy a box that someone left on the front porch. She looks inside but won't let Simon see.

Later Lucy goes by to see Mike, and catches Sam,

Randy, and Jimmy pelting his trailer with eggs and toilet paper. Randy shouts that it's "payback time for all those kids you gobbled up, you mutant!" Lucy turns the garden hose on them and runs them off. She finds Mike inside, shivering and terrified.

When it's time for the parties, Matt shows up at Roxanne's in a hobo costume. He explains he just couldn't make the other costume work. Roxanne says she can't possibly be seen with someone dressed as a derelict. Matt protests: What about that story of Roxanne loving Cyrano in spite of his looks? "Oh, please," she says. "That was fiction." Matt gets angry and leaves.

At the last minute Mary whips up a new costume for Ruthie made out of a mop—she's happy to go as Happy the dog!

Meanwhile, Eric visits Henry Bernard's house with the coonskin cap and apologizes for hitting him. Henry invites him in for coffee.

Everyone is having fun at the church carnival when Matt shows up, explaining that the dance didn't turn out to be what he expected. Ruthie shows everyone the butterfly painted on her cheek. "Lucy's friend did it." Matt says he's a big guy in a Frankenstein costume, and he can really paint. Eric shows up wearing his coonskin cap. When they all compare notes about Mary, they discover she's not at the carnival or the dance. Annie smiles. She knows where Mary is.

Mary's at home gobbling ice cream. Then she goes off for a long soak in a bubble bath. When her friend Valerie calls, she tells her it's great. In a house full of seven people, this is the only night of the year she gets to be alone.

Back at the carnival, they announce that the winner of the pumpkin-carving contest is . . . Lucy Camden! But Lucy announces that she didn't really carve her pumpkin. The real artist is her friend Mike Mitchell! She leads him to the front so everyone can see that appearances can be deceiving: Mike is not frightening after all.

Season 1: Episode 7

What Will People Say?

**written by Brenda Hampton;
directed by Duwayne Dunham**

Annie and the kids spot Eric going into a motel with an attractive woman, and even Annie struggles to keep trusting him when the rumors fly. Simon makes a fool of himself over a girl. Annie helps Mary's new boyfriend, Richard, with his secret problem.

"Look! There's Daddy!" Ruthie shouts. On the way home from school, Annie and the kids see Eric walk into a hotel room with an attractive young woman. "I'm sure it has something to do with the church," Annie insists brightly. But Simon is suspicious.

The truth is that Eric has booked a hotel room for Abby Morris, a battered woman, but now she's having second thoughts about leaving her husband. She says it's her fault her husband abuses her because she doesn't keep the house clean enough and doesn't know how to please him. Eric tries to get her to go to an abused women's shelter for counseling. But Abby refuses; she doesn't want anyone else to know about her problems.

Later Matt has a talk with Mary about her new boyfriend, Richard, who has a reputation as a ladies' man. He's not happy with her answer that Richard is also a "great kisser." Richard stops by, and Mary goes out with him to toss the football around. Eric tells Annie that he thinks Mary should be spending more time on schoolwork and less time on boys. Annie suggests that they let Mary go out on one weekend date and have one study date during the week. Eric agrees.

Upstairs, Simon tells Ruthie he's in love with a new girl named Gabrielle and swears her to secrecy. But at dinner he lets the name Gabrielle slip out. Ruthie tells her dad, "Maybe Simon will tell you who Gabrielle is if you tell us who the woman was at the motel." After dinner Annie insists that she knows Eric's work is confidential. But he hears a hint of suspicion in her voice.

The next day Simon writes Gabrielle a love note, but before he can give it to her, a big bully grabs it on the playground and reads it out loud. Mortified, Gabrielle runs away. Simon is so embarrassed that the next day he pretends to be sick. Annie realizes he's faking but lets him stay home anyway.

When Eric overhears Mary and Lucy talking about boys, Mary snaps at him, "You know, you're really getting good at sneaking around, aren't you?" Eric asks Lucy if she's mad at him, too, but she says she's just curious about his relationship with the woman. He reminds her that he can't discuss his counseling or people would no longer trust him.

Soon after, Jake Morris shows up and accuses Eric of having an affair with his wife, Abby. Eric says he has heard the rumors, too, and wonders where they started. Then Jake apologizes. He says it's not the first time Abby has done this. He says she makes up crazy stories to get sympathy from a man as a way to start an affair. "I'm surprised you haven't divorced her," Eric says in surprise. Jake says he doesn't believe in divorce and that he keeps trying to get her to see a therapist, but she always quits. He blames it on the fact that she grew up with an abusive father. Eric is again surprised; he says Abby told him her father died when she was young. Jake says no, but he's sure she wishes he had. Eric suggests that maybe Jake could use some counseling, but Jake insists he's fine. He just wants Abby to get better. He just wants things to work out. Eric wonders who is telling the truth.

That afternoon Simon walks in on Mary and Richard's "study date," but it looks more like a make-out session. Richard is having a hard time studying anyway. Then Annie interrupts to talk to Mary about her math teacher, who called to say Mary's grades have been slipping and that she didn't get a test paper signed. While Mary goes up to get it, Annie takes the opportunity to talk with Richard and discovers what his real problem is—he can't read well, but he hides it because he's ashamed. Annie fixes him up with a retired teacher who didn't learn to read until she was forty. She'll really understand his problem.

Eric follows Jake to the motel, where he pretends he's meeting his wife so he can find out what room she's in. Eric tells him to leave or he'll call the police. Then Eric spots Matt hiding behind a palm tree. Matt's embarrassed to be caught trailing his dad, but Eric says it's okay. He likes that Matt is looking out for his mom.

At home, Simon tries to get Ruthie to hit him on the head and knock him out so he won't have to go to school. But when Lucy overhears, she tells Simon not to worry. By tomorrow the kids will have forgotten all about the love letter.

When Eric comes home late, he decides it's time to tell Annie the truth—especially now that Abby has given him permission to do so. When Annie first learns that Abby has been abused, she is surprised, then realizes it all makes sense. Abby always turned down invitations to join in church activities, as if she feared that she would face disapproval from someone.

At school the next day, the bully starts teasing Simon about being "love sick." But when the boy jumps down off a wall, his pants rip. The kids howl with laughter, and the bully gets a taste of his own medicine. But instead of joining in, Simon takes off his jacket and gives it to the boy to tie around his waist to cover up the rip. The bully is surprised by Simon's kindness. "Don't worry, pal," Simon tells him. "After tomorrow, they'll forget all about it."

As the kids come home from school, Eric shows up with Abby, and Annie greets her warmly. Abby reveals that she's decided to go to New York to stay with her sister. Jake shows up demanding to see his wife. "She's my wife!" he shouts from outside. "She'll do whatever I tell her to do!" Matt calls the police, and they soon arrive to arrest Jake on charges of spousal abuse. Abby is trembling; will she have the strength to start a new life? Annie assures her that she does, and promises that they'll always be there to help her.

25

See No Evil, Hear No Evil, Speak No Evil

written by Catherine LePard; directed by Harry Harris

Matt and Annie get robbed at gunpoint, and the thief takes Annie's wedding rings. Mary is pressured by the girls on her basketball team to get a tattoo. Simon and Ruthie come down with the chicken pox. Jimmy Moon breaks up with Lucy.

Season 1: Episode 8

Matt and Annie are driving along a dark street, but the speakers on the new CD player Annie installed don't sound right, so she tells Matt to pull over. As she sticks her head under the dash, a man sticks a gun up to Matt's head. He shouts at them to hand over their wallets and jewelry. When Annie struggles to get her wedding rings off, the robber reaches in to yank them off. Annie gets a glimpse of the unusual tattoo on his forearm.

Back home they give a description to the police. Matt and Annie both insist that they're fine, just tired. Annie goes to check on Ruthie, who's in bed with the chicken pox. She reassures Ruthie and Simon that the robber only took things, things that can be replaced, and reassures Ruthie that she's still married, even though her wedding rings were stolen. She tells Simon the scuba mask he's wearing is not going to keep him from getting chicken pox, since he was probably exposed at Sunday school.

When Eric goes to tell the girls good night, he finds Lucy dressed in a tight, sexy miniskirt. She explains that she's running for class president and insists she needs to dress in a way to get people's attention when she makes her speech. Eric reminds her it's what she says that should get their attention and offers to help her write an "electric" speech. Trying to change the subject, Lucy blurts out that Mary's getting a tattoo. Unprepared, Mary sputters that she was just thinking about it, since all the girls on the basketball team are getting one. But Eric declares their house "a tattoo-free zone."

The next morning, when the kids get in the car to go to school, Matt just sits there, staring into space like a zombie. Matt admits to Eric that he feels guilty about doing nothing during the robbery. He doesn't feel as if he's ever going to be the same again. Eric reminds him that he's just been through a terrifying trauma and that the most important thing is that he and Annie are safe. He suggests that Matt go talk to someone at Victim's Support and adds that it's a good day for a sick day; he'll drive Lucy and Mary to school. He adds that Simon's come down with the chicken pox, too.

At school, Lucy is upset to learn that Jimmy Moon is running against her for class president. He says it's not personal.

At church, the choir talks to Eric about getting rid of Mrs. Hinkle, the organist. They say she plays like she has mittens on. When he hears the older woman play a couple of bars of "Turkey in the Straw" in the middle of "Rock of Ages," Eric agrees to help.

That night, as Eric and Annie share their day, she still insists she's feeling okay about the robbery. But when she goes down

to get them a bedtime snack, she nervously checks all the locks, then curls up on the floor next to Happy by the front door.

The next day Eric gently tries to talk to Mrs. Hinkle about retirement, saying "it would be selfish to continue to ask for more from someone who has given so much." "Are you firing me?" she asks. Eric's embarrassed, but Mrs. Hinkle just thanks him and asks if she can play one more Sunday. He agrees. Then Jimmy Moon comes to see Eric and reveals that he wants to break up with Lucy. But he doesn't want to hurt her feelings, he explains, and asks for Eric's help. Eric feels uncomfortable with the request and says this is something Jimmy needs to learn to do by himself.

As Annie and Mary leave the supermarket, a stranger rushes up to them in the parking lot. Annie screams at him to get away. Mary realizes the man was behind them in the checkout line and only wants to return Annie's sunglasses, which she left behind.

At home, Annie finally admits that she's not fine. She believes the robbery was her fault because she hadn't fixed the speaker wires properly in the first place. "I can't get the image of that gun next to my son out of my head." Eric tells her that what matters is that they're both safe. Annie nods, but adds, "I don't know how to stop being afraid." When the phone rings, Annie answers, and it's the police. They have a man in custody and want her to come down tomorrow to see if she can identify him. "Sure," she says. But when she hangs up, she tells Eric it was a wrong number.

Eric takes Lucy on errands so he can talk to her about Jimmy. When they return, Jimmy is there and apologizes for not talking to her himself. He says he's withdrawing from the campaign because he values their relationship. Lucy says she is, too, hoping for a kiss. But Jimmy just shakes her hand.

Eric gets a call from the police station, then asks Annie why she didn't show up for the lineup. It doesn't take long for Eric to realize that Annie was afraid. He takes Annie and Matt to the police station, but they're unable to identify the robber since they never saw his face. Back home, they find Mary shooting baskets and realize she has a tattoo on her leg. Her parents are upset until Mary smiles and reveals that it's a removable decal. But this reminds Annie that their robber had a tattoo. They return to the police station and have the suspects roll up their sleeves. She and Matt instantly identify him.

At church on Sunday, Mrs. Hinkle plays beautifully. After the service she thanks Eric. She'd wanted some time off for years, but felt she couldn't just walk away from the church. Getting fired made everything all right. After the church clears, Eric tells Annie a friend gave him something to give her, "so you wouldn't have to be afraid ever again." Then he slips Simon's Red Lightning ring onto her finger.

Last Call for Aunt Julie

written by Ron Zimmerman; directed by Joel J. Feigenbaum

The Camdens are thrilled to have Aunt Julie visit—until her alcoholism threatens to ruin their Thanksgiving.

The Camdens are so excited that Aunt Julie has finally arrived to stay with them for Thanksgiving. She's brought all the kids presents—everything from a doll for Ruthie to bags of makeup for Mary and Lucy. Matt shows her to his room, which he's given up for her visit. Then he asks her if she'd mind if he went on a free ski trip Wednesday, adding that he'll be back before she leaves. Julie guesses there's a girl involved, and says, "All right! Have fun!" As soon as Matt leaves, Julie digs through her luggage, pulls out a bottle of vodka, and takes a long, urgent drink.

At dinner Eric and Annie announce they've decided to let the kids do things with their friends after Thanksgiving, if they choose, and that Matt can go on the ski trip. Simon notices that Aunt Julie is on her third glass of wine. Eric apologizes for rushing off to a deacon's meeting.

Free of the kids, Annie and Julie have a talk. Annie reveals that she's a little depressed because Thanksgiving was her mother's favorite holiday, and she misses her. Julie confesses that she's been feeling depressed herself and is tired of everything, in fact. When Annie goes upstairs to put the kids to bed, Julie searches the liquor cabinet, then pours herself a coffee mug full of port wine.

While getting ready for bed, Eric confesses he's a little nervous about giving a sermon with Julie in the audience. Annie wonders if he thought she drank too much at dinner.

At church, Eric preaches on the importance of sharing and being thankful for what we have, even if it's less than what others have. He says he's thankful for his sister visiting from New York. Suddenly Julie spills the contents of her purse and finds the whole congregation looking at her. Eric saves the moment by claiming that she is not only his younger sister, but also the family klutz. That afternoon Annie calls Brian, Julie's longtime boyfriend, to say they're sorry he couldn't come. Brian reveals he broke off their relationship. Even worse, he tells Annie that Julie was fired from her job.

Downstairs, Simon is playing Batman with Ruthie. As Julie goes to open the liquor cabinet, Simon steals the key and races off with it. Julie playfully tries to get it back. When tickling doesn't get her the key, Julie loses her temper and shouts, "Gimme that damn key!" Ruthie starts crying as Julie begins to choke Simon. "Aunt Julie, you're hurting me!" Simon cries. Annie rushes in and shoves Julie away. "Get out of this house now!" she yells, and Julie runs off.

After a seven-hour search Eric finally finds Julie getting drunk in a saloon. She struggles against him, but he manages to drag her out,

At home, Annie is explaining to her children that Aunt Julie is sick with a disease called alcoholism. "People who have it often hurt the people they love the most," Annie says, and adds that they're going to put her in a hospital. Matt worries that it doesn't seem right to send her away when she needs them the most. But Mary is angry; she doesn't care if she ever sees Aunt Julie again. Lucy is in tears because their first Thanksgiving without Grandma has turned out so horribly.

When Eric brings Julie home, there's an awful scene. Still drunk, Julie sobs and apologizes pathetically. Afraid of losing her temper, Annie tells Eric to take her upstairs "and stay with her or lock her in her room."

Matt tells Lucy and Mary they all need to cancel their Thanksgiving plans so they can help Aunt Julie. But Mary is still too mad at her for hurting Simon. Matt insists she didn't mean it, she's sick. Mary says she's embarrassed Aunt Julie is part of the family, and Matt angrily replies that right now, he's embarrassed that Mary's part of the family.

Meanwhile, Eric tells Annie he doesn't want to send Julie to a treatment center. He wants to keep her at their home to help her through her first days of withdrawal. Annie reluctantly agrees, but she tells him the safety of the kids comes first and that "you're on your own."

Simon and Ruthie return their presents to Aunt Julie, and she cries as she clutches the doll she gave Ruthie.

The next morning Julie says she's better. She wants Eric to lend her money so she can fly home. But Eric knows she'll just go home and drink. She demands that he put her into a hospital, but he fears she would just check herself out. Julie gets angry and starts calling Eric "the high and mighty reverend."

Matt goes up to give his father a break and sit with Aunt Julie, and she tells him she's recovered. They commiserate on how tough Eric can be. Then Julie uses the moment to try to talk Matt into bringing her one little beer. When he refuses, she explodes: "You make me sick!" she shouts. She orders him to get out. Once outside, Matt sinks to the floor, cring-

ing as he hears his favorite aunt rant and rave about how ungrateful he is.

Later, as Eric sits with her, Julie bolts up out of bed, screaming that she can't breathe. Annie races in, and Eric explains that Julie is having the D.T.s. She starts shaking and shouting and crying that it hurts, then begins hallucinating that she sees rats everywhere. Eric and Annie hold on to her so she won't hurt herself. "We're gonna get you through this," Annie tells her. When morning comes, Eric and Annie are huddled under a blanket as Julie sleeps peacefully in the bed.

When they go downstairs, Annie and Eric find the kids preparing Grandma's recipes for Thanksgiving dinner. Annie tells the kids they should go ahead with their own plans and she'll take over. But the kids want to finish what they started. They send their parents off for a shower and a nap. Only Mary is still angry. Matt tells her everyone's trying to work past the problems and have a happy Thanksgiving. Mary snaps that she's entitled to her own feelings. Matt replies that if she's ever in trouble, he hopes someone will be kinder to her than she's been to Aunt Julie.

Upstairs Julie calls Halpern House and identifies herself as the sister of Reverend Camden, who does counseling there. She arranges to check herself in the next day. When she hangs up, Mary is standing in the doorway. Mary asks if she's going to join them for Thanksgiving dinner. But Julie shakes her head, thinking that the kids all hate her. She sees that Mary has her bag of cosmetics and assumes Mary's returning her present, too. But instead, Mary reveals that she's come to do a little makeover. . . .

When Eric and Annie come down later, the dinner looks wonderful—even if they can't identify all the foods! They all sit down, and then Mary brings Julie in, all spruced up. The girls run over and hug her and compliment her. "Are you all better now?" Simon asks. "No," Julie admits, "but I've made a start." Annie says grace, giving thanks that "He filled the pain of her mother's loss with the joy that comes from helping others in need." Then, with all the wineglasses filled with water, the Camden family happily digs into a wonderful Thanksgiving dinner.

Now You See Me

written by Charles Lazer; directed by Harvey Laidman

Simon's trying to become invisible through mind control. Matt has a new girlfriend, but does she really like him—or his family? Eric and Annie help the girl deal with divorcing parents, and make time to rekindle their own romance. Mary puts down Lucy for trying out for the cheerleading team.

Season 1: Episode 10

It's Sunday morning in the Camden house. Simon is upstairs practicing a new skill—invisibility, which he believes he can achieve "thanks to Ninja mind control." Matt's in front of the mirror, working on hair control because he's taking a date to church. Mary frowns when Lucy says she's interested in trying out for the cheerleading squad. "Cheerleading is stupid," Mary says. According to her definition, it's not a sport. Then Matt comes out of the bathroom and nearly runs Simon over. "Didn't see you," he says, to Simon's delight.

After church Matt introduces his date, Tia, to Eric and Annie. Impressed, Annie invites Tia to dinner. Then Simon catches a ride home with Matt and Tia, where he tells her about his quest for invisibility. Tia says she thinks it can be done.

At home, Annie and Eric prepare dinner together. Annie comments that watching Matt and Tia together reminds her of old times with Eric. Romantic times.

Out in the backyard, Lucy asks Mary to help her practice for cheerleading, but instead Mary gives her a big lecture about how cheerleading "trivializes" women and women's sports. Tia joins them and says she always thought it would be wonderful to have brothers and sisters.

At the dinner table, Tia asks Eric to recite again the lines from Robert Frost's poem "The Homecoming" that he used in his sermon: "Home is the place where when you have to go there, they have to take you in." When he does, tears well in Tia's eyes and she abruptly excuses herself from the table and hurries to the living room. Matt follows her and discovers why the poem touched her so deeply: Tia's parents are going through a divorce. She tells Matt he doesn't realize how lucky he is to have such a wonderful family.

The next day Matt drops Tia off at her dad's, where he's surprised to learn she has her own car. Tia invites him in and tells him that her dad is away, but Matt says he needs to go home to study. When he invites her to join him, she says she'll drive herself over.

At Lucy's school, she overhears a couple of girls saying that she doesn't have the skills to make the cheerleading team. Hurt and embarrassed, she races out to meet Matt, who's picking her up. She confesses how hurt she is that her friends think she can't make the team. But Matt reassures her that, with some helpful training from him, she can do miracles. Just then Simon pops up from behind her seat, boasting that he was invisible. Lucy's angry that he overheard her private conversation with Matt.

That evening Annie opens the door to find Tia with her

mom, Ellen, who's talking business on a cell phone. Ellen finishes her call first, then greets Annie, explaining that she's constantly working because she's in real estate. She's quick to let Annie know that she's relocating to a singles' apartment and would appreciate an introduction to any single men Annie and Eric might know through the church. Tia is embarrassed by her mother's frankness that she's already looking for a new husband.

Later Eric picks up Mary at basketball practice and suggests that Mary go a little easier on Lucy when it comes to cheerleading. After all, when it comes to sports, Lucy is Mary's biggest fan.

At the house, Matt and Tia study in the living room until Eric and Annie stick their heads in and say good night—a polite signal that it's time for Tia to go. Matt and Tia kiss good night, then Tia leaves. But at 2:30 in the morning, the phone rings. It's Tia's father, Bob Jackson, and he tells Eric that Tia never came home. Eric and Annie search the house, then notice her car parked in the driveway. They find Tia sleeping in her car. "I was going to drive home in the morning," Tia says, and explains that by then, her dad's date for the evening would be gone. Eric asks her if she's told her dad how she feels about his dates staying over, but Tia says she doubts he'd care what she thinks. Annie makes up a bed on the couch for Tia while Eric phones her dad.

The next morning Eric makes an appointment to see Tia's dad. They meet in Jackson's posh law office, but they're constantly interrupted by phone calls and never get to talk. Jackson suggests they make another appointment, and suddenly Eric better understands how Tia must feel around her parents: practically "invisible."

Matt watches Lucy work on her cheerleading routines after school, then goes home to discover Tia hanging out with Mary. She's even given her an expensive leather jacket, explaining that her mom bought it for her but it doesn't fit. When Matt runs into Simon upstairs, Simon suggests that maybe Tia doesn't just like Matt, she likes being a part of their family—and maybe Tia wants to be adopted. Matt realizes this may be the truth.

The next day the Camdens all attend cheerleading tryouts to cheer Lucy on. The thing Lucy's been worrying about, her small size and light weight, turns out to be an advantage—an invisible talent—when the team forms a human pyramid, with her on top.

Later, at the house, Annie has invited Tia's mother, Ellen, over to meet someone. Then the doorbell rings, and the person Eric brings into the room is Bob Jackson. Then Tia enters, and Eric explains that both parents need to be reintroduced to her.

Tia uses the opportunity to tell them that even though they are divorcing, she still loves them both. Eric reminds Ellen and Bob how important it is to make sure their child feels loved, regardless of their feelings toward each other. Ellen and Bob admit that he's right, and for the first time in years, it seems, Ellen and Bob agree on something.

Upstairs, Lucy shows Mary her cheerleading sweater. And Mary makes a peace offering to Lucy: a sports bra to wear while she's cheerleading.

After Tia and her parents leave, Annie and Eric spread a blanket on the rooftop and open a picnic basket containing champagne and glasses. Eric strums an old tune from their courting days on his guitar—visibly rekindling the affection he and Annie share in their marriage.

With a Little Help from My Friends

written by Brenda Hampton & Jack LoGiudice; directed by Burt Brinckerhoff

Matt helps Mrs. Bink, but she makes him keep it a secret. Eric helps out a church family who's lost everything. Lucy's angry that she can't have a boy-girl party for her thirteenth birthday, and Happy finally has puppies!

Season 1: Episode 11

"It probably has something to do with a girl," Simon says when Eric expresses disappointment at Matt's absence from church services. In a way, Simon's right, but the girl is an elderly Mrs. Bink, who has asked for Matt's help at her house. While Matt stands on a stepladder, replacing a lightbulb, Mrs. Bink swears him to secrecy about her need for help. She doesn't want anyone to think she's ready for an old folks' home.

The next day, Happy barks at the door from outside, and Simon lets her in, upset that she's out alone when she's expecting puppies any minute. But Annie reassures him: Dogs don't need to birth puppies in a hospital, like humans. They know instinctively what to do.

Meanwhile, Lucy is brooding on the phone. She commiserates with her boyfriend, Jimmy Moon, that her mom and dad won't allow a boy-girl party on her thirteenth birthday. When she gets to school, she finds out that their mutual friend Dwight is planning a party for the same day, which happens to be his birthday, too—a remarkable coincidence.

Matt evades Eric and Annie's questions about why he wasn't in church the day before and asks his parents to trust him. Seeing Matt's discomfort, Eric changes the subject to Steve, a church member whose family is going through some very tough times financially. Annie comments with a smile that Eric has been breaking things at church so that he can pay Steve to fix them.

At the high school, someone identifying herself as "Aunt Gladys" calls the principal's office for Matt Camden and claims that it's an emergency. Matt discovers that it's just Mrs. Gladys Bink. Mrs. Brogan, the office secretary, insists that Matt go, and take Mary with him, since it's a family matter. When Matt and Mary arrive at Mrs. Bink's, they find she doesn't remember why she called. Matt wants to get his dad involved in finding help for Mrs. Bink, but she balks, fearing she'll be placed in an institution.

After school Dwight comes by to ask Annie's permission to have Lucy attend his birthday party—she ought to be there, he explains, because he's Jimmy Moon's best friend. He explains that she already said no at school because of a conflict in her family schedule that day. Lucy comes home and feels humiliated to find that Dwight is trying to trick her into coming, and she runs upstairs. Annie asks Matt and Mary to help talk her into going.

Later Eric gets a call from the high school about "Aunt Gladys," and Matt and Mary have to confess they left school to help a friend, although they don't want to identify her beyond that. Eric and Annie discuss the situation and decide not to press for now.

Meanwhile, Happy's had puppies!

Upstairs Mary tries to convince Lucy to go to Dwight's party, but Lucy says it's no fun to go to someone else's party on your own birthday. Besides, she's decided they're not part of the "cool" group. If she was having a party, she'd invite all the cool kids.

Mrs. Bink calls the house and asks Matt to help her get a can from a top shelf; he tells her it'll have to wait until after school because he's already in trouble for cutting classes. Mrs. Bink says she'll manage, hangs up, and pushes a rickety stepladder across the floor. She climbs it, reaches for the can, and falls.

Eric visits Steve, whose family is living in a van because they lost their house. He turns down Eric's offer to stay at the Camdens, asking only to be remembered in prayer. Eric is impressed that, even after losing his job and his home, Steve hasn't lost his faith.

At the supper table that night, Lucy tells the family she declined Dwight's invitation by phone and has sadly decided to forfeit any kind of celebration for her birthday. Comparing Lucy's problems to those of Steve's family, living in a van, Eric loses his temper momentarily. Then the phone rings—it's a call from the hospital for Matt; Mrs. Bink has been admitted.

Annie and Eric hurry to the hospital with Matt, who explains her situation and the reason for his mysterious behavior. At the emergency room, Dr. Weisman tells them the main problem with Mrs. Bink is the way she's mixing medications. Suddenly Eric gets an idea; he convinces Mrs. Bink to take in Steve's family in exchange for some help around the house.

Once Mrs. Bink is home from the hospital, it doesn't take too long for her and Steve's family to take to one another. Mrs. Bink even comes up with the idea of converting her garage into an apartment for them, so they won't have to live in the van.

Meanwhile, Lucy gets a surprise at school: Dwight's party was intended for her all along—but now it's off because she refused to go! Jimmy says he's going over to poor Dwight's after school anyway. Lucy says they can both come to her house, but Jimmy figures Dwight wouldn't be interested and counters, "You wouldn't come to his house."

That night the Camdens have a quiet dinner at home, and then Annie sends Lucy into the living room for cake and a big surprise. All her friends from school are there! The party Dwight planned is on again, at the Camdens!

Later, after the party, Lucy lies in bed thinking. A funny thing happened, which she tells Mary: "Dwight told me he loves me." Lucy's not sure how she feels about it, but Mary assures her it'll all work out.

Suddenly the whole Camden family is in the room, with gifts for Lucy. "I thought the party was my gift," Lucy says, but she's ecstatic to realize there's more. But after opening all the presents, she realizes the best gift of all are the people around her.

Season 1: Episode 12

The Camdens are at the airport, awaiting the arrival of Eric's parents, Grandma Ruth and the Colonel, who are coming for a one-week stay. Ironically, while everyone pretends they're glad to get together, no one on either side of the family is really comfortable with the visit.

Once they're home, Matt coaches the younger children out in the garage on how to "survive" the week ahead: "Never make eye contact, keep moving, and never show fear." The same rules you'd follow with attack dogs, in other words.

Privately, the Colonel complains to Ruth how the Camden kids "push the envelope on perky." He and Ruth are both grateful when Annie invites them to accompany her to the hardware store. It's not a totally clean getaway from the kids, however, as Lucy invites herself along.

At the hardware store, Annie notices an unusual necklace worn by the owner, the widow Emma Hutton. It's two gold rings on a chain, and, oddly, they look very much like a pair that was taken from Annie in an armed robbery several months ago. Annie asks about the rings, which Emma says were a gift from her son. They leave, but Annie remains convinced the rings are hers. Grandma Ruth figures the hardware store owner's son was the armed robber.

At Eric's office, the Colonel pays a visit to inquire about Julie, his daughter. Eric says she's making progress at a rehab center, where she's being treated for alcoholism. "It's a good thing you kids never tried the Marine Corps," the Colonel comments. "You wouldn't have lasted two minutes." Then he spots a pair of feet below a rack of choir gowns. He pulls the gowns back to reveal George, an orphan who has run away from several foster homes. Concerned, Eric invites the boy to stay at the Camden house until alternative arrangements can be made.

The Colonel is surprisingly friendly toward the boy, who he regards as a "tough survivalist." Privately, with Ruth, he even discusses adopting George. Coincidentally, Eric and Annie are discussing the same thing downstairs. They even call a family meeting in the garage to see what the kids think.

Meanwhile, George knows what's going on. He mentions it to the Colonel, who finds the idea of Eric and Annie adopting George totally impractical—they already have their hands full. He says as much to Eric, privately, and they argue over the style of parenting that the Colonel used on Eric and Julie. Then the Colonel and Ruth leave in a borrowed car, to do some "errands."

They're not gone long when Annie gets the idea they've gone

Seven Is Enough

written by Ron Zimmerman & Catherine LePard; directed by Harry Harris

Eric's parents come to visit, opening up old wounds—especially when the two households make separate plans to adopt an orphan named George. A woman at the hardware store is wearing presents from her son, and Annie's convinced they're her stolen wedding rings.

back to the hardware store for her rings—it would be just like Ruth and the Colonel to "take charge." She sends Eric over, and although he doesn't find Ruth and the Colonel, he does get a look at the necklace and has a word with Emma. But the widow is adamant about keeping the beloved gift from her son.

Meanwhile, Ruth and the Colonel have indeed taken charge, but of a different matter. They've gone to the Kensington Home to discuss the adoption of George. Mrs. Kleric is very encouraging.

Later, Ruth and the Colonel announce their plans at the Camden's supper table. Eric objects strongly, criticizing the Colonel's "tough love" style, on which he blames his sister Julie's alcoholism. Both men storm out, and Annie is blunt with Ruth

heartbroken, but the Colonel says it's for the best. Here, he says, George can follow the example of Eric and, with luck, grow up to be just like him. Eric and Annie overhear him from the hallway.

Meanwhile, Matt's at the hardware store, telling Emma about the robbery and how it affected his mother. She is moved by his words, and at last turns the rings over to him.

Back at the house, Grandma Ruth shares something with Lucy— the Colonel's first love letter to her, saved in a yellowing envelope.

As the Colonel and Ruth prepare to go, Eric comes to them and hands over George's adoption papers. The boy is delighted. It's a happy ending after all.

Then, from out of the blue, a man from the mall arrives with news: Simon Camden has won a Viper sports car in a drawing! But

about her feelings: "You're not terribly supportive, and it shows in a lot of hurtful ways," Annie says. "You're a little distant and opinionated, your jokes are cruel, you're formidable and awfully tough on people." She also comments that Lucy has recently lost her other grandmother and so has been trying hard to bond with Ruth, but with no luck. Ruth thanks her for her honesty and says she'll try to do better, starting with showing more kindness to Lucy.

Upstairs, the Colonel tells George he's leaving. George is

when the man realizes that Simon is underage, and thus disqualified, Simon convinces him to let Eric take him for a drive around the block.

"I can't believe I'll be teaching you to drive soon," Eric says to Simon.

"Your brother, too," Simon says. "George is your brother now, right?"

"Now that you mention it, I guess he is," Eric says, dazed.

"Poor George," Simon quips.

America's Most Wanted

written by Brenda Hampton;
directed by Mark Jean

Eric's upset that nobody knows how
to sing "The Star-Spangled Banner"
anymore. Mary gives in to a class
ritual and steals a glass from
a local restaurant—but Matt takes
the fall and goes to court.
Lucy cheats in English by recycling
one of Mary's old essays.

Annie's reading Ruthie a bedtime story when Eric returns from a Golden Gloves boxing tournament. He's really upset that when "The Star-Spangled Banner" was played, no one seemed to know the words. It's a sign, he tells Annie, that the country's "basic moral fiber is being ripped and torn to shreds."

Once in bed, Ruthie tells Simon she has to learn "The Star-Stapled Banner" as soon as possible. "Piece of cake," Simon says, and begins the song: "Oh, say can you see . . ." Ruthie doesn't get it: "Who's Jose? . . . *Jose,* can you see?" Simon groans.

The next morning Annie gets up early and makes pancakes. At the table, Matt asks permission for Mary and himself to have dinner at the Varsity restaurant with John and Keesha Hamilton. Lucy, who isn't invited, calls it a classic case of "middle child left-out syndrome." As it turns out, she couldn't go even if she was invited—she hasn't even started her essay for Mrs. Penn's English class, and it's due the next day.

Meanwhile Simon's "Star-Spangled Banner" lessons continue with "what so proudly we hailed." Ruthie won't say "hail" because "it's a bad word." Simon tries to explain it's not *hell,* as in "Go to hell." Eric hears the last part and glares at his son, who tries to explain. Happily for Simon, Matt calls out that it's time to go to school.

Later, outside the high school gym, Mary is reminded by her teammate Corey that there's just one day left to participate in the "Great Theft" ritual—a ritual in which students are supposed to steal something from the Varsity restaurant. Top "honors" go for glasses bearing the Varsity logo. John and Keesha have agreed to go to dinner with Matt and Mary to help cover for Mary.

After school, before she and Matt leave for the Varsity, Mary gives Lucy an essay she wrote for Mrs. Penn when she was in the eighth grade. "Use all the same quotes and the references. Just write a new essay," she says, which will allow Lucy to skip the research work at the library. Later, at the restaurant, Mary nervously puts a glass in her purse. With Matt, John, and Keesha covering for her, she manages to leave without getting caught.

Things start to catch up with everyone the next day, though. Eric spots the glass in the kitchen, and Matt, cornered, takes the blame. Mary feels guilty about it, on top of feeling ashamed for being pressured to steal in the first place. Meanwhile, Lucy feels guilty for turning in a rewrite of Mary's old essay to Mrs. Penn.

Eric advises Matt to return the stolen glass to the Varsity's manager, Mr. Ryland, with an apology—which he does. But

Mr. Ryland is unsympathetic. He is so upset about the rash of stealing by other students that he decides to make an example of Matt, and he presses charges!

Later, Annie discovers Lucy's deception and advises her to confess to her teacher. Mrs. Penn is more forgiving and decides to give Lucy a second chance at writing her own essay. Lucy is pleased.

Eric goes to the Varsity on Matt's behalf, but Mr. Ryland is adamant in his decision to press charges. In the meantime, Matt goes to the Reverend Hamilton for advice and asks him not to reveal Mary's secret to their dad. But Reverend Hamilton tells Matt that, eventually, it will all come out anyway. Matt promises that he'll set things straight after the hearing. The reverend agrees to keep their secret, and he suggests he might be able to help at the hearing, although Matt can't imagine how.

In the courtroom, Judge Carnes presides over Matt's case. Before Matt can say anything, Eric interrupts on his behalf, which annoys the judge. Things aren't looking good when suddenly Mary makes a surprise confession. The judge looks to Annie and Eric, but the shock is evident on their faces.

Suddenly into the courtroom march dozens of kids, Mary's classmates and teammates, bearing boxes of glassware and other objects stolen from the Varsity. It's evident that everyone's decided to do the right thing and return what they've taken. Eric asks the judge and Mr. Ryland to be lenient—as long as the tableware is returned and the kids agree to do some work at the Varsity without pay. After the judge explains that it will take many trials to deal with all the evidence and defendants, and the proceeding could take weeks, Mr. Ryland reluctantly agrees to drop the charges.

Back at the house, there's one more surprise waiting for Eric, but this time the surprise is delightful: Ruthie sings a rousing "Star-Spangled Banner" perfectly, word for word. By the look on Eric's face, it's clear that he has reconsidered his earlier pronouncement: maybe the moral fiber isn't being ripped and torn to shreds after all.

Happy's Valentine

written by Brenda Hampton;
directed by David Semel

Season 1: Episode 14

Annie and Eric are invited by Patricia and Morgan Hamilton to go on a Valentine's Day overnight camping trip. Annie's all for it, despite Eric's reservations and the wrench it throws into the older kids' plans: Matt and John Hamilton have already planned for a double date, and Mary's invited two friends over to watch videos. But despite these complications, Annie's mind is made up.

At school, Matt and John try to foist responsibility for entertaining the younger kids off on Mary and Keesha Hamilton, but without success. So all the older kids have to pitch in. Matt and Mary decide the best plan is to divide and conquer: Matt, John, and their dates will get the den, while Mary and her friends will get the living room; Lucy will have to take Simon, Ruthie, and Nigel Hamilton along with her and Jimmy to the movies. Lucy agrees to the plan *after* they pay a ten-dollar bribe.

In the meantime, Simon packs Happy's puppies in a box for the trip to Dwight's house, which will be their new home. Then Annie and Eric congratulate Simon on his maturity about letting the puppies go, but they caution him about Happy. "Keep an eye on her," Annie says. "Make sure she doesn't go out looking for the puppies."

With no other alternative, Lucy makes baby-sitting plans with Jimmy; they decide to go to a multiplex where there's an animation retrospective that Simon, Ruthie, and Nigel would probably like. Coincidentally, there's a movie that *they* might like at the adjoining theater!

Dwight and his mom arrive and take the puppies, whom Dwight considers naming "Simon" and "Ruthie." Annie and Eric leave with Patricia and Morgan. Soon Jimmy arrives, and he and Lucy take Simon, Nigel, and Ruthie to the multiplex.

At the campground, Eric and Morgan are complaining about the inconveniences of camping when Morgan's beeper goes off. After Eric produces a cell phone on which Morgan can return the call, Morgan hands the phone to Patricia, who walks off a ways for privacy. Annoyed, Morgan reveals that it's a Valentine's Day phone call from her first husband. They married right out of high school and divorced after a year, but Morgan complains that the man still calls on their "anniversary."

Back at the Camden house, there's a party in full swing. The friends whom Mary invited brought their boyfriends, and Matt, John, and their dates have joined in, too. It's a good thing Matt and John are there, because a little supervision is definitely needed when Matt spots one of the boys with a

Valentine's Day plans go awry when Eric takes the cell phone camping and the kids try to combine baby-sitting and a party. Happy gets hurt.

beer and John warns an older boy away from his sister, Keesha.

At the movies, Lucy and Jimmy exchange Valentines. Lucy's is romantic and says, "All my love on this first Valentine's Day together." Jimmy's, on the other hand, takes a different tone and reads, "If a pretty girl is like a melody, how come you're such a strain?" Jimmy explains he went with a light card, "since it was a heavy movie." Lucy is not amused.

Meanwhile, the mood at the campsite has chilled, and not because the sun has gone down. Patricia goes to bed, and Eric apologizes to Morgan for bringing the phone. He thought he'd call the kids, he explains, but now he doesn't want to make them feel as if he doesn't trust them. Morgan suggests they call Sergeant Michaels and ask him to drive by the house.

At the animation retrospective, Simon and Nigel throw popcorn until an usher spots them and escorts them out. Then he helps Simon find Lucy, just as Jimmy's about to give her a Valentine's kiss.

Meanwhile, Sergeant Michaels is at the door of the Camden house, looking on with disapproval at some of the boys drinking beer—one of them his own son. Then he tells Matt shocking news: Happy was found in the street in front of the house—she's been hit by a car!

Although Eric and Annie are having a great time, they decide that, just to be safe, they'll phone home and check on the kids. But just as Eric hands her the phone, it rings, and it's Sergeant Michaels. He tells Annie the bad news: Matt and Mary are at the animal hospital with Happy, who has been hit by a car. The emergency only exacerbates the tension between Patricia and Morgan as the campers pack up and leave.

According to the vet's advice, Matt and Mary return home, where it's Matt's unpleasant duty to tell Simon what happened. "I hate you!" Simon screams at Matt. "You were supposed to be watching her!" But what can Matt say or do? He agrees to drive Simon to the animal hospital.

That's where Annie, Eric, and the others find them—Matt looking remorseful and Simon asleep on the table with Happy. Eric and Annie agree to hold off until morning on disciplining the many children involved with the night's escapades. It's not until several hours later, at daybreak, that they know Happy's condition.

"You're going to have to watch her closely for the next twenty-four hours," the doctor says, but then he confirms she's going to be all right after all. The family gathers around to breathe a sigh of relief, their exasperations and guilts mixed with welcome exclamations of joy.

disapproves. Mary tells him that she's turned Michael down, but that it's none of his business.

Across town, Eric and Lucy are driving Lucy's friend Suzanne home after dinner at the Camdens. They arrive and wait for her to go inside her house, but she waves them on, explaining she has to use the back door to avoid tripping an alarm. They drive away, then return when Lucy discovers Suzanne's notebook still in the car. Oddly, they find Suzanne still waiting outside her home. Eric and Lucy get the feeling something isn't right.

The next morning Lucy tells Eric he should find out about Suzanne, but he's reluctant to pry when their beliefs about the situation are based only on gut feelings. Meanwhile, at the breakfast table, Ruthie's usual appetite is missing—and

Brave New World

written by Catherine LePard; directed by Harvey Laidman

Ruthie starts preschool, Lucy's friend Suzanne reunites with her father, and Mary's nemesis, Michael Towner, gets a head-dunk in the toilet.

Simon expertly identifies her condition as preschool "first-day jitters."

At school Lucy's concern about Suzanne grows when they meet in science lab later that day. For one thing, Suzanne is wearing the same shirt Lucy loaned her the day before at the house, when Suzanne spilled something on herself at dinner. Suzanne explains that her mom couldn't get their dry cleaning on account of car trouble. Then Lucy says she called Suzanne after they dropped her off, but Suzanne's mother said she wasn't home yet. Suzanne shrugs it off. "My mom's sort of a flake," she says.

At the high school, Mary hears from her friend Corey that Michael Towner has written some explicit graffiti about her in the boys' bathroom. Mary waits for the halls to clear, then slips inside and discovers it on one of the stall walls. It reads: "You're always sure to score with Mary Camden, she likes it one on one." As she cringes at the graffiti, she hears male voices approaching. Ducking into a stall, Mary hears that one of the voices belongs to Matt. When he sees the graffiti, he snaps, "I'm going to kill that guy."

After school, Lucy and Jimmy tail Suzanne to a low-income housing development—not at all the same building at which Lucy and her dad dropped Suzanne the night before. But Lucy finds Suzanne's name on the mailbox and decides this must be her real home. And the woman wearing a uniform who goes into the apartment—Suzanne's mother?—doesn't seem "flaky" at all.

At home, Mary asks Matt to forge Eric's signature on a tardy slip. She explains she got it hiding in the bathroom, where she happened to overhear his threat toward Michael Towner. "I can handle him on my own," she assures him.

In the kitchen, Eric and Annie marvel at the form Ruthie brought home from preschool for their signature: a notice prohibiting "firearms, knives, razors, blackjacks, chains, or whips" at preschool. Then Simon comes in and asks Annie not to kiss him good-bye on school grounds anymore as it makes him look like a "mama's boy" in front of his friends. Ruthie comes in, shocked to learn there's preschool again. Angry at Simon for not telling her, she hits him in the arm. Eric and Annie are shocked and demand to know where she learned that: At school, Ruthie says, and adds that she's never going back.

Lucy interrupts Eric in his study to tell him what she found out about Suzanne's "double address," prompting Eric to visit Suzanne's mother the next day. As it turns out, there's a simple explanation: Suzanne's mom, Pam, and dad, Bill, have divorced, forcing Pam to get a job as a maid. Because Bill doesn't pay child support or alimony, the government-sponsored housing they live in is all they can afford. Unfortunately, Suzanne comes home before Eric has had a chance to leave, and she is embarrassed.

When Simon learns that Ruthie has made a new friend at preschool who's a *boy*, he worries about what kind of influence this person, whose name is Skyler, might have on his sister. It's a lot like the way Matt feels toward Mary—their argument over what to do about Michael Towner continues.

Eric visits Suzanne's dad, where he works at a used-car dealership. Bill Sanders is defensive when Eric questions him about child support, and the meeting ends on a sour note. Later Eric and Lucy run into Bill again at the pool hall. Bill accuses Eric of flaunting what a proper father-daughter relationship should be, then challenges Eric to a game of pool for money. At first, Eric refuses, then changes his mind when Lucy puts in her allowance money to help match Bill's impressive bet. Eric quickly wins a substantial amount, which he intends to take to Suzanne's mother. At home, he tells Annie that the money is almost like "child support" from Bill.

That's exactly what the money becomes when Eric finds Bill on the steps to Pam's apartment. He's had a change of heart and wants to see Suzanne. Eric gives Sanders the money to deliver himself, and the effect on Suzanne is worth ten times as much. To her, it's a sign that her dad really loves her.

At the high school the next day, Mary and two girlfriends follow Michael into the boys' bathroom and corner him, demanding that he mark through his graffiti about Mary. He scoffs and lets the pen she tosses at him fall to the floor. When he bends down to pick it up to return as a "parting gift," Mary dunks his head in a toilet and flushes—a show that's a big hit with the crowd that's gathered behind her in the bathroom!

At the Camden house, Simon meets Skyler and, more important, Skyler's older sister. As suddenly as Simon disapproved, now he's all for Ruthie's new friendship.

Later, at a meeting in the high school principal's office, Michael Towner's parents threaten to file assault charges against Mary. In response, Miss Russell asks Mary if she wants to file sexual harassment charges against Michael. When Michael's father alleges that Miss Russell is biased, she responds by claiming that sexual harassment was responsible for the entire confrontation, and that if the behavior continues, the punishment will be severe.

On their way out of the office, Eric tells Mary, "There's always going to be somebody who'll try to take your dignity and self-esteem. Just never let them take your voice."

Season 1: Episode 16

Mary stays after school for being tardy and meets Camille, who's there for smoking in the boy's locker room! Camille invites her to go to the mall later. Mary agrees to ask her parents, and Camille says it's time she "loosened up the reins a bit."

At home, a taxi brings a surprise visitor—Tom Harrison, a former assistant to Eric. When he pays the driver, Tom accidentally drops a fifty-dollar bill on the ground.

Over coffee, Tom tells Eric he is tired of his job as assistant pastor in Denver and asks whether Eric needs anyone. Eric says no, for budgetary reasons. When Tom is out of the room, he tells Annie he never liked Tom, that he seems to be hiding something. But Annie has already invited Tom to stay at their house while he's in town.

Lucy comes in for a talk with Eric. He tells her that at thirteen, she is eligible to begin her confirmation classes.

Outside, Simon and Ruthie find the money Tom dropped. They immediately begin to make spending plans.

Mary arrives home and asks for permission to go to the mall. Annie, who thinks she's just come from basketball practice, says okay. Privately, Matt cautions her about "wild" Camille.

Lucy talks to Tom about her confirmation class and he

Choices

written by Sue Tenney; directed by Kevin Inch

Mary chooses a friend from after-school detention. Simon and Ruthie select a pair of pesky ferrets for pets. An old acquaintance of Eric's reveals a deep secret and decides not to give up on himself.

advises her to choose her religion carefully. She is surprised to think there is more than one option.

In the hallway, Simon and Ruthie beg Eric to take them to the mall. Matt overhears and mentions that he is taking Mary and Camille there—maybe Simon and Ruthie can go along with them. Eric likes that idea; Mary is furious with Matt over suggesting it. Meanwhile, in the kitchen, Tom starts to talk to Annie about a problem, then decides not to. When she leaves the room, he takes a couple of pills from a bottle in his pocket. In the study, Lucy borrows a book on Buddhism from Eric, who is surprised to learn that Tom has suggested she examine other religions.

At the mall, Mary and Camille leave Simon and Ruthie in the pet store while they look at dresses in another shop. The pet store owner refuses to sell the young kids a pet without an adult, but Simon and Ruthie run into Ralph just outside, who is returning two ferrets. They buy them from him instead.

At home, Eric asks Annie along on a visit to a parishioner named Judy Calloway. She hasn't attended church services since her husband committed suicide six months before. Tom remembers them, and Eric invites him to come along with him and Annie. Tom says he has a problem with such situations, and he goes off to bed. Eric and Annie are puzzled.

Matt brings everybody home from the mall, unaware that Simon and Lucy are carrying ferrets with them. Mary goes upstairs and confides in Lucy her plans to sneak out to a frat party with Camille. She persuades Lucy to help her distract Matt so she can get out the door. Camille is waiting in her car, with a dress for Mary she has stolen from the shop in the mall.

Eric and Annie return home and ask Matt and Lucy about the other kids and Tom. Matt says Simon and Ruthie have been snacking a lot, and Tom's out on a walk. Lucy simply says Mary went straight upstairs after the mall trip, keeping her secret. Annie discovers chewed cereal boxes in the pantry and suspects they have mice.

At Eddie's Pool Parlor, Tom has several soft drinks and then discovers his fifty-dollar bill is missing.

At the fraternity house, Camille gets a sexy kiss from a boy named Jason, then introduces Mary to Max. As they open beers, Mary is shocked to find out the "frat party" is just "for the four of them." Then Camille and Jason head upstairs, leaving Mary and Max alone.

Back at the house, Simon and Ruthie are stunned to discover the ferrets are missing from their box. Annie notices Happy acting strangely excited and wonders if it has anything to do with the "mice" in the kitchen.

Downstairs, Eric momentarily thinks he spots a couple of rats running by. Lucy comes in to borrow a book on Quaker beliefs. She worries that Eric might be offended, but he assures her he doesn't want her to feel pressured into his way of thinking.

At the frat house, Mary asks Camille to drive her home. Camille isn't ready to go and insists Max do it. He's had a few beers, though, and is in no condition to drive. Mary calls home and gets Lucy.

Annie screams when she sees ferrets in her lingerie drawer! Simon, Ruthie, and Happy rush in, and the kids confess they bought the ferrets to raise more and "pay their way through college." Matt interrupts to borrow the car because Lucy just got a call from a girl they know who got in a jam and needs a ride home from a certain party. Annie says okay.

Eric finds Tom at the church, praying. He tells Eric it seems God has put him "on hold," and explains his problem in Denver. Tom secretly suffers from epilepsy and had a massive seizure in church, badly scaring the congregation. Eric feels terrible about distrusting Tom and offers him a job at Glenoak, if that's what he wants. But Eric also thinks Tom should think twice about leaving the Denver job over having a seizure.

Matt arrives at the fraternity house and puts both Mary and Camille, who has been drinking, in his car. He takes both girls home.

Eric and Tom return home and hear about the ferrets, which Annie has managed to capture. They're in a strong box, with air holes, ready to be taken back to the store. When Tom hears how the kids bought them with their "found money," he doesn't say he lost fifty dollars in the driveway. But he does ask if he can take the ferrets with him when he returns to Denver.

Mary and Matt enter, and Mary confesses everything to Annie. Annie's really mad and puts Mary on restriction from phone calls, TV, and social activities for a month. Lucy gets two weeks for being an accomplice.

A little while later Mary goes to Matt's room to thank him for helping her. He warns her about associating with kids like Camille, and promises he'll be watching her from now on. Eric overhears from the hallway and nods approvingly. Then he sticks his head in the girls' room and says good night to Lucy. When he says "Goodnight, Mary" and Lucy fakes for Mary, who's still in Matt's room, Eric gives her a stern look. She tells Eric she'll be in confirmation class bright and early Sunday.

In the church, Tom rehearses a sermon that he expects to deliver when he gets back to Denver. Present for the rehearsal are the Camdens and Judy Calloway, who has decided to start attending church again.

Eric is very glad Tom paid them a visit after all.

Faith, Hope, and the Bottom Line

written by Catherine LePard; directed by Burt Brinckerhoff

Season 1: Episode 17

Eric is at the Glenoak Community Job Fair, interviewing for a new church organist. He meets Ron Kramer, who seems perfect for the job. Ron is surprised: most people are turned off by the part of his application that reads "training at Wilder Correctional Facility." Eric assures Ron that this is not a problem for him.

The problem for Eric is the Vestry meeting he's late for. He's up for the job of treasurer, and the committee is waiting at his house. Annie makes excuses, but finally one of the members, Lou Dalton, loses patience and nominates Annie for Eric's position. Before she knows it, she's the new treasurer.

The next morning, as Annie is making school lunches beside a stack of church paperwork, Eric wonders if she can manage both church and family responsibilities. As proof of Annie's already busy schedule, Ruthie complains that she's got the wrong dessert in her lunch, and Simon needs a ride to the doctor's office after school for the tetanus shot before he plays Little League. Annie reminds Eric that the last treasurer had a full-time job, too.

Eric says he can take Simon for his shot, but Simon com-

plains, "You hum and tap your foot real fast" in the waiting room, which makes him extra nervous. He prefers Matt, who may be nervous, too, but "hums better."

Upstairs, Simon's real reason for preferring Matt to Eric comes out: They can skip the doctor's office by checking the "yes" box beside "tetanus shot" on the Little League application. Meanwhile, Mary tells Lucy her true motive for agreeing to tutor Lucy's boyfriend, Jimmy Moon, in science—she wants him free to keep Lucy occupied this summer, not stuck in summer school.

Later that morning Ron Kramer auditions at the church. He plays well, and everybody likes him—except Lou Dalton, who doesn't trust him because he's served time. Eric insists the man was honest enough to list it on his application, and deserves a second chance.

That afternoon Matt and Simon are in the waiting room at the doctor's office, feeling uncomfortable. Simon thinks perhaps the office thermostat is broken, which is why the boys decide to leave and put the tetanus shot off until the next day.

At the church Lou Dalton discovers Ron Kramer trying to dislodge the front doors, which are actually locked. Embarrassed, Ron explains he was only coming back to borrow a hymnal so he could practice. Lou, who's been lobbying

Annie becomes church treasurer, and the tight budget becomes a test of faith. Eric tries to hire an ex-prisoner as church organist. Matt and Simon face tetanus shots. Lucy becomes jealous when Mary tutors Jimmy Moon. Ruthie learns emergency numbers in preschool.

the Vestry to install a new security system—instead of hiring a new organist—is suspicious. He finds Eric in a church office and warns him that by supporting Ron, Eric may be putting his own job at risk.

Saturday morning Annie rushes to complete the church budget while Eric does after-breakfast cleanup. He's curious about whether Annie's made room in the budget for an organist, but she won't say. She surprises Eric, too, when she says she agrees with Lou that a full-time organist is not a church necessity.

Upstairs, Matt looks for Simon. It's time to go to the doctor, but Simon claims that his door is jammed and he can't get out. Ruthie, who's been memorizing emergency telephone numbers in preschool, calls 911. Minutes later two policemen arrive and pound on Simon's door. Simon moves the chair that's holding his bedroom door closed and opens up to find two large policemen staring down at him. The police remind Ruthie that emergency numbers are only for emergencies, and Simon and Matt promptly head for the doctor's office. Once there, Matt is stunned to hear that he needs a booster shot, too, and begins to protest loudly until . . . he discovers the nurse has already given him the shot. Simon smiles and hands his big brother a sucker.

Downstairs, Jimmy Moon arrives with a prepared statement for Lucy. She's become jealous of him and Mary spending time together in their tutoring sessions. But Jimmy says that she should have had more faith in him and Mary. Lucy agrees.

In the kitchen Simon tosses an empty pizza box into the trash, complaining that if his mother had a "real" job, they could eat like kings every day. Eric reprimands him by saying Annie *does* have a real job: taking care of a home, six people, and a dog seven days a week, twenty-four hours a day. Matt asks Eric if he hired Ron Kramer. Eric replies that he left a message and can only hope that Ron shows up for Sunday service.

Early Sunday morning Annie gives the treasurer's report and suggestions regarding the church's very tight budget. In her opinion, "the greatest risk we face is the danger of losing our faith in others." They must not, she tells the congregation, sacrifice their mission to lend a "helping hand to those in need, for the sake of building maintenance." She continues by saying, "With this budget, we decide what kind of people we want to be." Eric and the rest of the family grin proudly.

Then the choir marches in and begins to sing. No organ music is heard, though, until the last minute—when Ron rushes in from a late city bus. As music fills the church, even Lou Dalton has to agree that Ron deserves a second chance.

It's About George . . ..

**written by Ron Zimmerman;
directed by Harry Harris**

Eric's alcoholic sister, Julie, is
released from the rehab center,
but the stress of a visit from their
parents threatens her sobriety. Eric
discovers George's birth father, and
the crisis that ensues helps Julie
rediscover her father, the Colonel.

Season 1: Episode 18

Eric's sister, Julie, is ready to be released from the Halpern House Rehab Center, where she's been treated for alcoholism. She's greeted there by her parents, Ruth and the Colonel, their newly adopted son, George, plus Annie and Matt. George is only ten, but he tells his new sister that she can always count on him.

At the pool hall, Eric is shooting a game with Eddie, the owner. Eric's waiting to meet Will Grayson, an ex–undercover cop who is coming out of hiding after ten years in a witness protection program. He arrives and asks Eric to help him find his son, who was placed in the Kensington Home orphanage after his wife died in childbirth. The boy's name, he reveals, was George. Eric is stunned. He worries that Will's son and George may be one and the same.

At the Camden house, Lucy, Matt, and Mary improvise a skit about their grandparents, the Colonel and Ruth, for Lucy's boyfriend, Jimmy Moon. The performance portrays the grandparents as strict and severe, which makes Jimmy extra nervous about meeting them.

The group arrives home from the rehab center and sets Julie up in Lucy and Mary's bedroom. The two sisters plan to sleep on the floor so Ruthie and Aunt Julie can use the beds. George, meanwhile, is using Ruthie's bunk—sharing the room with Simon—while the Colonel and Grandma Ruth move into Eric and Annie's room. Even Eric and Annie have to adjust, and are sharing a single bed in Matt's room.

Later Annie takes everyone to the garage to see the fishing boat she's building for the Colonel and George. But when she unveils it, everyone laughs at how small it is—everyone but George and the Colonel. The Colonel tells an old war story about a homemade Jeep top that everyone poked fun at . . . until it saved his life in Korea. Annie is grateful for his unexpected insight.

That night Eric tells Annie about Will Grayson's search for his son, and that he's both worried and convinced it's George.

The next day the Colonel and Grandma Ruth are introduced to Jimmy Moon, who is as nervous as a new recruit before a commanding officer. Just for fun, the grandparents play their roles to the hilt, all the way to the command "Dismissed!" After Lucy and Jimmy run out of the room,

unaware that it was a joke, the Colonel and Ruth burst into laughter. But their mood changes abruptly when Eric takes them to the study and tells them about Will. The news is so upsetting to them that the Colonel storms out of the room and Ruth actually slaps Eric. Then Eric discovers George in the room and realizes that he's heard every word. But George, as always, takes the situation in stride.

Eric takes George to the pool hall for a meeting with Will. It seems to go well until Eric dismisses George briefly so he and Will can have a little "grown-up talk." That's when George disappears. Eric finds him at church, where the Colonel first discovered him, and they have a talk. George explains that he doesn't want to choose sides; he likes his adoptive parents and his blood father as well. He asks Eric to take him back to the orphanage. But Eric responds that, while George faces a tough decision, the two will get through it together.

Back home, Eric's news is hitting everyone hard. Confused and upset, Grandma Ruth blames Julie for everything: if she hadn't gone into rehab, they would never have come to visit, which would have kept them from finding George. After Ruth walks out of the room, Julie reaches for a drink. But Matt comes in and stops her. He points out the kitchen window—the Colonel sits dejected in Annie's unfinished boat. Matt tells Julie, "That's what you need," a warm relationship with her dad, not a temporary high from alcohol. Julie pours out the drink she almost took, then joins her dad in the boat.

Finally Eric calls a family meeting in his study and presents a bold plan: He suggests that his parents let George and his real father, Will, come live in the guest house on their property back East. The Colonel snorts that the neighbors will think they're running some kind of commune! But Ruth insists that it's a wonderful idea. George will fly back with the Colonel and Ruth. Will volunteers to strap the boat to his car and drive it cross-country. And he invites Julie to ride along with him.

Annie and Eric have one thing they want Julie to see before she goes: Mary and Matt's "famous" impersonation of Grandma Ruth and the Colonel. Reluctantly they agree, then discover their grandparents have crept up to watch! But as it turns out, the "stern" grandparents have mellowed out more than anyone could have expected: The Colonel and Ruth break out into laughter and wrap their grandchildren in warm hugs.

Say Good-bye

**written by Brenda Hampton
& Sue Tenney;
directed by Gabrielle Beaumont**

Ruthie's invisible friend, Hoowie,

disappears after Simon

"sits on him." Annie's newly divorced

friend Rachel shows up and makes a

pass at Matt. Lucy's best friend,

Suzanne, announces she's moving.

And Mary gets a chance to

sing at a local coffeehouse.

Season 1: Episode 19

In the kitchen, Ruthie reminds Annie to put out breakfast for her invisible friend, Hoowie, too. The phone rings, and an old high school chum of Annie's, Rachel, is on the line. She tells Annie that she's divorced—again—and has rented a place in town. They make plans to get together. Then Annie hangs up to settle a quarrel between Ruthie and Simon—Simon just sat on Ruthie's invisible friend. "Now Hoowie's gone forever!" Ruthie cries.

That night a glamorous Rachel shows up at the door. When Matt answers, she at first mistakes him for Eric. She meets the Camdens and reveals that they'll practically be neighbors, since her place is so close by. She and Annie leave for a restaurant.

Upstairs, Simon tries to console Ruthie: "Maybe Hoowie isn't gone. Maybe he's at the airport loading luggage." But Ruthie rejects this idea—that was his old job. Eric tries to cheer Ruthie up about Hoowie, too, and gets more details about him: He's married to an astronaut who's in the space shuttle. In the backyard, Matt suggests he or Mary fix Rachel up with the coach at the high school.

Meanwhile, Lucy has received a call from her friend Suzanne—her mom has a good job interview coming up. Later Suzanne comes over to thank Eric for his part in helping her mom and dad, who are separated, to start talking again. When Matt offers to drive Suzanne home, they meet Annie and Rachel coming in, and Rachel bums a ride. After dropping Suzanne off, Matt heads for Rachel's. When they get to her apartment, alone, she invites Matt in. He declines but gets cornered into a "date" to see a band the following night.

The next morning Simon tells Lucy he heard Hoowie snoring in the night, but she won't believe him. "Hoowie's gone," she insists.

At school, Suzanne is missing. Lucy doesn't hear from her until that night, when she learns that Suzanne is, in fact, moving.

That night Mary invites herself along on Matt and Rachel's secret "date," and to Matt's relief, she is given permission to go. As it turns out, Rachel is a friend of the band. When their singer doesn't show, Rachel convinces Mary to take her place. Finally alone with Matt, Rachel drags him onto the dance floor, but Matt is uncomfortable with her overly flirtatious attentions.

When they get home, Mary scolds Matt for behaving

romantically toward Rachel—only to discover that Eric is sitting quietly at the kitchen table and has heard everything. Eric takes Matt aside, and Matt tells him what happened: "It was Rachel hitting on me, not the other way around." Eric tells Matt, who's just seventeen, to make it clear to Rachel that he's not interested.

The next morning Annie learns that Mary sang with the band, and disapproves when she learns Mary has been invited back to perform in another gig. Eric suggests he and Annie go to the show.

Upstairs, Ruthie and Simon continue to worry over Hoowie. Simon's been setting traps for him, but he doesn't think Ruthie appreciates it. Meanwhile, Lucy's depressed about separating from Suzanne when she moves. Annie sends her off with two pieces of leftover cake when Eric and Ruthie enter with news: There will be a farewell party for Hoowie that night.

While the kids are at school, Rachel shows up at the house to use the washing machine. She mentions to Annie that Matt made a pass at her but that Annie shouldn't worry—it was all very flattering to her. Annie is stunned. After school she confronts Matt, who apologizes—which only seems to confirm the charge.

Upstairs, Mary tries to console Lucy over losing her friend, while Simon tries to do the same for Ruthie, who's lost Hoowie. But a wonderful surprise is in store when Suzanne makes a surprise visit. She came to see Lucy one more time before moving, and to attend Hoowie's farewell. Ice cream is dished out, Eric gives a warm speech about the invisible man, and then—

"There he is!" Ruthie cries. Her invisible friend is back!

In the kitchen, Rachel, who has taken to heart the part of Eric's speech which dealt with dishonesty, privately apologizes to Annie for claiming that Matt made the pass. Instead, she acknowledges, she made the pass. After explaining that she's rebounding from her divorce, and found the young man's attentions flattering, Annie insists that she apologize to Matt, too.

In the foyer, Suzanne makes her own confession: She kissed Lucy's boyfriend, Jimmy Moon—back when they were in kindergarten. Lucy says it's okay, then mutters, "He's a dead man."

In the kitchen, Rachel apologizes to Matt for coming on to a teenager. Matt advises her to be less hard on herself—after all, he's learned in health class that going through a divorce is almost as emotionally disturbing as losing a parent. Matt starts to put his arm around her—then thinks better of it and shakes her hand.

At the coffeehouse, Eric and Annie go to Mary's show. She's a hit, especially with the men in the audience. To Mom and Dad it's a reminder that their fourteen-year-old is growing up, and they try their best to lean back and enjoy the show.

Dangerous Liaisons, Part 1

teleplay by Brenda Hampton & Ron Zimmerman; story by Brenda Hampton; directed by Harvey Laidman

Season 1: Episode 20

Grandpa Charles, Annie's dad, is flying from Arizona to visit the Camdens. It's his first visit since his wife, Annie's mom, died. Unknown to the Camdens, he's bringing his new girlfriend, Ginger. But he promises her that his family will love her just as they loved his wife.

While Annie and some of the younger kids get the house ready for Grandpa's visit, Eric and Matt wait at the airport for his plane. Matt asks an attractive stranger for change for a dollar, but she just smiles and keeps going. Matt is embarrassed to think she figured his question was a pick-up line.

Back at the house, Lucy thinks about coloring her hair blond, like the cover girl of a magazine she's confiscated from Simon. Simon points out the blond hair-coloring sample already inserted in her magazine.

Meanwhile, at the city park, Mary and Ruthie meet a young man named Wilson, who's with a one-and-a-half-year-old boy named Billy. Ruthie and Billy play, and before long, Wilson asks Mary for a date that night. "I'll have to ask my parents," Mary says, and gives him her phone number.

At home, Annie is stunned when Eric and Matt arrive not only with Grandpa, but with Grandpa's new *girlfriend*. As the family gets to know her over lunch, they find that Ginger seems very nice. But Annie is resentful that her father would be dating so soon after her mother's death. Later Simon learns from Grandpa that Ginger's family felt the same resentment about Grandpa. But Grandpa assures Simon that "no one can take the place of someone who's passed away."

That night, as Matt drives Grandpa and Ginger to their hotel, he spots the girl from the airport entering a house. Grandpa encourages Matt to stop and go to the door. The girl's mother introduces her as Heather, but does so in sign language. Matt realizes that's why she didn't answer him at the airport! Unfazed by the complication, Matt invites Heather, through her mom, to a party later that night.

Back at the house, Annie backs out of a dinner date she and Eric had with Grandpa, explaining that if he didn't feel the need to warn her about Ginger, she doesn't need to inform him that she's not coming to dinner. Then Wilson arrives, ready to take Mary out. Because it's a first date, Eric interviews Wilson in the foyer and is pleased when the responsible-sounding young man offers Eric his beeper number. Upstairs, Matt asks Simon if he can teach him any sign language from *Sesame Street*. Meanwhile, Lucy has tried the magazine hair-color sample—and her hair looks awful!

Later, Matt takes Heather to the party, but the date ends when she leaves the room in tears over some crude mock "sign language" gestures made by other boys. Across town Mary's date goes just as poorly when she trades insults with some bullies at the pool hall who make fun of Wilson. As it turns out, the fight she puts up hurts Wilson's pride—and he abruptly takes her home. Soon, everybody's home again, where Lucy continues to fret about her new hair color.

At last something good happens: Toward the end of the night, Ginger arrives at the front door to see if she can patch things up with Annie a little bit, and they make some progress.

The next day at church Mary is overjoyed to see Wilson attending with the same toddler she met in the park. Annie gets introduced to Wilson and Billy, then heads into the church. Alone with Mary, Wilson confesses that Billy is not his brother, but his son.

Suddenly Annie sees her dad and Ginger arrive and take a seat in the pews. Angry and frustrated, she turns and marches away from the sanctuary. Upset over her own situation, as well as Annie's, Mary runs out of the church and yells, "Mom! Wait!"

Annie turns just in time to see Mary running across the street after her—but it's too late. Car tires screech—Mary is hit by a car! Annie screams her daughter's name at the sight of Mary's body lying unconscious in the street.

After a car strikes Mary in front of the church, she waits at the hospital to undergo emergency surgery on her knee. Annie and Eric are with her, but they've told Matt and the other kids to stay at the house. Lucy's boyfriend, Jimmy Moon, shows up to find out about Mary's condition and practically goes into shock himself—over Lucy's new hair color. Eric calls and tells Matt the kids need a distraction. He tells Matt to take everyone to "that new café on Tenth Street."

Wilson shows up at the hospital to check on Mary. Grandpa shows up, too, just in time to hear Wilson lie to the receptionist that he is Mary's brother in order to get a report on her condition. Grandpa doesn't reveal the lie, though, and Wilson offers to pick up some take-out food for the Camdens while they await news from the doctor.

In the waiting room, Annie and Grandpa argue about Ginger. "I've seen you kinder and more polite to strangers than you were to Ginger," he scolds. Eric interrupts to say Mary is out of surgery, and Annie rushes down the hall to her room.

Matt and the other kids discover that the new café on Tenth Street is run entirely by people who are deaf. Looking around at the patrons signing to one another, Matt shakes his head. "Even with Mary in the hospital, Dad can find a way to teach me a lesson," he says.

Annie and Eric learn from Dr. Wolf that Mary will need some physical therapy but will recover. Wilson arrives with their take-out, and Mary, glad to see him, says she hopes his son, Billy, wasn't frightened. Eric and Annie figure she's still woozy from the operation. Why else would she call Billy Wilson's "son"?

At the Tenth Street Cafe, Matt spots Heather. He gathers his courage, asks a waiter how to sign "I'm sorry," and then signs his apology to Heather. Ruthie, who knows American Sign Language much better, from *Sesame Street*, signs "I love you" between them, and Heather smiles.

Once they're all home, Matt helps Lucy recover from Jimmy Moon's disapproval when he says he thinks her new hair color is "sexy." Pretty soon she's confident enough to tell Jimmy that if he doesn't like her hair, she'll find someone else who does.

At the hospital, Grandpa visits Mary and reveals that Ginger's gone home to Phoenix. He runs into the Camdens' friend Mrs. Bink, who offers him a ride back to his hotel. She tells him that when her husband died, she didn't remarry because of her daughter's wishes, and it was a big mistake. "She'll come around," she says of Annie. "Follow your heart."

Dangerous Liaisons, Part 2

teleplay by Brenda Hampton
& Catherine LePard;
story by Brenda Hampton;
directed by Harvey Laidman

Mary undergoes surgery,
Ginger goes home early, Matt
slugs Michael Towner, and Lucy
breaks up with Jimmy Moon.
And there's *still* a happy ending!

At the hospital, Mary receives a bouquet of flowers from Wilson, and Mary admits to Annie that she has the feeling that he's rather special. In the meantime, Wilson visits Eric at the church office and tells him all about his teenage marriage, which ended when Billy was born and his wife died. Eric is stunned, and unsure how to respond to Wilson's request that, in spite of these complications, he wants to continue to date Mary.

At the high school, Heather stops by to see Matt and ask about Mary. A fellow student, Michael Towner, shows up concerned about Mary, too. Then he reveals that he was the one driving the car that hit her. Unable to control his anger, Matt throws a punch that lands Michael on the floor. He looks around for Heather, but she's driven away.

At the Camdens', Grandpa tells Annie that he's on his way back to Phoenix. "I love you," he says, "but I can't let you run off Ginger like Mrs. Bink's daughter did." Annie replies, "I'm so sorry. I love you, too." The two share a warm hug.

A short while later Annie phones Mrs. Bink to say thank you, even though she thinks that "daughter" story was all made up. It was, Mrs. Bink admits, but adds that it worked—didn't it?

At the hospital, Michael Towner visits Mary and apologizes for the accident, but Mary doesn't blame him. Wilson arrives after that and tells Mary about his visit with her dad. "Our biggest problem is my mom," Mary tells him. "She's a lot tougher."

At the café on Tenth Street, Matt waits for Heather. He knows she was frightened by the way he punched Michael Towner, and he's not sure she'll come. To his relief, she does— and surprises him by speaking. She admits that speaking makes her nervous because she's unable to hear her own voice. She hands Matt her address and says that maybe they should get to know each other first by writing letters. Then she gets in her car and drives away.

Back at the house, Lucy is crying over the news that Jimmy Moon is now going out with Ashley. "You deserve better than him," Simon assures her. It's one thing to have a fight, he says, and quite another to fight and refuse to make up, as Jimmy has done.

The next day Mary is due home from the hospital, and everyone's at the house to greet her. Even Ginger, who flew all the way back from Phoenix, at Annie's request, and Heather, who has thought twice about the restriction she placed on her relationship with Matt.

Everyone rejoices as Mary comes home, and Wilson passes her the basketball. To everyone's delight, she throws a shot at the basketball hoop. Eric reveals to Annie that Dr. Wolf has warned him that Mary's road to recovery will be much more difficult than any of them expects. Annie's worried, but after a moment responds with confidence, "What do doctors know? She's playing basketball right now." The smile and look of determination on Mary's face tells Annie that if anybody can make a comeback from an injury like this, Mary can.

Season 2

It's a season of beginnings and endings. Eric and Annie become "newlyweds" for the second time. Matt's romance with Heather comes to a close; Annie starts a new business making muffins. Eric tries a new diet, and Mary gets off her crutches. While Lucy learns about death when a friend passes away, Simon is taught about the Holocaust. The Camden kids learn about drugs, and Matt decides to leave for a summer job. The Camden house is kind of like the weather: if you don't like what's happening at the moment, stick around, things are bound to change!

Don't Take My Love Away

written by Brenda Hampton; directed by Burt Brinckerhoff

Eric helps a woman who wants to talk with her husband's murderer. He and Annie celebrate their anniversary by getting married. Matt struggles to tell Heather good-bye; Lucy mourns her breakup with Jimmy; Ruthie tries to scare Simon so he won't move out of their room; and Mary is afraid to give up her crutches.

Nora Chambers stops by Eric's office and says her wedding anniversary is coming up. "Mine, too," Eric says, smiling. "This Saturday Annie and I have been married nineteen years." Nora sadly reminds her pastor that hers would have been twenty-five, but her husband, James, was murdered three years ago. She never got to talk to the teenager who killed her husband. She has written him many letters, but he has never responded. Eric promises to help.

When Nora leaves, Eric suddenly has an idea. He calls Annie and tells her he's coming home. "Something's up with Dad," Simon reports to all the kids, and they stampede downstairs just in time to see Eric rush in, drop to one knee, and say, "Annie, will you marry me?" The kids are flabbergasted. Weren't their parents already married?!

Later, in their bedroom, Eric and Annie—who are, of course, legally married—plan the big dream wedding they never had for this coming Saturday. Simon interrupts, worried the plans will prevent his mom from fixing up his new attic bedroom. "I can't go to junior high school and still be sharing a room with my little sister," he says. "Word would get around." Annie assures him she can have it ready. Then Ruthie comes in and reports that none of the other kids want to go to the wedding; it's the last weekend of the summer, and they all have other plans. Eric informs her that all the Camden kids have to go. Annie wonders if they're crazy to plan this ceremony. Yeah, Eric replies, but seeing Nora Chambers reminded him that "life is short, and we shouldn't put things off that we've always wanted to do."

When Mary comes home from her date with Wilson, he encourages her to try to walk without crutches, but she snaps at him and hurries inside. Upstairs, she finds Lucy crying—she can't face going back to school with everyone knowing that Jimmy is dating her former best friend, Ashley. "That's what life is all about," Mary snaps, "disappointment and failure. So get used to it."

Sitting in the car in front of Heather's house, Matt tells her he doesn't want her to go back to school. Just as they're about to kiss, somebody pounds on the hood of the car. It's a guy, and Matt is stunned when Heather jumps out and hugs him. It's the friend Heather told him is staying with her a few days before they drive back to school together. Matt hadn't realized her "friend" was a guy.

The next day Wilson drops by to take Mary to the pool to exercise her injured knee, but she doesn't want to go. Ruthie tells Matt she thinks Simon is moving out of her room because he doesn't like her anymore. Matt says it's just because he's growing up, but he gives her an idea that might keep Simon from leaving.

At the detention center, Eric tries to talk to Martin, the teen who murdered Nora's husband, but Martin snaps that he's paying his debt to society and doesn't owe Nora anything. He's had a bad life, a bad mother, no father. He was raised by a TV. "And all I learned from TV was how to kill people."

At home, Lucy calls Jimmy Moon to invite him to her parents' wedding. When he reminds her he's with Ashley now, Lucy winds up inviting her, too, then hangs up, frustrated. That's not what she meant to do! In a rotten mood, she and Mary try on their "stupid dresses" their mom is making them wear.

Ruthie puts her and Matt's plan into action: she warns Simon that there is a ghost in his new attic bedroom. She tells him what Matt told her to say: that the woman who died and willed the house to the church died right here, in the attic! Ruthie tries not to giggle as Simon seems to fall for her story.

When Eric comes home, he finds Lucy and Mary arguing as Annie makes adjustments to their dresses. He tells them that the wedding is supposed to be a happy event. Mary says she hopes her parents are having fun, because the rest of the family is not. Annie is getting fed up with the girls feeling sorry for themselves. First, she makes Lucy call and "uninvite" Jimmy and Ashley. Lucy leaves a message on his answering machine, but adds that Jimmy can come alone if he wants to. Then Annie makes Mary sit down with Wilson, who's been so supportive all summer, to work out their problems. Wilson is confused by Mary's hostile attitude until, in tears, she confesses she's tired of using crutches, adding, "But I'm afraid if I don't, I might fall."

That night Simon creeps up to the attic with Happy, trying to reassure himself about the ghost. When Annie comes in, they scare each other half to death. Annie tells him the ghost story isn't true, but Simon decides to move back in with Ruthie anyway.

Later Eric gets a call from Martin's social worker. He's agreed to see Nora Chambers tomorrow, Saturday. Eric promises to be

there, even though he's got a wedding to attend. The next morning, just as he's leaving, a package arrives. It's the "wedding present" Eric arranged for Annie. Inside is a note from her father: "I should never have let nineteen years go by without apologizing for everything we did to make you call off the first wedding. Congratulations on your anniversary!" Inside is Annie's mother's wedding dress—the one she was supposed to wear the first time but didn't. Annie's eyes fill with tears.

At the detention center, Eric and Nora meet with Martin. Martin says he never meant to kill anybody, but during the robbery her husband got in the way, trying to protect the store manager. It helps Nora to learn that her husband died a hero. As she leaves, she tells Martin she forgives him. Martin yells at her that he didn't ask for her forgiveness. But as Eric leaves, Martin asks, "Do you think God will forgive me?" Eric replies, "You better pray that he does."

Waiting at the church, Mary and Lucy, dressed in their frilly pink dresses, get in an argument that ends in a shoving match. Mary's crutches tumble to the floor—and so do the girls. Annie and Matt break up the fight with word that Eric has arrived.

Ruthie goes down the aisle wearing a pint-sized tuxedo and tossing flower petals, followed by Mary, without her crutches, leaning on Lucy's arm. When Lucy sees that Jimmy didn't come, Mary tells her, "He has no idea what he lost." At the front of the church, Eric is puzzled by his daughters' slightly rumpled appearance. Simon whispers, "You missed a great chick fight!" But when Annie walks down the aisle, beautiful in her mother's dress, Eric and the children struggle to hold back tears of joy.

It's the first day of school, and Eric announces he's taking the day off to spend it with his "wife for life" in their now quiet house.

But not all the Camdens are so cheerful. Lucy didn't sleep well worrying about the first day of high school, and the possibility of running into Jimmy Moon and his new girlfriend, Ashley. Ruthie's worried about first grade because of "snakes"— Simon told her they use them to clean the toilets and they sometimes crawl out. Matt asks Mary if she's okay about not being on the high school basketball team, but she insists she'll make it back on the team soon. Eric wonders why Matt is wearing Eric's jacket. Matt replies that it's *his* jacket; Eric borrowed it and never returned it. Simon decides he needs more in his lunch, so he digs around in the fridge and finds a large piece of leftover chicken. Annie puts a small knife and fork into his lunch bag so he can cut it up. At last Annie sends them all off with a lunch, a smile, and a kiss. When the house is silent at last, she and Eric toast each other with orange juice.

At school, Ruthie is upset when her strict first-grade teacher, Mrs. Rainy, makes her take off her backwards baseball cap because the school does not allow "gang clothing or insignia." At junior high school, Simon is upset to learn that he and his friend Nigel have different homerooms, and he spends the morning dodging a bully named Buck. At the high school, Lucy is frantically trying to work the combination on her locker, when Ashley and Jimmy show up. Jimmy tells Lucy she looks as if she's going to "throw up." Totally humiliated, she walks past Mary, muttering that "you'd think that having Dad as a minister, God wouldn't hate me so much." But Mary has problems of her own. She's stuck showing around a new boy named Marcus, who's developing an instant crush on her. Meanwhile, Matt is bummed out to discover his favorite English teacher has been replaced by gruff Mr. Koper, who seems to take an instant dislike to Matt.

At home, Eric is snoozing on the couch, and Annie is watching soaps, when Sergeant Michaels calls—a young man from Eric's church is about to jump from a rooftop. Word quickly spreads at the junior and senior high schools: the boy is a freshman named Peter McKinley. When Eric and Annie arrive at the scene, they meet Peter's mother, June, a single mother who admits she and her son don't always see eye to eye. The boy shouts down that if they let his mother come up, he'll jump. Annie takes June for a walk so Eric can counsel the boy. But Peter refuses to come down.

See You in September

teleplay by Christopher Bird; story by Brenda Hampton; directed by David Semel

Eric and Annie plan to celebrate the first day of school by taking the day off. A teenage member of their church threatens to jump off a roof. And all five Camden kids get in trouble at school.

Meanwhile, Ruthie's in trouble at recess when she puts her hat back on, "gangster style," and three other kids copy her. Mrs. Rainy makes her stay in from recess. Later she gets in trouble for nearly flushing her cap down the toilet when she and a classmate named Lynn try to deal with the "snakes."

At lunchtime, Simon and Nigel get in trouble when they sit at the table Buck claims is "his." When Buck bullies them about what's in their lunches, Simon offers to share his chicken. But when he takes out the knife and fork to cut it in half, a cafeteria monitor orders Simon to the office. The charge? Carrying a concealed weapon—the knife—in his lunch box.

Meanwhile, Lucy's arm is in pain from carrying her books around all day, since she can't get her lock open.

to make her listen. She takes his hand and says now she's listening, really listening.

Mary and Lucy are waiting outside the principal's office for Matt when Mr. Koper approaches Mary. He says he'll be the new coach when Coach Mayfield leaves at the end of the year. When Mary tells him she's not on the team because of her injury, he offers to help her work on her knee after school every day. When Ms. Russell comes out with Matt, she quips that she's giving them all a special family rate—they all get a one-day suspension. Then she gives Lucy a new lock with a simple "two-two-two" combination. And she casually mentions to Lucy that Ashley slipped in some spilled spaghetti in the cafeteria, exposing her underwear. At Lucy's

When Principal Russell sees Mary give Lucy an aspirin, they're both in trouble because it violates school rules: students are not allowed to possess or take any medications without written permission. Even worse, Jimmy and Ashley have witnessed Lucy getting in trouble.

Matt gets busted, too, when Mr. Koper hears a beeper go off in Matt's pocket. Matt realizes it belongs to his father; he must have left it in the jacket when he borrowed it. Matt tries to explain, but Koper won't listen and confiscates it as "drug paraphernalia."

Meanwhile, Mrs. McKinley has decided to go up on the roof and confront her son. As Eric and Annie follow to try to avert a crisis, Peter shouts at his mother that she never listens to what he says or how he feels. She's always trying to make him different, and he's tired of being a geek and not fitting in. He admits he never intended to jump and only wanted

smile, Ms. Russell promises that "there will be better days ahead."

As Eric and Annie head home, Sergeant Michaels tells them that school authorities have been trying to beep him all day: all five of his kids were involved in some minor disciplinary problems. At home, the kids try to explain that all their problems were accidental or well intended. But Eric can't get their "sentences" lifted. When Ruthie explains that she can't wear her cap anymore, Simon says he'll take it, and he slips it on his head. He can't understand why that sends Ruthie into a fit of the giggles. Lucy tells Eric about the rumors about Peter McKinley, and Eric instead says that Peter actually chased a burglar to the roof and held him at bay until the SWAT team arrived. The kids are impressed, and only Matt questions Eric's wild story. But Eric just winks and tells Matt to spread it around anyway.

No one goes grocery shopping with Annie; she prefers to do it alone. But now Lucy has a school assignment to plan a month's worth of meals for a family of four and actually shop for it using seventy-five dollars a week. Annie agrees to help her. Lucy wants to go and buy whatever looks good; Annie stresses the importance of planning and preparing a list to avoid going over budget.

Meanwhile, Simon and Ruthie spy on Matt writing a letter in the living room. When he goes out, they sneak in and read it. It's a love letter to Matt's girlfriend, Heather, and is signed: "I love you." They don't realize Matt sees them. Then Mary catches them and says they shouldn't read other people's letters. But Simon blurts out what was in it and asks Mary if her boyfriend, Wilson, has ever used the "L" word with her. Mary just glares and walks away. In the kitchen, Mary asks her mother, "How long were you and Dad together before he said it to you?" Annie answers, "About a year." But Eric insists, "Not until after we were married!"

When Annie and Lucy are at the grocery store shopping, Annie explains why she likes to shop alone. It's not that the kids bother her or slow her down. "When I shop for food, I take my time," she says. "I think of all of us around the dinner

I Love You

written by Brenda Hampton; directed by Gabrielle Beaumont

Simon and Ruthie sneak a peek at a love letter Matt wrote to his girl-friend. Then Eric finds an even more shocking one and worries: Are Matt and Heather secretly married? Lucy tries to help a friend whose mother has never said "I love you."

table, laughing and talking. I kind of get lost in the experience. It's kind of a Zen thing." Lucy is impressed. But suddenly she spots a classmate named Laurie, shopping with her mom, doing the same assignment. Only they're not having a nice mother-daughter moment. The mom is yelling. "If you weren't so stupid, then you would have done this on your own before I came home. Do you ever consider how hard I work?" Laurie is nearly in tears, especially when she realizes Lucy has overheard. Annie introduces herself and says she'd be glad to have Laurie join them, then come home to work on the project with Lucy. The mom calms down and thanks Annie.

Matt gets a phone call from a friend who needs a ride to the garage where his car is being repaired. Eric gives him permission to provide the ride. But when Matt hangs up, he reveals the fact that the garage is two hours away. Eric's not happy about that, especially when Matt wants a twenty-dollar advance on his allowance for gas.

Later Ruthie lures Simon down to the living room to read another letter she saw Matt write. But when they get there, they see that Eric has beaten them to it. They're stunned as they hear him read aloud: "Dear Mrs. Matt Camden." When Annie gets home, Eric tells her he thinks Matt is married. Annie sinks into a chair as Eric reads the letter—sentences like, "I can hardly wait until we can tell everyone we are husband and wife" and "I have a hard time keeping our marriage a secret." It's signed, "Yours forever, your husband, Matt." Annie is stunned. Eric is angry: How can he take care of a wife and family when he's only seventeen? he complains. How can he support a family when he has to borrow twenty bucks for gas? "Family?" Annie gasps. She hadn't even thought of that. But Matt won't be home for hours. So they call Heather's mother and invite her over for coffee.

Lucy comes down and asks if Laurie can spend the night. Too distracted to disagree, Eric agrees to go over and get her things. Annie privately tells him to keep an eye out for any signs of child abuse. When he gets there, Laurie's mom, Carol, opens the door. She's pleasant and friendly and apologizes for the scene at the store. Suddenly an old woman shouts profanities at Carol for opening the door to a stranger. "You're such an idiot sometimes. It's a wonder you don't get us all killed." Carol introduces the woman as her mother. When Eric comes home and tells Annie, they agree that since Carol gets yelled at by her mother, that's probably the reason she verbally abuses Laurie the same way. It's a cycle that's hard to break. But Annie is worried it's destroying Laurie's self-esteem.

When Heather's mother, Donna, arrives at the Camden house, Eric and Annie show her the letter. She's shocked, too, and very upset. After Annie shows her the way to the upstairs bathroom so she can splash some water on her face, she hands out hugs and an "I love you" to all the kids—even Laurie. When Annie leaves, Laurie's eyes fill with tears and she tells Lucy, "No one has ever said 'I love you' to me before." Lucy can't believe it.

On a date at the pool hall, Mary has been trying all night to get Wilson to tell her that he loves her. When Mary finally says, "I love you," Wilson only says "thank you"—which makes Mary really mad. But Wilson says he's not ready. "Saying I love you is a commitment," he says, and they're too young. And he's said it to only one person: Billy's mother. When he gets up to call home to check on Billy, Matt shows up, back from helping out his friend. Mary tells him what she's been up to, and how his letter to Heather started it all. At his surprised look, she explains that she caught Simon and Ruthie reading his letter. He admits that Heather's the only girl he's ever told "I love you." Mary asks him if he'd marry Heather. Matt says yes, then says, "I've been dying to tell someone this all night. . . ."

As the parents wait for Matt to come home, they grow more and more upset. "I can't believe your son talked my daughter into something so stupid," Donna says. Annie gets mad and insists her son would never pressure anyone into doing something they didn't want to do. In the middle of it all, Matt and Mary come home, and the parents ask to speak to Matt alone. Eric first apologizes for invading Matt's privacy by reading the letter, but he says they have to talk about it. Matt shrugs. "It's a joke. I wrote it because I caught Simon and Ruthie reading my mail again. I thought I'd scare them a little." Relieved, the parents burst into laughter. After Donna leaves, Eric and Annie ask Matt if he's thinking about marriage. Matt says of course not, he's only seventeen. Mary overhears and reminds him of what he said in the pool hall. "Do I ever tell Mom and Dad everything?" he replies. Coming up the stairs, Annie and Eric overhear. "Can we pretend we never heard that?" Eric moans to Annie.

The next day Eric offers to drive Laurie home. When they get there, she tells him how she noticed that everyone at the Camden house says "I love you"—a phrase she's never heard her mother say. Laurie wants to say it to her mother, but she's afraid. Eric counsels her to try, warning her that her mom might not know how to say it back yet. Maybe she never heard it as a child, he explains. When Carol opens the door, Laurie says she had a great time, but that she missed her mom. Carol's surprised smile gives Laurie the courage to say, "Mom . . . I love you." After a tough pause, Carol says, "I love you, too, honey, I love you, too."

Simon is concerned about a newspaper report about a cult leader who convinced thirty-eight people to kill themselves so they could get on a UFO with him. Eric tries to explain that when you're with a group of people who believe something, you can start to believe what they do. "So it's kinda like church," Simon says. No, Eric says. The difference is that cults shut themselves off from the rest of the world. The people at church want to be a part of the community and respect other people's beliefs. Eric suggests that Simon try an experiment to see if he can make people believe he's shrinking. He should ask Ruthie to help. Simon is excited. When Matt comes in, Simon looks at him funny and says Matt looks taller. When Matt says he's not, Simon shakes his head and says, "Then I must be shrinking."

At school, Matt, Mary, Lucy, and some friends are having lunch. A classmate named Shelby, who is slowly eating an orange, suddenly rushes off. A friend named Melissa says Shelby has bulimia, a disorder where girls throw up food on purpose to keep from getting fat. Matt and Mary don't believe her. But Lucy, who knows Shelby from algebra, decides to invite her over to study and have dinner the next night—to see what happens. Mary privately accuses Lucy of being "catty and nosy." Lucy argues that she's concerned and not afraid to get involved.

Meanwhile, Mrs. Bink tells Eric that her long-time friend, Mrs. Hinkle, has suddenly put her house up for sale and moved to a retirement home without letting her know. She's worried the woman's children forced her to do it, and she asks Eric to take her to the retirement home to check on her. Eric agrees, but when they get there, the receptionist says Mrs. Hinkle has asked not to be disturbed. So they leave her a note asking her to call.

In the living room after school, Ruthie and Simon try several tricks to convince everyone he's shrinking: they stick phone books under the couch so Simon's feet dangle when Matt comes in. Simon pretends not to be able to reach a glass in the kitchen. "You need to see a doctor," Ruthie says.

When Mrs. Hinkle doesn't call, Mrs. Bink gets Eric to accompany her in sneaking past security to see her. Once there, they discover the room is nothing like the horrific quarters Mrs. Bink imagined. In fact, it's beautiful, and Mrs. Hinkle insists she's happy. Mrs. Bink still doesn't buy it. They leave, not seeing Mrs. Hinkle sag against the closed door, looking homesick.

Says Who?

written by Catherine LePard; directed by Harvey Laidman

Simon tries to convince his family he's shrinking. Lucy tries to find out if a classmate is really bulimic. Eric helps elderly parishioner Mrs. Bink find out why her friend Mrs. Hinkle suddenly moved into a retirement home.

Annie finally asks Simon and Ruthie what they're up to, and they cave in and tell her about their experiment. Simon begs her not to tell. But outside Matt overhears him and grins.

That afternoon while studying, Lucy asks Shelby if she'd like a snack, and Shelby asks her where the bathroom is. In the kitchen, Annie overhears Lucy talking to Mary about it and scolds them both for trying to confirm a rumor like this. Bulimia is a serious, life-threatening health problem, she tells them, and Lucy doesn't have the training to treat it.

Meanwhile, Eric stops by the open house at Mrs. Hinkle's old home and meets her children, Dana and Kevin. They seem nice, and say all the right things—in fact, they use the exact same words Mrs. Hinkle did about why she moved out, as if they had brainwashed or coached her. Eric has a funny feeling and picks up Mrs. Bink on his way back to the retirement center. Once there Mrs. Bink confronts her friend, and Mrs. Hinkle finally confesses: Both her kids need money, and even though she didn't really want to move, she decided she had to sell the house to help them. She blames herself for being such a poor mother that they always run to her for help. Eric says it's not too late to change her mind.

At home, Simon goes to his clothes closet and finds that he can't reach his clothes bar. Matt comes in and says now he thinks Simon is right, he does seem smaller. When he leaves, Simon is happy. They convinced Matt! Then he looks at a poster of a race car on his wall—it's higher than before—and gasps, "I *am* shrinking. For real!" Annie tries to convince him it's impossible, but he won't believe her—until Matt comes in and tells him he found out about the experiment. He told everyone in the family. And they've all been trying to trick him. They raised the bar in his closet, moved his poster, and lowered the cuffs on his pants. Annie, not happy that Matt has tricked his little brother, insists that he take Simon to the doctor to prove he's okay.

Eric drives Mrs. Bink and Mrs. Hinkle to her home, where Mrs. Hinkle informs her children that she's changed her mind. She's *not* selling her house. They try to talk her out of it: she's too old to live alone; what if someone tries to break in her house and rob her or hurt her? Mrs. Hinkle replies, "Do you think some stranger could hurt me worse than my own children trying to scare me out of my house so they can pay off their credit cards and travel?" They leave in a huff. Eric removes the sign.

At home, Matt comes back with Simon from the doctor's and reveals that Simon's not the same size. He's an inch and a half taller! Simon is thrilled.

At dinner, Shelby excuses herself from the table. Worried,

Annie goes up to check on her. But in the bathroom Annie discovers that Shelby isn't throwing up, she's brushing her teeth, because she has braces. But she tells Annie she knows what she was thinking. She knows all the kids at school think she's bulimic. It's not true, but it's better than the truth: Her mom's welfare got cut off, and now they're so poor they don't have enough to eat. Annie promises not to tell anyone, not even Lucy and Mary, but she insists on getting her address for the church's "Meals on Wheels" program. No one needs to know.

Back downstairs in the kitchen, Lucy helps Annie prepare ice cream for dessert. Annie tells Lucy simply that Shelby is not bulimic. When Mary later asks Lucy what she's going to tell her friends, she says, "that Shelby's nice and funny and really good at algebra."

Eric comes home as Matt and Simon are taking out the trash, and they tell him what happened with the experiment. Eric says that when you love and trust someone, it makes you vulnerable. And he tells Matt he shouldn't abuse that trust. Matt promises. Then Simon stares at Matt's hair. He says it looks thinner. Matt freaks out until he realizes Simon's playing with his head again.

Who Knew?

**written by Greg Plageman;
directed by
Gabrielle Beaumont**

**The Camden family's trust for one
another is tested when Matt brings
home some marijuana, Eric
questions all the kids about drug
use, and Annie reveals a secret
about her past. Simon tries to teach
Ruthie how to do her own laundry.**

Season 2: Episode 26

At school Matt's friend Mitch invites him to a party where the kid's parents are out of town. Matt declines, and Mitch laughs. He forgot about Matt pining for Heather. So he stuffs something into Matt's hand, "to tide you over for the weekend." It's a marijuana cigarette. Before Matt can react Mitch disappears, so Matt quickly hides the joint in his jacket pocket. When he gets home, he leans over to pet Happy and doesn't see the joint fall to the floor. As he heads to the kitchen, Happy picks up the joint and trots off.

In the kitchen, Simon complains to Annie that it's not cool to get picked up by his mom anymore, and he wants to wait for Matt. Annie tells Simon and Matt that Ruthie's teacher expressed concern at the PTA meeting the night before. Ruthie wore the same shirt for three days. Annie says she explained to her that Ruthie is now dressing herself. Simon complains that she's sleeping in it, too. Ruthie explains that she sleeps in it so that when she wakes up she's already dressed. Annie tells Simon to help her with the Camden rule: If you're old enough to dress yourself, you're old enough to do laundry. He takes her off for laundry lessons.

Mary comes in and asks if Wilson can come over that evening. She also asks for eyedrops, complaining that the incense Lucy spread around the room is making her eyes red and itchy. Lucy comes in dressed all in black with colored yarn braided into her hair. She wants to know if her new boyfriend, Rod, can come over, since she's not allowed to date yet. Annie's worried when she hears Rod has a mustache and drives a moped.

When Eric comes home, he's greeted by Happy, who presents him with the marijuana. Eric is stunned. When he goes in, everyone can tell something's up—especially when he says no friends can come over tonight. He notices that Matt is gobbling down cookies—has he got the marijuana munchies? When he takes Annie upstairs, he shows her the joint. Annie is shocked. Eric thinks a certain cookie-munching teenager is the culprit. Annie says he doesn't have proof. It could belong to any one of their kids, or any one of their friends. For example, Annie points out that Mary's eyes are red, Lucy's dressing in black and has a new older boyfriend, and Simon's just started junior high school, where he's likely to be approached by kids with drugs. Annie asks how Eric counsels other families with this problem. Eric explains that he suggests they talk casually to the kids about drugs, with the hopes that the guilty party will confess. Taking his own advice to heart, Eric decides to allow their kids' friends to come over so they can talk to them, too. Eric gives Annie the "evidence," and she hides it in her dresser drawer under some scarves.

Meanwhile, working on her new fashion look in her room, Lucy decides her all-black outfit needs some color. She goes into her mom's room to borrow a scarf from her dresser and discovers the joint. "Mom and Dad are smoking pot!" she exclaims. Down the hall, Matt hears her say the word *pot* and checks his pockets. He panics—the joint is missing! Matt calls his friend Mitch and asks him to pick him up so he can get out of the house. Annie is suspicious of his change in plans. Meanwhile, Eric has begun questioning the other kids, assuring them that they can come to him with any problems. Lucy and Mary ask, "Is everything okay with you and Mom?"

Then Rod, Lucy's new boyfriend, shows up. He is wearing a Rastafarian T-shirt and sporting a mustache and a bike helmet. Eric begins to question Matt about Rod: Would *he* know how to tell if the kid is smoking pot? The exchange gets a little heated until Annie interrupts. When Eric and Annie are alone, Eric shouts, "I knew someday he'd do something stupid." But Annie has a confession to make: The summer before she went off to college, she experimented with pot. Eric stares at her in disbelief. His trust in her is broken—not so much because she tried pot, but because she's kept this secret from him all these years. Later Eric asks Wilson if he thinks Rod might use drugs. Wilson admits that he doesn't know and can only judge for himself; he adds that since he became a teenage father, his parents no longer trust him. They give him a drug test every few months. Alone with Wilson, Mary is angry at him for giving her dad ideas.

Annie goes out where Matt is shooting baskets and tells him about something stupid she did. One summer she smoked pot with a friend and her friend's boyfriend. One night the boy left stoned and died in a car accident. It was a wake-up call for Annie. She never smoked again, but always felt partly responsible for his death. "I'm telling you this because if you're using drugs, I want you to stop. If anything like that happened to you, I could never forgive myself." She says she doesn't want to accuse her children, but Matt says, "Funny. Sounds like I'm already guilty."

Ruthie runs in to show her dad her new "pink laundry"—she's washed everything with a red sock that ran. Eric smiles and sends her up to put it away, while all the other kids are herded into the living room for a family meeting. Eric bluntly tells the kids he found marijuana in the house. Mary and Lucy interrupt to say that they found a joint in Annie's drawer. Eric holds it up. It's the same one he and Annie found. Finally Matt confesses: "It's mine." Simon is totally shocked and upset and rushes out before Matt can say anything else. Eric sends the girls upstairs, too, then Eric explodes so Matt doesn't have a chance to explain. "Please explain to us how anyone could be so stupid as to do drugs in the first place?" Eric shouts. Angry that his parents don't trust him, Matt snaps, "I don't know, Dad. Why don't you ask Mom?" Eric demands an apology, but Matt hears a car horn and dashes out to leave with his friends.

Upstairs, Ruthie doesn't understand all the anger and shouting. Simon says it's because "our older brother is a big jerk and a major loser." Ruthie doesn't understand, but says, "I love Matt, and he loves me." Mary and Lucy can't believe Matt is using pot, because he never hangs out with those kids at school.

Out with his friends, Matt suddenly tells them to stop the car. They hassle him, but he gets out of the car anyway.

At home, Annie and Eric wonder how this could have happened to their family when they've talked to their kids over and over about the dangers of drugs. Annie laments that it's hard to imagine when you're young how the choices you make will come back to haunt you. Eric wonders if he and Matt will ever be able to trust each other again. They decide they need to get out, go for a ride. They ask Mary to watch the kids. Eric goes where he often goes when he doesn't have answers: the church. As he and Annie slip inside, they find Matt kneeling in the candlelit sanctuary, praying: He swears that he has never smoked pot and knows he made a mistake in bringing the joint home. "I'm so sorry. . . . It was so stupid. . . . I don't know how they're ever going to trust me again if they won't even listen to me." He stops when he hears Annie sobbing softly. "What are you doing here?" he asks them. And Annie replies, "Trying to figure out a way to get our son back." As the three embrace, Matt says he's sorry, and Eric promises, "We'll talk, okay? And this time I'll listen."

Breaking Up Is Hard to Do

written by Brenda Hampton; directed by Harry Harris

Matt gets a "Dear John" letter from Heather and heads for Philadelphia to change her mind. Lucy falls for a heartbreaker. Simon goes steady for the first time. Ruthie gets busted for "sexual harassment." And Wilson breaks up with Mary.

Matt's suddenly trying to borrow money from all the other Camden kids, but he won't tell them why. Secretly he makes a phone call to an airline, then disappears.

Meanwhile, Lucy walks in on her parents kissing over ice cream and complains about all the kissing going on while she has no love in her life. Even Mary and Wilson, she adds, haven't "come up for air" in half an hour. This grabs their attention, and, after assuring Lucy that a nice boy will come along, Eric goes to check on Mary and Wilson. He's a little worried that their relationship is getting too physical. Mary protests that they're just in the "kissing phase" of their relationship and they're not doing anything wrong. Wilson seems to side with her dad and says they can stop and play cards. When Eric leaves, Wilson says he's got a kid and he understands why it would make her parents nervous. Mary says, "It'd be really great if you could just be a regular guy instead of always acting like somebody's parent." Wilson answers, "I *am* somebody's parent."

Meanwhile, Simon gets a phone call and learns that his best friend, Nigel, now has a steady girlfriend. Simon moans that he's the only guy in sixth grade who doesn't have a girlfriend. Ruthie encourages him to call a girl named Cheryl whom he likes. Simon takes her advice, but when he hears the girl's voice on the phone, he totally freezes up.

Down in the kitchen, Annie finally gets a call from Matt. He tells her he got a "Dear John" letter from Heather, in which she explained that she'd met someone else. But when Annie tells him to come home to talk about it, she gets some shocking news. He loves Heather and wants to marry her someday, so he can't let it end. "I'm going to Philadelphia," he says. "I'll call you when I get there."

The next morning Eric and Annie check with the airlines, but there's no record of Matt getting off an airplane in Philadelphia. Annie feels that Eric blames her for not stopping Matt, but she asks him if she'd written him a "Dear John" letter, would he have let her go?

At school Lucy notices a handsome boy whose locker is next to hers. He introduces himself as Charlie Banks and seems to be interested in her. When he leaves, Mary comes over and warns Lucy that he's a notorious flirt and heartbreaker. Lucy doesn't care.

At the junior high school, Nigel ignores Simon because he's too busy with his girlfriend, Myra. Simon tries to speak to Cheryl but discovers she has a boyfriend. Back at his locker, a girl named Janice asks him if he'd like to go steady. Simon is delighted; the two join hands and walk off down the hall.

Ruthie and her friends are playing "Xena: Warrior Princess" on the playground. When they capture a boy named Ricky, he says he'll kiss them if they don't let him go. Ruthie stands her ground and gets kissed, then kisses him back—which gets her in trouble with Mrs. Rainy, who sends a note home to her parents.

Out on the road Matt has enough money to fly to Indianapolis, then enough cash to take a bus to Pittsburgh. From there he tries to hitchhike to Philadelphia. Back home, his parents worry because he hasn't called.

Meanwhile, Lucy gets a phone call from Charlie, but he only asks her to deliver a note to a girl named Rita. Lucy is at first disappointed; then she realizes that he may be breaking up with her. Simon gets a call from Janice. Downstairs, Eric keeps picking up the phone when it rings, hoping it's a call from Matt. Instead, he's uncovering new layers of his children's lives. He is getting more and more upset, worried about Lucy's "boyfriend" and about an eleven-year-old boy going steady. Annie reassures him that at Simon's age it's all very innocent.

Going into her room, Ruthie drops the note from her teacher. Simon picks it up and reads it and asks her about the kissing incident. She explains she was waiting until after Matt calls, so their parents will be in a better mood. Then Simon asks Ruthie if she has any jewelry he can give Janice to prove his affection for her. Ruthie suggests that he give Janice his "Red Lightning" ring, but Simon scoffs—he can't give her his most valuable possession!

In the midst of all this confusion, Wilson drops by, and Eric tells him it's a bad time. Mary is upset that her father is taking his feelings about Matt out on her. She says it means he doesn't trust her. Eric says he does trust her. "I just don't trust him or any other guy." Then Wilson knocks again and says he has something to tell Mary that can't wait. Eric allows them to sit out on the porch swing. Mary is delighted, but when she leans in to kiss him, he announces that he thinks they're getting too serious and that they should see other people. He doesn't want their strong feelings to get out of hand; he doesn't want to go through fatherhood again at his age. Mary is angry that he doesn't trust her to control herself. Wilson gives her a good-bye hug, and Mary goes back inside in tears.

The next morning Eric and Annie find out about the letter from Ruthie's teacher. Mrs. Rainy feels that the incident could be considered "sexual harassment." The Camdens think that's a bit over the top, but they advise Ruthie not to do any more kissing until she's at least "twenty or thirty." Ruthie promises. As Mary sits down to breakfast, she angrily tells her parents that Wilson broke up with her because of what Eric said. She hopes one day to have a boyfriend who won't do everything her dad says. But upstairs she confesses to Lucy that she's actually interested in seeing what it's like to kiss other boys. Lucy warns her to stay away from Charlie Banks. Simon interrupts for advice on breaking up. He's desperate to break up with "telephone girl" Janice, who's calling him all the time and trying to run his life. But he doesn't want to hurt her feelings because then no one will ever want to go steady with him again.

Meanwhile, Matt has reached Philadelphia and talked things out with Heather. He's met her new boyfriend, Mason, who seems nice, and Heather is kind but honest: She's sure she's in love with Mason and that they are more suited for each other. His sister is deaf and he signs, and it just feels right. Matt says he feels *he's* the right guy for her, he loves her, and he wants to marry her someday. Heather says she can't help the way she feels. Sadly, Matt goes to the bus station, where his parents have promised to buy him a return ticket; it'll take three and a half days to get home.

At school, Lucy delivers Charlie's note to Rita. Charlie thanks Lucy and says he owes her, then asks if there's anything he can do in return for her. Lucy pulls him to the side and asks if he'll be the first boy to give her a kiss. Charlie declines; he says it would ruin their friendship. But he grins and calls her Peaches, for her peaches-and-cream complexion, and tells her to hang in there. The right guy will come along.

In another school hallway, Janice tells Simon that her parents want Simon and his parents to come over for dinner. After agonizing over how to end the "affair," Simon finally blurts out that they're breaking up. But before he can even make up an excuse, she says, "Who cares?" and asks the first boy she sees, "Hey, want to go steady?"

When Matt reaches the bus station, he's upset to discover that there's no bus ticket waiting for him, like his dad promised on the phone. But when he goes to sit in the waiting room, he's surprised to see his father walking toward him—holding out two plane tickets. "I couldn't let you spend three days on a bus with a broken heart," he says. "Let's go home."

Girls Just Want to Have Fun

written by Catherine LePard;
directed by
Joel J. Feigenbaum

Simon no longer trusts Matt after
he tells their parents a secret.
The Camdens try to help Simon's
friend Stan, whose sister might
be in a gang. Lucy gets in trouble
when she tries out a new look at
the mall with her "cool" friends.

Season 2: Episode 28

In the middle of the night Eric and Annie hear screams. They race into Simon's room and find that his friend Stan, who's sleeping over, is having a nightmare. When Annie asks him about his bad dream, Simon quickly explains that the boys were telling scary stories before they went to bed. When the parents leave, Stan thanks Simon for making up something and not telling the real reason. "You're not gonna tell anyone, right?" he asks. Simon promises.

The next morning Stan's sister is late to pick him up, like always. "I wish I didn't have to go home," he says. Simon invites him to spend the night again, and assures him they're going to figure out a solution to his problem.

When Stan's sister Karen shows up, she's really bossy to him. Matt asks her about the B on her belt buckle. She says it's for her nickname, Babydoll. When she and Stan leave, she asks him if he told Simon anything. Stan looks away and swears he didn't. She warns him he'd better not.

Meanwhile, Lucy is planning a trip to the mall with her cool new friends, Terri and Lauren. When Mary asks to come along, Lucy says she's not invited. Then Mary catches Lucy stuffing some clothing and makeup into a zippered bag. Mary demands to know what's going on so she can be prepared to deal with whatever stupid thing Lucy's doing. But Lucy tells her it's none of her business.

At the mall, Lucy and her friends duck into the ladies' room and soon emerge wearing too much makeup and not enough clothes. They synchronize their watches so they can be back in time to change before their moms come to pick them up.

Meanwhile, Matt goes to Simon's room to talk to him about his friend. Matt says he's seen the same "B" Karen has on her belt buckle at school tattooed onto the arms of some kids who hang out in a gang called Blackburn 16. Under pressure, Simon finally admits that Stan told him, but that he gave his solemn promise not to tell anybody. He panics when Matt says it's very serious and they have to go tell their dad. Simon shouts, "I trusted you!" Then adds, "I wish you weren't my brother!" Matt is torn, but feels he has to tell his parents.

Just then Stan's mother calls, asking if it's really okay for Stan to spend the night again. This is news to Annie, but she says they'd love to have him. Eric goes out to talk to Simon about the news Matt just shared, but Simon insists that Matt betrayed him and made him look like a traitor. "I'll never trust him again," he says. But Eric confirms that Matt was right about coming to Eric: Matt is older and can see the situation is far too complex for Stan or Simon to handle alone. Eric tells Annie he's going to see what Sergeant Michaels has on the gang, then head over to Stan's house.

Later Annie tells Mary to find Ruthie so they can go pick up Lucy and her friends. But Mary's worried for Lucy, because it's much earlier than Annie agreed to arrive, and Mary procrastinates by not finding Ruthie during a game of hide-and-seek.

When Eric visits Stan's parents, Joe and Joan, they say they can't believe their daughter is in a gang. They say they trust their daughter and don't even know what to look for. Eric suggests that often a kid in this kind of trouble will have gang paraphernalia in her room; they go search Karen's room but find nothing. Joe and Joan assume there's no truth to Stan's story, and though they appreciate Eric's concern, they're happy that they were right about their daughter.

At the mall, Lucy and her friends are flirting with a twentysomething security guard. When Annie drives into the parking lot, Mary volunteers to jump out and find the girls while Annie parks the car—it's the only plan she can think of; she's sure Lucy is up to something. Annie agrees, but adds that she will meet them inside at the food court. Inside, Mary spots the girls and tells the guard, "They're fourteen. Get lost." Lucy is outraged and says Mary betrayed her. Mary tells her she's really being stupid, and if she was really betraying her, she'd just let their mom find her. "Mom's here?" Lucy gulps. "Thanks for the warning." Unfortunately, Annie spots Lucy before the girls have a chance to change. At home, an angry Annie grounds Lucy for a month and tells her they've lost something important: "I trusted you, and you betrayed that trust." "Can we ever get it back?" Lucy asks. Her mom replies, "With some work, we'll get it back. Eventually."

When Stan comes over, he confronts Simon by saying, "You told, didn't you?" Simon tries to explain how he told Matt and Matt told his parents. "But I didn't tell him everything." When they go upstairs, Matt sits up from where he's been lying on the couch. He's heard the boys' conversation, and so has Eric. Eric has a hunch and leaves to check it out.

Annie answers the door and finds Karen outside. The girl explains that Stan left his sleepover stuff in the car. Annie casually asks her about the B on her buckle, then tells her that the son of a woman at her church had the same B tattooed on his knuckles. Karen snaps that her life is none of Annie's business. Annie tries to talk to her about how dangerous gangs are and tells her that Stan loves her. But Karen insists that her friends would never hurt her or betray her, and she can handle anything. Annie says that's good, because she'll need all her strength to handle the choice she's made.

Upstairs, Matt tells Stan that he pressured Simon into

revealing some of their secret and confirms that Simon really wanted to keep it. Simon thinks his brother is cool again.

At Stan's house, Eric has told Joe and Joan his idea, and he watches as they search Stan's room. They're stunned by what they find hidden under Stan's mattress: homemade knives, chains, plus marijuana and pills. Just then Karen shows up, and her parents ask her, "How could you do this to us?" They exclaim that they both work hard so they can afford for their kids to live in better neighborhoods and attend safer schools. They threaten to move or send Stan to live with his grandparents. Karen tells them they're overreacting, and she says she'll get out of the gang. Eric warns her that it's not that easy; the other gang members will see it as a betrayal and will seek revenge. Joan wants to call the police; Karen protests and says her friends will want their stuff back. She says Eric's seen too many movies and snaps that they don't need his help.

Later the Camden girls are playing basketball against the Camden boys and Stan when Annie gets a phone call. Karen has been beaten up by her gang and is in the hospital. Eric drives Stan to the hospital, where they find his parents at Karen's bedside. Karen says she tried to quit the gang, but they wouldn't let her. And then she asks Eric if he can help her get into one of those safe havens he told her about. As Eric leaves, he hears a public service announcement on a patient's TV: "It's ten o'clock. Do you know where your children are?"

Do Something

written by Naomi Janzen;
directed by Tony Mordente

Annie goes into the muffin business,
Annie goes out of the muffin
business. Simon goes into the
greeting card business, and Ruthie
buys him out. Matt gets a job and
loses it, on purpose.

Season 2: Episode 29

Outside the church, Simon hawks greeting cards, which he signed up to sell through an ad in a comic book, until Eric puts a stop to it. Inside the church, at the refreshment table, Annie gets a business offer from parishioner David Friel to supply her muffins to his chain of bake shops. She declines, to Lucy and Mary's surprise.

Congregation members Emory and Nell tell Eric someone is needed to sit with their son, Steve, who is in bed at the hospital with a terminal illness. Matt tries to step forward, but Eric blocks him and says he'll try to find someone qualified.

At home, Lucy and Mary tell Eric about the offer Annie got and urge him to be more supportive. They believe that Annie's role as a housewife, and her lack of a professional career, has lowered her self-esteem. Meanwhile, Matt tells Eric he took the job caring for Steve, which angers Eric. He points out that Matt's been fired seven times already, and this is the hardest job yet. Before he commits, Eric wants Matt to visit Steve at the hospital.

Out in the yard, Annie cuts flowers with Ruthie, who's trying to understand the principles of business. Annie gives her an assignment: use $40 that Annie will loan her to buy all of Simon's greeting cards, then resell them at a profit. Delighted with the idea, Ruthie turns Eric into her first customer; he finds the lesson amusing. Annie takes offense, thinking he's ridiculing her business sense. Eric apologizes and offers to help more around the house so Annie can pursue the baked-goods deal with David Friel.

At the hospital Matt meets Steve, and they hit it off when Matt shows his familiarity with the action hero The Tick. Later, Matt borrows some of Simon's Tick comics for Steve. In the meantime, Simon, after receiving the $40 from Ruthie, mails in the money order to receive his coveted award: a Tick action hero! But Ruthie bursts his bubble when she says it could take six weeks to arrive.

Downstairs, David Friel visits Annie to work out the details of the muffin deal. Annie insists that his bakery use the same high-quality ingredients that she uses at home, even though they may be more expensive. David agrees to having a thirty-day trial period in which Annie will be doing all the baking at home. She gets to choose the ingredients, and they will be delivered in the morning. The first order is for thirty dozen muffins.

Matt takes the job sitting with Steve. The first day Steve asks Matt what he thinks it's like to die. Matt says it might be like when Steve was younger and woke up in his parent's bed. At first it was scary, not knowing where he was, then everything was all right. Steve likes the comparison. He tells Matt that before he dies, he wants just one day outside. He reveals that his parents don't allow it because they are worried, but he believes he can persuade Matt to help him. For Matt, this would mean getting fired.

Very early the next morning, Annie's up baking and answering the door for a delivery truck arriving to pick up muffins. Eric tumbles out of bed and finds Matt already leaving to spend time with Steve before school. Simon's up, too, counting the money in Ruthie's piggy bank, incredulous at the profit she's made on "his" cards. Ruthie giggles under the covers; she calls the mark-up her "loophole."

Later, at the hospital, Matt asks a doctor about Steve's condition, and whether or not going outside would be harmful. The doctor says there's little risk healthwise; the reason for the parents' rule is that Steve wouldn't have help close by should anything go wrong. Although Matt knows the decision really belongs to Steve's parents, he decides to grant Steve's wish—to play baseball one more time—that day. A few hours later, everyone is searching for them.

Back at the house, the pace of the muffin-baking operation, in addition to her family responsibilities, is getting to Annie. When Mary exclaims that she's proud of Annie for taking on a career, Annie explodes unexpectedly: her feelings of self-worth are *not* dependent on having a successful business career—she's already the family bookkeeper, banker, nurse, carpenter, psychologist, plumber, dog-walker, maid, and chef. As abruptly as she entered the muffin-baking business, she quits it.

Eric and Steve's parents search for Matt and Steve. Finally they find them at the local baseball field, running the bases in Steve's wheelchair. Despite the risk Matt took, it is evident to everyone that the results are positive for both boys. Eric is proud of Matt's sensitivity, and Steve's parents decide he should come home from the hospital. Matt's out of a job again, but he feels that, somehow, caring for Steve may have in some way guided him toward a career path.

At home, Ruthie shows Simon what she bought with her greeting card profits: a Tick action figure that's much bigger than the one Simon got from the greeting card company. It's a gift for Simon, and she still has $10 left over!

I Hate You

written by Brenda Hampton
& Eleah Horwitz;
directed by Burt Brinckerhoff

Matt's new date says Mary and Lucy hate her for no reason. Ruthie says she hates her mom for making her clean the walls in her room. But it's Simon who learns about real hate—the kind their neighbor suffered in the Holocaust.

Eric takes Simon on a house call, and they brainstorm ideas for Simon's history project on the way. Simon is considering interviewing people with the question "Where were you when JFK was shot?" although he admits it's not very original. They stop at the home of Mrs. Kerjesz. When she reaches on a high shelf to retrieve a gift for Simon, he notices numbers tattooed on her arm. When he asks her about them, she abruptly ushers him and his father out of her house.

At home, Eric explains that Mrs. Kerjesz was imprisoned during the Holocaust. Eric briefly describes what the Holocaust was: During a time of depression, when Germans were hungry and angry, Adolf Hitler used propaganda to convince his people to blame their problems on Jews, intellectuals, Gypsies, homosexuals, and Communists. Simon decides he wants to interview Mrs. Kerjesz for his history project. Out of respect for her privacy, Eric tells Simon that it's not a good idea.

The next day Matt waits in the living room for his date, Joanne, to arrive. Also waiting expectantly are all the other kids in the family, who are curious. Annie takes pity on Matt and ushers the others upstairs. But as soon as Joanne arrives, Mary and Lucy come up with a scheme. They send Ruthie downstairs to pretend to be looking for her invisible friend, Hoowie. Then Mary and Lucy go downstairs, pretending to be looking for Ruthie. Matt guides Joanne to the door, and they make a quick exit. Mary and Lucy giggle and make some catty remarks about Joanne's "perfect figure, perfect blond hair, and perfect walk."

Annie comes in and orders Ruthie upstairs to her room. She's discovered that Ruthie has drawn all over her walls. Annie tells her to get a bucket of soapy water and start scrubbing. Ruthie says she hates her mother. Annie goes off down the hall, so hurt by Ruthie's words that tears fill her eyes.

The next day at school, Lucy and Mary spot Joanne greeting Matt with a kiss. Lucy says she probably gets "perfect grades," too, and pokes fun at her by imitating her walk—but she doesn't realize Joanne has seen her.

At the middle school, Simon's classmates take turns announcing their project titles. There are quite a few "Where were you when JFK was shot?" projects in the works, he finds. When it's Simon's turn, all he can think about is Mrs. Kerjesz. He says that he's doing his project on the Holocaust. One girl says her grandmother survived the concentration camps. But a boy named Larry says his dad told him all that was just made up. The teacher is very enthusiastic about the idea. Simon just hopes he hasn't promised more than he can deliver.

That night Eric makes supper while Annie helps Ruthie clean the crayon on the wall of her room. During the cleanup, they argue again.

When Matt comes home, he's worried about Eric doing the cooking because he's invited Joanne over for supper. Annie reassures him that she's done all the prep work and dinner will be fine.

Meanwhile, Simon takes Happy for a walk and stops at Mrs. Kerjesz's house, although it appears no one's home. When Eric discovers him on the way back, looking guilty, he reminds Simon that he's been told not to bother Mrs. Kerjesz.

Joanne has arrived for dinner and heads into the kitchen with an offer to help. But when she hears Mary and Lucy joking around, making fun of her for being "Miss Perfect," Joanne quietly changes her mind.

The next day Joanne acts cool toward Matt; she finally confesses that she feels his sisters hate her. Matt is upset as he watches her hurry off.

At Mrs. Kerjesz's house, Eric apologizes for Simon's unannounced visit the night before, and he tries to explain the reason for the intrusion. When Mrs. Kerjesz hears that one of Simon's classmates has been told by his father that the Holocaust story is all made up, she decides Simon is old enough to hear the truth.

That afternoon at home, Matt confronts Lucy and Mary about making fun of Joanne. They insist they don't really hate her and realize that they got carried away with their joking around. When Annie finds out, she insists that they apologize to Joanne in person. Then Ruthie tells Annie she's sorry, too, for saying she hated her mom. Annie accepts her apology, but says the pain caused by cruel words doesn't go away so easily. She explains to Ruthie that we should all be very careful about what we say to others.

When Eric takes Simon to Mrs. Kerjesz's house, Simon listens to her story with tears in his eyes. The next day at school, Simon gives his report, but says he felt the story should be told by Mrs. Kerjesz herself. Then Mrs. Kerjesz retells her tragic story: her whole family was executed in prison camp gas chambers. As a child, she saw the smoke rising from the ovens where their bodies were incinerated afterward. Tears stream down the faces of the children, and even Larry's father is deeply moved. Mrs. Kerjesz ends her statement with a simple plea: It is wrong to hate. And we all need to live in peace.

Truth or Dare

**written by Brenda Hampton
& Eleah Horwitz;
directed by Les Sheldon**

Season 2: Episode 31

When Eric has trouble getting into some old jeans, he and Annie decide to change their diet and start jogging.

After school, Mary asks Matt to suggest to a boy she admires, Brian Keys, that she'd like to go out with him. Matt complies, and even promises to loan Brian $20 for expenses. Later, Mary does a similar favor for Lucy when she nudges a popular classmate of Lucy's, Beverly, to invite her to her sleepover.

At home, Simon kids Eric about his too-tight jeans. Annie tries to get Ruthie to sign up for swim class at the Y, but she won't. Simon offers to give her lessons in the bathtub.

Matt borrows the $20 for Brian from Simon. Simon expects the money back from Matt, along with $2 interest.

Annie asks Lucy about Beverly, which puts Lucy on the defensive. Beverly is the leader of the "in group" that Lucy thinks she wants to be part of. Then Annie checks on Ruthie, who's in the bathroom. She says she's taking a bath, but she's really getting ready for swim class. A few minutes later Simon goes in to give her the first lesson.

Downstairs, Brian Keys arrives for his date money from Matt and a few pointers about taking Mary out—what to do,

when to come home, and what kind of good-night kiss is appropriate. Matt says "on the cheek." Brian's clearly unsure about the whole thing.

Brian takes Mary to the pool hall, where the conversation sputters along slowly until Brian brings up his science project, a frog dissection. Soon they discover a common interest in the medical channel on TV, and Brian offers to help Mary with her chemistry class.

Back at the house, Eric asks Matt to smuggle in a couple of cheeseburgers; the weight-loss diet is starting to get to him, but he doesn't want Annie to know.

At Beverly's sleepover, Lucy learns they have a game planned. She's supposed to hide while they await the arrival of another girl, Shelby. Then everyone will talk about Lucy, to see what Shelby will say "behind Lucy's back."

Mary and Brian get back to the house from their date and exchange a warm and affectionate kiss on the front porch. Matt arrives just in time to see, and Mary slips into the house. Brian tells Matt he had a great time and is returning the $20 Matt paid him to date his sister. Mary overhears and runs upstairs in tears.

Shelby arrives at the sleepover and answers questions about Lucy in a way that is fair and friendly. But another girl named Jenny lets it slip that Lucy's invitation was by her sister Mary's request. Lucy emerges in tears, and everyone laughs at her except Shelby.

At home, Mary confronts Matt and Simon for bankrolling her a date. Then the phone rings and Lucy asks to be picked up from the sleepover. On the way out in the car, Eric and Annie bicker over the smuggled cheeseburgers. When Lucy gets back, she confronts Mary for setting up her sleepover invitation.

The next day, Eric forces down a breakfast grapefruit while eyeing the kids' pancakes. Upstairs, Annie discovers a swimming lesson in progress. She reprimands Simon for misleading Ruthie—she can't really learn to swim in a shallow bathtub.

Eric and Lucy go jogging in the park, where they stop for a hot dog and a shake. Shelby shows up to apologize to Lucy for what happened at the sleepover. Lucy feels better. Eric wonders how Shelby knew where to find them; it turns out Annie suggested the snack bar.

At the house, Simon levels with Ruthie. She needs real lessons if she wants to swim "over her head." Ruthie starts to feel better about taking lessons at the Y. Brian arrives and explains to Mary why he took the money from Matt—it was a loan for the dinner bill, not a fee for taking Mary out. Mary feels better.

Eric and Lucy return from the park. Eric is thirsty, from the hot dogs, he admits to Annie. They share a smile and a kiss. Upstairs, Mary asks Lucy to forgive her for prying into her party invitations.

Later Eric, Annie, and Simon take Ruthie to the Y for swim lessons. To everyone's surprise, she can dog paddle expertly, from her bathtub lessons. Simon beams.

That night Eric and Annie head for bed with a carton of low-fat milk and no-fat cookies. Minutes later there's a crash, and all the kids rush in. The bed is on the floor. Eric and Annie resolve to go right back on the diet and exercise program, starting the next day.

It's Thursday night, and Eric comes home from work with big news. Too bad everyone's too busy to stop and listen. Simon's practicing a magic trick, Lucy's on the phone, Matt and Mary are discussing basketball, and Ruthie's focus is on ice cream. Eric's news: This Sunday's church service will be on TV! Not only that, if attendance is large enough, it could become a regular weekly program.

The next day, it's Eric's turn to be extra busy, getting his sermon ready for the big day. Annie takes over all his office chores—everything from taking choir robes to the cleaners to clipping the hedges—so he can make it perfect. But Annie reminds him that he's written some of his best sermons while doing routine chores. At least he promises to put the roast in the oven for her.

At school, Lucy gets her history midterm grade. It's a D. The only good thing about a D is the sympathy and support she suddenly gets from the other low-scoring students, commonly known as the "loser" group. The bad thing is her paper has to be signed by a parent.

At high school Mary runs into her new basketball coach, Mr. Koper, who's been paying the injured athlete special attention. She tells him she's working hard on the physical therapy exercises he gave her so she can get back in the game as soon as possible after her accident. Down the hall, her teammates tell her that a transfer student named Diane will be trying out for the team.

At home in his study, Eric is trying so hard to write the perfect sermon that he can't think of anything to say. The kids come home from school and go about their business. Simon and Ruthie check out a new magic kit Simon ordered in the mail.

Lead, Follow, or Get Out of the Way

written by Greg Plageman; directed by Harvey Laidman

Eric's sermon is going to be on TV. Annie takes over Eric's extra church chores. Mary is jealous of a new girl on the basketball team. Lucy has trouble with history. Simon and Ruthie take up magic. The Colonel comes to the rescue.

Lucy heads for the telephone, and Matt tells her to make it short so she can study for history. Finally Annie drags in, worn out after spending the day doing Eric's chores, only to discover that Eric never put the roast in the oven, as he'd promised.

Upstairs, Ruthie resigns angrily from the job of Simon's "magician's assistant" when she finds out that he gets to wear a cape, while he says she must wear her old bathing suit.

At the high school, Mary is confused about why Coach Koper missed her physical therapy session in the workout room. She finds the answer in the gym: he and the rest of the basketball team are busy applauding the new student, Diane, as she shoots basket after basket. Mary can't help feeling demoted—and jealous.

Eric's "writer's block" spills over into Friday. By late afternoon he's resorted to "loosening up" by dancing to the radio. When Ruthie comes in and wants to join him, he confuses her by stopping abruptly and claiming that he's trying to write his sermon. Outside, Matt wonders aloud why Mary's shot-making abilities have gone downhill—isn't Coach Koper's physical therapy program supposed to be helping? To Matt's surprise, Mary storms into the house. He follows her, but neither of them hears overworked Annie ask for help setting the table.

Upstairs, Matt makes two surprising discoveries: Lucy is failing history, and Mary's quitting the basketball team. Annie hears it all from the hallway and bursts in, demanding full explanations from everyone. At the worst possible moment Simon sticks his head in to ask if anyone wants to see a "magic coin trick," and gets a resounding "NO!"

Downstairs, Eric's father calls long distance. Ruthie answers and gives the Colonel the whole story: Eric has a "block" in his head, Simon is into magic, Lucy is failing history, and Mary is quitting the basketball team. As soon as Ruthie hangs up, the Colonel throws a few things into an overnight bag and calls the airport.

On Saturday, just as Eric begins to compose his sermon, the doorbell rings: It's the Colonel. Eric claims that the last thing he needs now is more pressure. But the Colonel insists that humans work best under pressure, and he sends Eric off to his study. The Colonel then heads straight for the kitchen and starts cleaning. Mary and Matt come in and are happy to find the Colonel . . . who gives them both some advice. First, he agrees with Mary's decision not to play "second fiddle" to some new girl on the basketball team. Then, after she's gone, he reassures Matt she'll decide not to quit the team on her own—*after* she's gotten over her jealousy. He adds that it's important to know when to be helpful, and when to step aside.

Next, Lucy discovers the Colonel at the ironing board. "I'm not failing history," she whines. "I just got a D on a midterm." "Grab a sponge," he replies, enlisting her in kitchen cleanup. Utilizing the time it will take them to complete the household chores, the Colonel gives Lucy a history lesson by reviewing the last two hundred years. By the time the laundry is done, the kitchen is clean, and dinner is in the oven, the Colonel's teachings have spanned the American Revolution to Vietnam. The way he tutors gives Lucy a whole new perspective on her studies, and it helps her see that being popular with boys who are low-achievers isn't something she really wants. "One of the reasons my marriage has lasted so long is because your grandmother is the smartest person I know," he tells her.

When Annie comes home, she is delighted to find the house in order and dinner prepared. To top things off, Eric emerges from his study with "the best sermon I've written in years."

The next morning Eric has a full house for Sunday services as TV cameras scan the crowd. Mary catches sight of Diane slipping into a pew and fumes that her competition is now "plaguing" her in church. Matt opens a packet of breath mints, and Simon and Ruthie beg for one, too. As Eric welcomes the crowd, Simon shows Ruthie the "disappearing mint" trick. He pretends to hide it in his nose.

Eric extends a special welcome to his dad, the inspiration for the day's sermon. He admits it has taken him a lifetime to realize that, when his father speaks, it is wise to listen. He realizes now that he was fortunate to have a father who cared more about doing and teaching the right thing than simply winning the approval of his son. He says the Colonel is a man of action who has always liked to say "lead, follow, or get out of the way. . . ."

Suddenly a blood-curdling scream splits the air. Ruthie has tried to copy Simon's "disappearing mint" trick, but has actually shoved it up her nose—and now it's stuck! Television cameras rolling, Eric and Annie rush Ruthie to an exit. As the congregation slowly exits in confusion, Ruthie does blow out the mint.

In the sanctuary, Diane introduces herself to Mary. To Mary's surprise, they hit it off right away, exchanging injury stories. Diane says she's heard what a good player Mary is and is looking forward to seeing her on the court soon. Across the room Lucy says hi to her "low-achiever" friend, Todd. He asks if Lucy might be interested in getting together to study. She agrees, hoping Matt will lend a hand to them both.

Eric and Simon take Ruthie to the emergency room to have her nose checked. Simon apologizes for disrupting the service. But Eric explains that Ruthie's scream helped him to remember that his family is more important than anything else in his life. And that when it comes to what's important to him, it's his family that "leads." Everything else can "follow or get out of the way."

Rush to Judgment

**written by Christopher Bird;
directed by Neema Barnette**

Annie discovers a large sum of money missing from the church treasury. Coach Koper is rough on Matt in English class—but as Mary's coach, his "extra help" turns into inappropriate sexual advances. Simon and Ruthie suffer from too much golf.

Season 2: Episode 33

Sunday services end on a peaceful note, but it's shattered outside. At the front door, Eric is pressured by Lou, the church treasurer, to discontinue Wednesday chapel service for budgetary reasons. A few feet away, Mary gushes about the help Coach Koper has given her with her basketball injury. But when she leaves, Matt and Lucy bad-mouth Koper, who—as Matt's English teacher—recently gave him a bad grade. Meanwhile, Simon bugs Annie to take him to the driving range—he keeps a club with him at all times now, as he's learned every golfer should. Annie says no, but the urge to hit a few shots gets the best of Simon, and then, right in front of Dad and Lou, he drives one through Lou's windshield.

At home, as Annie looks through the church's budget book for a way to afford continued Wednesday services, she discovers a $2,500 error. She's certain it's a mistake, but Eric phones Lou to check things out. Lou's wife says he can't come to the phone and abruptly hangs up. Eric is mystified by how nervous she sounded.

Lucy goes to Matt's room, looking for a quiet place where she can study, in other words, away from Mary—who can't stop talking about how wonderful Coach Koper is.

Ruthie finds Simon in their room, eating supper alone as punishment for hitting a golf ball at church. Ruthie cringes when Simon spots a golf ball on the floor and the urge to hit away is overwhelming—but Happy snatches it before he can do anything.

Downstairs, Mary sets the table and continues to praise Coach Koper to Annie. Annie admits that she's happy Mary is so excited about her coach, but she wonders why Matt dislikes him so much. She says it's as if her kids are talking about two different people. Mary says Matt dislikes him because he's a tough English teacher.

In the study, Eric calls Lou about the missing $2,500, but Lou is evasive. He won't come to the house to discuss it, but promises to try in the morning. Eric suspects he's hiding something. The next day Lou shows up in Eric's office and confesses: He took the missing money. He refuses to explain, but insists he'll return it in a few days.

At school, Matt is frustrated that Mr. Koper continues to badger him, even when he says he's finished reading the assigned James Joyce book and has almost finished his paper. Instead of being pleased, Koper orders Matt to do an instant oral report. After class Matt catches up with Lucy and thanks her for an idea she gave him that helped in Mr. Koper's class. He asks her to pass the word to Mary to catch another ride home from basketball practice because he's leaving straight after school to work on his English paper. Down the hall, Lucy spots Mary. She's with Coach Koper, and it looks as if he has his arms around her! She delivers Matt's message, then darts off, unsure of what she's seen.

At home, Eric tells Annie that Lou has admitted he took the missing church money. Even though he said the money would be returned "in a couple of days," the action, Eric insists, still constitutes theft. He has blocked the church's bank account against any further withdrawals, just in case. And he says it troubles him that, in a way, he is "covering up" for Lou.

Upstairs, Lucy tells Mary she seems to have a "crush" on Coach Koper, which Mary denies. Matt overhears, and then, out in the hall, Lucy tells him about Coach Koper hugging Mary.

The next morning a golf ball crashes through Simon and Ruthie's bedroom window, from *inside* the room. Ruthie takes the blame to keep Simon out of trouble, but Eric takes Simon's clubs away and forbids both of them from playing golf for a month. But Eric can't help making a few practice strokes of his own, when he thinks the kids are gone.

Later, Lou arrives at Eric's office with the money he borrowed from the treasury, a bill for the windshield Simon broke, and news that he is resigning from his job and leaving the church. Eric tries to uncover the reason behind Lou's actions, but Lou won't talk and begs him not to press charges. Before Eric can answer, Lou hastily leaves.

At school, Matt confronts Coach Koper about hugging Mary. Both of them march angrily down the hall to have it out in the principal's office.

Back at the house, Annie tells Eric she saw Lou's wife walking arm-in-arm with another, younger man at the supermarket. Eric decides to pay the family a visit that night.

At school, Mary and Lucy are summoned to the principal's office and are surprised to find Matt there with Coach Koper. Ms. Russell explains that Matt accused the coach of inappropriate behavior toward Mary, and now wants the girls' side of the story. Mary is mortified at what Lucy has told Matt, insisting what she saw was a supportive hug after she broke her own mile record. Still, Ms. Russell will have to meet with a parent.

That night Eric and Annie discuss the situation that has developed with Mary and Coach Koper. Even though a background check done by Sergeant Michaels reveals that the teacher has a clean record, both Annie and Eric have a bad feeling about it.

Later Eric and Annie drop in on Lou and his wife at their house, right in the middle of an argument. The younger man from the supermarket is there, too—he turns out to be Louis, Lou's grown son. Lou reveals that Louis is severely autistic, which means "the slightest change in routine can throw him into violent outbursts." Unable to handle their son's illness, Lou and his wife put Louis in an institution at an early age. But now it has closed, and the family needed a deposit to put Louis in another care center. Lou cashed in his life insurance policy, but because the check wouldn't arrive for several weeks, he borrowed the money from the church treasury—intending to pay it back when his check arrived.

Later, back at home, Annie is approached by Simon and Ruthie. Simon confesses to breaking the window. Annie tells them both that the truth has a way of coming out in the end.

At the Wednesday chapel, Lou and his family show up. To Eric's relief, Lou has decided to stay, and the family has found care for their son through the social services contact Eric hooked them up with. Suddenly Annie has an uneasy feeling about Mary and rushes out of the church.

At school, Mary apologizes to Mr. Koper for the embarrassment Lucy and Matt may have caused him. He accepts, then eases up behind her, begins to massage her shoulders, then caresses her arms . . . Mary is confused and frightened and pulls away. Angered by her rejection, Mr. Koper begins to badger her, saying no one would believe her now if she complained about his advances. Just then Annie and Ms. Russell step through the doorway—they've heard everything. Ms. Russell immediately fires Koper and warns him that the one thing he needs now is a good lawyer. As he rushes off, Mary wonders how her mother suspected something was wrong. Annie replies that she just had a feeling, and that as she matures, Mary will learn to trust her feelings more.

Stuck in the Middle with You

written by Brenda Hampton; directed by Harry Harris

Eric opens a can of worms when he heads up group counseling sessions for young marrieds. Suddenly Lucy has two boyfriends, and her siblings bet on who she'll choose. Annie's father shows up with a new toupee—and no girlfriend.

Season 2: Episode 34

NEWS FLASH! EX-BOYFRIEND JIMMY MOON BREAKS UP WITH ASHLEY! Lucy instantly puts her new boyfriend, Rod, off and rushes home from school, eager to share the news. But Annie can't talk about it. She's on the phone with her dad, who has just broken up with his girlfriend, Ginger, and is planning a visit. Ruthie comes in with a shoe box containing two lizards that she got from her friend Ricky, whose mother wouldn't allow him to keep them.

At the church Eric struggles to get a conversation going at the new "counseling group for young marrieds." Annie enters and whispers to Eric the news about Grandpa and Ginger.

Back at the house, Lucy is on the phone with her friend Marah, digging for details on Jimmy Moon's breakup with Ashley. "How can Jimmy or Rod call you, if you're on the phone?" Mary says, hoping for some quiet time for study. "I'm playing hard to reach," Lucy informs her. In the meantime, both Rod and Jimmy try to call Lucy, but keep getting a busy signal.

In the hallway Matt and Mary meet and discuss who is better for Lucy: Rod or Jimmy. Simon asks if either would like to place a bet on who Lucy will pick. Matt bets on Jimmy, but Simon and Mary bet on Rod. Suddenly Ruthie rushes up with more big news: Lester the lizard is laying eggs!

At the church, Annie tells the counseling group about her marriage with Eric. At first, she says, they held their feelings in so they would get along. Eventually, everything came out, though. It would have been better, she says, if they had been forthcoming on a daily basis. Suddenly all the couples are complaining about their spouses, all at once. Excited that they're finally getting somewhere, Eric is disappointed to realize that he has to end the meeting because his time is up.

Annie goes home just in time to greet Grandpa at the front door—with his new full head of hair! At first, Simon and Ruthie aren't sure who he is.

The next morning, Simon and Ruthie ask Grandpa if his new toupee is making him popular with women. After they leave to get ready for school, Grandpa makes a bizarre announcement that stuns Annie and Eric. With the price of burial plots skyrocketing, he says, he's decided to give them two spots in the family plot, right next to Annie's mother and him.

At school, Rod tells Lucy he doesn't want to see her go back to the "Moon Man." Jimmy interrupts their exchange and says he hopes they can analyze their relationship and see if they have "barriers they can cross together."

Later, in another hall, Mary finds Matt spying on Lucy and Jimmy Moon. He's hoping they'll get back together before Lucy starts anything more serious with Rod. A few minutes later Rod himself appears and tells Matt and Mary how much he cares for Lucy. Matt says he finds Rod somewhat "mature" for Lucy, a description that only pleases Rod. This convinces Matt more than ever that he and Mary need to act quickly.

In the church parking lot, Annie and Eric struggle with Grandpa's "gift announcement." Eric always assumed they would be laid to rest at the century-old Camden plot in upstate New York. Then the second session of the "young marrieds" begins, and it's just as loud and bitter as the first meeting. Eric decides to switch topics— everyone will talk about his and Annie's burial plots. The discussion heats up, people take sides, and finally Annie boils over, accuses Eric of insulting her family, and storms out.

Rod arrives at the Camdens', wanting to talk with Simon, who is on his side in the Rod-Jimmy contest over Lucy. Then Jimmy arrives and sits down in another room with Matt. Meanwhile, Lucy's on the phone in her room, until Ruthie whispers to her that both boyfriends are presently in the house. It takes a few minutes, but when Lucy calms down at last, she is able to face both boys downstairs with a promise that she will make a decision soon. Listening in are Matt, Mary, Simon, Ruthie, and Grandpa. They take a vote on who will win, but Ruthie's stuck in the middle between the two young men.

The next day the Camdens are visited, one by one, by

members of the "young marrieds" counseling group. Into his study, Eric welcomes Michael, who wants to talk about Katie. At the back door, Annie greets Bonnie, who wants to talk about Kevin. At the front door, Grandpa meets Robert, who's worried about becoming a father.

Upstairs, Lucy scolds Matt and Simon for meddling in her love life. It's bad enough that Matt calls it a choice between "Dull and Weird," but it's worse when Lucy finds out they've all been betting on the outcome with Monopoly game money!

Away from the others, Annie reminds Lucy that if either boy is the *real* Mr. Right, he shouldn't be hard to recognize. Mary suggests Lucy dump them both and explains that it's great to have no commitments to anyone, to be able to dress any way she wants, and to be free to do anything she chooses. Lucy says that even when Mary did have a boyfriend, she was free to do what she chose. Mary says that perhaps Lucy could learn by her example.

Meanwhile, Rod and Jimmy separately consider what they'll have to do to make themselves more attractive to Lucy. Rod figures his mustache will have to go. Jimmy believes he'll have to "loosen up" a little, starting with some purple hair color.

In bed, Annie and Eric both agree that wherever they are buried is fine. At breakfast, Annie says Ginger's distaste for Grandpa's new hairpiece is normal, that he should lose it and go back to Ginger. He'll live longer if he's happy, she says, and Ginger makes him happy.

At church, Annie and Eric discover that the three couples seem to have made great progress in solving their problems, thanks to the Camdens' counseling session. And one woman even has news: She's expecting twins!

At school, Lucy tells Jimmy and Rod politely that she isn't ready to go steady with anyone right now. She needs to find herself first. Later, Matt and Mary both congratulate her: From the ashes of two breakups, Lucy is rising fast.

Season 2: Episode 35

To thank Eric for volunteering at the food bank, Mr. Harrison treats the Camdens to a free Sunday blue plate special lunch at his restaurant. After reprimanding the kids for their poor public behavior, Annie tells them that she spends her life serving them, and she intends to enjoy being served for once. To the kids' horror, Sunday's special is liver and onions. They choke it down, amid lots of complaining. Ruthie splatters ketchup on Lucy, who's wearing Mary's sweater.

The next day at breakfast, Annie confronts the kids about their lack of good manners. From now on, she says, she expects to hear "please" and "thank you" around the Camden house. But the kids don't take her seriously, and she exits in a huff. As soon as she leaves, Mary tosses a muffin across the table, and the group erupts with laughter.

Red Tape

written by Brenda Hampton; directed by Les Sheldon

Eric works at the food bank and helps a single-parent family with an IRS problem. Annie works on the kids' manners. Matt gets lots of attention from a personal ad he never placed. Happy gets a credit card.

At school, Mary and Lucy spot a classified ad in the student paper: "Wanted, a nice girl to share the senior year with. Signed, Matt." It's followed by their home phone number! Matt happens by, but neither girl lets on they saw *his* ad.

At home, Annie shows Happy the catalog and credit card they got in the mail addressed to Happy Camden. "Sorry, you'll have to use cash, like the rest of us," she says. The phone rings, and Annie takes a message for Matt.

At the food bank office, Eric is approached by a polite boy named Clarence Fields, who asks for Beanie Weenies, as he does every day. With the manager's okay, Eric gives the boy a can. The manager then asks Eric if he wants to follow the boy home and get his story—since Eric is a "nice guy, but a nosy guy." Eric follows the boy.

At home, Matt finds a whole stack of phone messages, but he doesn't recognize any of the names. He tells Annie that a strange thing has been happening: All day girls at school have been smiling at him and giggling.

Upstairs, Mary is insisting that Lucy carefully wash her ketchup-stained sweater when Matt walks in with his telephone messages. "You should have told us you were desperate," Mary says, instead of running an ad in the *Wildcat*. Matt is astonished, then angry. He didn't know anything about the ad, and he thinks Mary and Lucy are behind it.

Outside, Simon rescues Happy's catalog and credit card from the trash can and tells Happy it will be their little secret.

Meanwhile, Eric follows Clarence to a run-down apartment building. He knocks at the door that Clarence entered, and they talk, although Clarence keeps the security chain fastened. Clarence reveals that his mother will be home soon, and Eric says he'd like to wait outside and meet her.

At the Camden house, Simon dials the number on Happy's credit card just to fool around, and before he knows it, he's placed an order for overnight delivery. He calls back to cancel, but because he isn't eighteen, they won't follow his instructions.

In the laundry room, Mary removes her sweater from the dryer. All of sudden it's Ruthie's size.

Clarence's mother, Harriet, comes home to their apartment and whacks Eric over the head with her purse until Clarence explains who he is. She invites Eric in and explains their circumstances: her ex-husband ran off and left her with a huge tax bill that she must work off. As a result, she works weekdays as a science teacher and nights as a waitress—and has moved her son to this low-rent apartment. It sounds like unnecessary red tape to Eric, who promises to help by meeting with her contact, a "Mr. Smith."

The next day Eric visits the local IRS office personally and calls Harriet's contact with his cell phone. When he sees the collection agent who answers to Mr. Smith, he walks in and introduces himself.

Matt, meanwhile, visits the *Wildcat* office to find out who's behind the classified ad with his name and to ask for a printed apology. But Leonard explains that the person who submitted the ad is protected by the First Amendment from being revealed.

At home, Annie opens a package from the Eddie Bowzer Company containing "doggie rain boots." She calls the company to complain, but they're not very helpful, so Annie just informs them that her dog doesn't have any money to pay her credit card bill.

Meanwhile, at the mall, Lucy tries to get credit for the shrunken sweater, but she's turned away for not having a receipt.

At the IRS office, Eric and Mr. Smith are in a heated discussion over Harriet's tax bill when the agent clutches his chest and gasps. Eric dials 911 on his phone and asks for an ambulance for a heart attack victim. At the hospital, Mr. Smith is wheeled to a desk where Eric learns Mr. Smith needs proof of insurance to be admitted. Distraught over the new layer of red tape, Eric rushes back to the man's office to find his papers.

Back at the Camdens, Simon and Ruthie arrive after school and remember to say "please" and "thank you" when asking for a snack, as well as when Annie doesn't press for information about the Eddie Bowzer boots that "Happy ordered."

At the mall, Annie gets Mary's money back for the sweater—citing the fact that it was laundered according to its directions, and still shrunk two sizes—but only after making a scene that embarrasses the sales staff into taking back the merchandise.

Leonard, from the *Wildcat* newspaper, shows up at the house and admits to Matt that *he* put the ad in the paper to spark some interest. Matt forgives him and apologizes to his sisters for suspecting them. But there's a reason for his easy forgiveness: It got him a call from Deena Nash.

At the hospital, Eric gets Mr. Smith admitted and works on his conscience by actually bringing Harriet and Clarence in to meet him. After experiencing firsthand the life-changing effects of "red tape," Mr. Smith says to Harriet, "If the Big Auditor in the sky lets me live, I'll get your problem straightened out." The doctor says that as long as Mr. Smith gets a little exercise and changes his diet, he'll have every opportunity to do just that.

Season 2: Episode 36

Homecoming

**written by Catherine LePard;
directed by David J. Plenn**

**Mary's afraid to play in a real
basketball game again. Eric
laments that Mary never talks to
him anymore. Lucy's friend Suzanne
feels shy about going to the
homecoming dance. Simon worries
his science project isn't good
enough. Annie and Ruthie get lost
on a field trip to the museum.**

It's the homecoming basketball game, and the entire Camden family is present to root Mary on. Mary attempts to block a jump shot when her injured knee gives and she collapses to the floor—then she wakes up in bed at home. It was just a bad dream.

The next morning Lucy chooses an outfit for school while talking on the phone with her friend Suzanne, who recently moved away. Neither has a date for the homecoming dance, so they agree to go together, although Suzanne feels shy about returning to her old school. In a bad mood, Mary closes the closet door on Lucy, but Lucy just keeps talking.

At the breakfast table, Ruthie mimics her dad, reading the paper, eating toast, and sipping her "coffee." Simon enters with a model of the solar system that's made from a bicycle wheel with doll heads for the planets. Eric and Ruthie head upstairs to finish getting ready to go. Annie enters the kitchen next, worried about the time; Ruthie has a first-grade field trip to the museum this morning, and Annie has volunteered to be a chaperone. Ruthie, she explains, is scared of getting lost in the museum.

Upstairs, Eric offers Mary a ride to school, but she declines, saying that she's fine. Eric confides to Matt that he wishes Mary would talk to him like she used to. Matt responds that she doesn't talk to anyone anymore.

Downstairs, Lucy is just starting to tell her mom about Mary's self-doubts about starting basketball again when Mary walks in. She passes on breakfast and complains about not having a date for the homecoming dance. Matt comes in, says he doesn't have a date either, and suggests they hang out together, but Mary doesn't seem to care. When she leaves, Matt admits to Annie he's been turning down dates so he can look after Mary.

Across town, Suzanne tells her mother her ride to school is out front and her mother calls good-bye. Actually, Suzanne hides in the bushes until her mother leaves, then gets on a city bus.

Later, at the museum, Ruthie and Annie take a side trip away from the regular school tour to another exhibit hall they think will be more interesting. They have so much fun that before they know what happened, the school group leaves without them. Worried Ruthie might be upset, Annie "covers" for them and Ruthie never even realizes they got lost.

At the elementary school, Simon watches his friend Nick botch his astronomy presentation, which gives him the jitters about his own project. He tells Ms. Hunter he's not ready, and she asks him to come in during his free period to discuss it. Simon goes to the school counselor and begs to be placed in another class. But the counselor convinces Simon to try Ms. Hunter for a few more days. He agrees, then asks to be sent home early. But he gets turned down because children are sent home only for sickness or if a parent arrives to pick them up. Simon heads for the school nurse's office.

At high school, Matt tries to cheer Mary up, but to no avail. She even turns down lunch with her basketball teammates and blows off her teammate Diane, who tries to commiserate with her about her injury and fears.

At the Camdens' house, Suzanne shows up to share a ride with Lucy, but everyone's gone except Eric. She's obviously troubled, so Eric offers her a ride, but he's unable to find out much.

At school, Lucy begs Matt not to force her and Suzanne to ride to the dance with Eric. Matt considers her request, then discovers Simon in the nurse's office. Simon explains why he's there: Ms. Hunter hates him, and he's afraid to make his presentation. What he doesn't know is Ms. Hunter overhears everything from the hall. Still, Simon convinces the nurse he needs to spend the rest of the day in her office.

After school Matt picks Mary up in front, where she's getting some advice from her ex-boyfriend Richard on how to handle pregame jitters. He tells her that everyone has fear—he may not have the physical fears she has, but he certainly has personal ones. He asks if she has a date to the dance, and she says no.

Finally everyone gets back to the house, including Suzanne, who hangs out with Lucy in her room until supper, admitting to Lucy that she thinks Matt is a "dream date." Later she pretends to call her mother and leave a message. But Annie and Eric sense something is wrong, and when they use the redial feature on the phone, they discover she didn't call home at all. Then they discover that she's run away from home; she's stressed about her mom's new boyfriend, who has a couple of daughters of his own.

In the kitchen, Matt tells Eric and Annie that Richard cheered Mary up. After Matt leaves, Eric admits that he wishes

he were the one Mary confided in. Annie says there will be many more "Richards" in Mary's life, and Eric must accept the fact that Mary is growing up.

Annie goes to Simon's room with Jell-O, not pizza, for supper—because he's "sick." Unfortunately, he's heard about the field trip and asks Ruthie what it was like to get "lost" from the rest of the class, blowing Annie's "cover" story. Annie then tells Simon that she knows he's afraid of his science teacher and project, and that if he continues to run from things he's scared of, he'll miss out on a lot of great things in life.

Later, Diane arrives to pick Mary up for the game. The family sends her off with encouragement. Eric goes upstairs to tell Suzanne how much they enjoy having her around and that he's sure her mother misses her. Encouraged, she picks up the phone, obviously to call home and patch things up with her mom.

In their room, Ruthie is watching Simon tinker with his solar system model when Annie sticks her head in with some news. Ms. Hunter has come to their house for a visit. She confesses that she's been strict because his class is the first class she has ever taught, and she was afraid of being too easy on them. She and Simon work things out.

At the gym, the family watches the game from the bleachers. Richard comes and sits with them. At first Mary plays timidly. Her friend Diane keeps passing her the ball, but Mary passes it on to someone else, afraid to try a shot. Then Mary's knee gives out, and she falls. But after a moment of thought, she takes Diane's hand to get up. The next time Diane passes her the ball, Mary shoots—and makes the basket!

Already feeling great, Mary is surprised and charmed when Richard asks her to the dance over the PA system. She tells her family she was afraid to admit, even to herself, that she was scared to play in the game. But now she's glad. At Annie's suggestion, Matt gets two dates: Lucy and an elated Suzanne. Matt begrudgingly agrees but insists he won't dance. Annie and Eric smile—they know he will.

It Takes a Village

written by Sue Tenney; directed by Burt Brinckerhoff

Friday night! Eric and his friend Morgan sneak out to confront Morgan's wife's ex-husband. Matt and John sneak out to a jazz club. Lucy and Mary sneak out on dates. But before the night is over, everybody will be held accountable to the moms!

Season 2: Episode 37

The weekend is here, and Annie figured on a big Camden-Hamilton double-family Friday-night bash. That's not going to happen, though. At the breakfast table, Eric tells Annie he would prefer an adult "boys' night out" with Morgan Hamilton instead of a family get-together. When Annie counters that they should all spend the time together, since Matt and John will be leaving for college soon, Eric retorts that the kids will all have their own Friday-night plans anyway. He's right.

At school, Morgan's son John talks Matt into going off with him to the jazz club, while Keesha Hamilton wants Lucy to *pretend* they have a movie date, so she can sneak out with her boyfriend. Meanwhile, Lynn Hamilton can't go out, as she's only in kindergarten. But she and Ruthie both *wish* they had a date with their new substitute teacher, Mr. Lim. As for Nigel Hamilton and Simon, they have been invited to a "make-out" party. And Lucy's classmate Scott Smith has plans for a study date with her at the Camden house.

After school Annie accepts everybody's cancellations for the family night one by one. Meanwhile, over at the Hamiltons', Patricia Hamilton goes through the same process. Everybody seems to have plans of their own.

But it's even more complicated than that. Scott Smith arrives to tutor Lucy, but when he catches Mary alone, he confesses his study date with Lucy was just a ploy to meet Mary. He asks her out for later that night, and Mary agrees to go to the movies with him—even though an anxious Lucy already warned Mary that Scott is only fourteen. Eric and Morgan have a secret as well: their boys' night out is really a prearranged meeting with Patricia's ex-husband. Morgan wants him to quit making his annual "anniversary" Valentine's Day call to his wife, which always starts a fight.

Matt, John, and Mary, in Annie's car, drop Simon and Nigel off at the make-out party house; the boys are extra-prepared with lots of cologne, aftershave, breath mints, and lip balm. Next Mary gets left at the multiplex theater where she secretly expects to meet Scott. Little does she know Lucy and Keesha have already gone inside with Keesha's boyfriend and Brian, another date he brought along for Lucy. Matt and John go on to the jazz club.

Annie and Patricia take Ruthie and Lynn to a restaurant. Annie discovers Ruthie is wearing a bra and learns that she's trying to look more mature for Mr. Lim—and has disregarded the jealous friction it's causing between her and Lynn.

At the jazz club, to Matt's surprise, John is called to the stage to sing! It turns out he's actually very good.

At the pool hall, Eric finds out that Morgan knows all about his son singing at the Mint, and that he's even been offered a record contract. The two men discuss their sons' futures, and their desires for their sons to go to a state school that is close to home. Finally, worried that Patricia's ex-husband is a no-show, Eric suggests they leave. But then a man in a wheelchair approaches and introduces himself as Kevin, Patricia's ex-husband. Morgan is shocked to learn that he was injured in Vietnam after his divorce from Patricia, and also discovers that Kevin never told Patricia of the injury. Although Kevin is happily married to a nurse he met while recovering, he calls Patricia to remember a more carefree time. Morgan's anger and suspicions fade away.

At the make-out party, Simon and classmate Laura Cummings share their first innocent kiss in the "make-out closet"—and are immediately discovered by one of the parents.

Across town, Annie and Patricia take Ruthie and Lynn to the movies, where they are annoyed to see two young couples making out a few rows in front of them. After discussing the punishment they would give if those children were their own, they realize that half of one couple is Lucy, and half of the other is Keesha! They interrupt the smooching verbally from their seats, and the girls exchange anxious glances. In yet another row Mary, with Scott, sees it all and slumps out of sight.

Back at the Camden house, Annie and Patricia enter with Keesha, Lucy, Ruthie, and Lynn. Ruthie and Lynn, excited by the night's events, are on good terms again. But Keesha and Lucy are only worried about what their dads will do when they find out about their behavior at the movies. Annie and Patricia

refuse to cover up for them because they never hide things from their husbands.

Later Matt and John pick up Nigel and Simon, and discover that Simon is never allowed back on account of getting caught in the make-out closet. Matt suggests that he won't tell their parents if Simon divulges all the details of the night's events!

At the Camden house, Eric and Morgan show up with Kevin. Patricia is happy to see Kevin, and a little skeptical of Morgan, who was obviously hiding something from her. After a short visit Kevin leaves, and Eric and Morgan sit down with Annie and Patricia to explain.

At the theater, Scott tries to kiss Mary, who instead offers him her hand to shake. The two agree that the date wasn't such a good idea. As it turns out, Matt and John have witnessed the exchange. They pick her up in the car and tease her about dating someone Lucy's age. She makes a deal with them: if they quit teasing, she'll tell them the gossip about Lucy and Keesha. The boys agree, and share what happened with Nigel and Simon.

When they get home, Mary kids Simon about the make-out party. Then the phone rings, and it's Scott for Mary; Simon takes advantage of this information and kids Mary about dating a fourteen-year-old.

Meanwhile, Eric, Morgan, Annie, and Patricia go upstairs to eavesdrop as Matt and John lecture Keesha and Lucy about their make-out sessions in the theater. Eric and Morgan look at their wives, who failed to share this information.

It took a while, but everyone finally made it to the big Camden-Hamilton double-family get-together after all—and all the secrets came out!

Nothing Endures
But Change

written by Heather Conkie;
directed by Stephen Collins

Lucy gets an invitation to have pizza
with two rebellious friends, then
blames herself for the tragic car
accident that claims her friend's
life. Mary agrees to baby-sit for
Wilson. Simon moves into Matt's old
room, and Matt moves into the attic.

Season 2: Episode 38

At school Lucy is excited to get an invitation to go out for pizza
that night with her friend Sarah Foster and Sarah's big sister,
Jen. Jen has a new car, and Sarah reveals a secret: Jen sometimes lets her drive, even though she isn't even old enough to
have a learner's permit yet. Lucy says she'll have to get permission from her parents to go out, and Sarah suggests she ask
Mary to come along, too, to help convince her parents.

A few steps away Lucy runs into Mary and asks her to
come, but Mary turns down the invitation since she doesn't
know the girls. Lucy feels betrayed because Annie won't let
Lucy go alone with kids she doesn't know. After much hag-
gling, she finally convinces Mary to go. But as she's getting
ready, the phone rings. It's Wilson for Mary, and she's ecstatic
to hear from her old boyfriend. But joy turns to disappointment when she realizes he wants her to baby-sit while he goes
to a school dance. Nonetheless, she agrees to watch Billy. Lucy
is outraged that Mary is backing out of her plans and storms
out. She runs into Matt, who says he'll fix things with Mom
and Dad—he can drop Lucy off and pick her up at the pizza
place. Downstairs, it takes some persuading, but at last Annie
and Eric give in.

Meanwhile, Simon is complaining that Ruthie damaged his
volcano science project when she moved it to make room for a
house for her puppets. Annie sees that the room isn't big
enough for the both of them, and suggests that Simon could
move into the attic. Simon and Ruthie enthusiastically agree to
the plan. But once up there, Simon worries that it's too far away
from everyone else.

Meanwhile, Lucy calls Sarah to tell her she can go, only to
discover they've changed their plans. They're going to a burger joint thirty miles out, but it's no problem: they'll just pick
Lucy up at the pizza place and go from there. Her parents will
never know. Lucy is happy to be going but troubled by her
deception. Still, when Matt drops her off at the pizza place, she
doesn't confide the new plan. Matt says he'll be back at 9:00
sharp to pick her up.

At her baby-sitting job, Mary finds Wilson looking terribly
handsome in a tuxedo and wishes she were going out with him,
especially after he leaves and Billy starts to cry!

At home, Eric and Annie are reminiscing about their children growing up in this house when Matt rushes in. There's
been a car accident—Jen and Sarah were involved. But he can't
find Lucy and doesn't know if she's with them.

In all the commotion, Simon asks Matt if he can have his

room. Simon is surprised that Matt readily agrees, as he'll be going off to college soon anyway.

Annie rushes to the scene and finds Lucy, who's still waiting outside the pizza restaurant. She never got picked up and she's trying to explain what she was doing when Annie delivers the news: Sarah and Jen were in a wreck. Sarah, who was driving, is dead, and Jen is hurt. Crying, Lucy stumbles into her mother's arms. Annie shares her daughter's tears, but hers are tears of grief mixed with tears of relief that Lucy is safe.

Meanwhile, Mary is having trouble with Billy when Wilson comes home early from the dance because he didn't enjoy his date. After he puts Billy to bed, he and Mary talk—and it's obvious they both are still attracted to each other.

Eric goes with Sergeant Michaels to the Foster house with the unenviable task of informing them of their daughters' accident.

During the next few days Eric tells Annie he's disappointed he couldn't get Lucy to go to Sarah's funeral. And they're worried, not sure how to help her. Upstairs, Matt has a different reaction: he's very upset with Lucy, he confesses to Mary. She deceived him and . . . "Lucy could have been in that car."

Lucy overhears and comes in crying. She says she knows what could have happened, and she blames herself for Sarah's death. If Jen and Sarah hadn't been on their way to pick her up, none of this would have happened. Lucy flees the room in hysterics. Matt and Mary run after her and assure her the accident is not her fault. But Lucy won't listen. When Eric and Annie come upstairs to check on the noise, Lucy confesses that she knew that Jen let Sarah drive sometimes. If only she'd told a grown-up, she says, someone would have stopped them. And Sarah would still be alive. None of the Camdens can talk Lucy out of these ideas; all they can do is hold her while she cries.

Later Mary answers the door and is delighted to see Wilson. But he hasn't come to see Mary. He's come to see Lucy. He wants to talk to someone. "Why can't you talk to me?" Mary fumes. "Because," Wilson says, "you're not in the Club." When Lucy comes down to the living room, Wilson hugs her, then they sit down to talk. Wilson explains that they both belong to a Club—of people who have lost someone they loved. He knows what it's like to lose someone close, because his own young wife died in childbirth. It makes you afraid to be close to others, the way he's afraid to be close to Mary. He adds that it helps him to be a good father to Billy. When Lucy complains that she doesn't have anything like that, Wilson disagrees: she has her family. Then Wilson convinces Lucy to go with him to "Our House," a counseling group for people who have lost loved ones.

Once at Our House, Lucy learns from the members that there are no easy solutions to dealing with such a loss. Slowly Lucy begins to deal with the fact that her life will go on, and that she should be happy to be alive.

Back home, Lucy checks on Matt, who is settling into the attic. When she sees Mary, she assures her that Wilson likes her and she should call him. Down the hall, Ruthie and Simon are slowly but surely adjusting to their new separate rooms, and Simon senses that he's leaving his childhood behind. When Lucy goes to the linen closet to get Matt a blanket, she runs into her parents. She hugs them, then hurries upstairs to help Matt. Reassured that Lucy is doing better, Annie and Eric look around their house, where their children are quickly growing up, and wistfully realize that nothing endures but change. Lucky for them, they have love to see them through.

Time to Leave the Nest

written by
Stephanie Simpson;
directed by Tony Mordente

Simon finds a little girl who's lost. Eric tries to help her and her alcoholic father. Annie referees a fight between Mary and Lucy over territory in the bedroom. Matt says he needs personal space and has an older woman sleep over.

At the breakfast table, Eric and Annie enjoy a quiet moment . . . until Matt comes in with the mail. One letter is for Matt, and he learns he's been accepted to college. But rather than share the details, he runs upstairs. Eric hopes the acceptance letter came from a local, and less expensive, college; a pricey out-of-state school has already accepted him.

Upstairs, Lucy breaks off her phone call to wrest her diary away from Mary. Then, back in the kitchen, Simon enters with a new friend: a little girl dressed in rags and covered with dirt. "Can I keep her?" he wants to know. His parents are stunned.

Later, Sergeant Michaels visits with Eric and Simon about the girl. He and Eric have a hard time convincing Simon that she needs to be returned to her parents. Simon argues with their logic: any parents who would neglect their child this way should have no rights over her.

Upstairs, Annie cleans the little girl up, brushes her hair, and offers her a dress. The girl is clearly happy with the attention, but she doesn't speak.

Meanwhile, Lucy runs a strip of black tape down the center of the room that she and Mary share, dividing it between them and warning Mary not to cross the line. Ruthie walks in, glad to have a room of her own since Simon moved to another one. Lucy says the new girl will probably be put in Ruthie's room, if she stays.

Downstairs, Matt warns Annie that he's having a date over to the house and would like some privacy in his room. Annie agrees reluctantly, then tells Eric about it. They think Matt may be using his lack of "personal space" at the house as an excuse for going away to an out-of-state college. They agree to pass Matt's "test" by staying out of his way.

Eric goes to the police station and meets Joe James, a dirty, drunken, and screaming man who is looking for his daughter, Sarah. As it turns out, Sarah is the girl Simon found. Joe passes out, and they remove him to the hospital. Later Eric learns from Joe that no one knows where Sarah's mother is, and that Joe is all the family she has.

Matt arrives at the house with his date, Molly, who tells Annie that she's twenty-three years old. Annie invites them to watch a movie with her and Eric, but they decline and head upstairs. A few minutes later they're up in Matt's room, kissing, when Ruthie barges in and asks if she can hang out. Molly immediately says okay, to Matt's disappointment.

Lucy and Mary continue to feud in their room. When Lucy asks Mary if she saw Matt and his date, Mary tells Lucy the tape line is a sound barrier, too; so if she has anything to say, just "write it in your diary" and she will read it later! Annie comes upstairs to break up the fight and removes the tape line. She then retrieves Ruthie from Matt's room, where Molly was teaching her to dance.

Eric finds Simon and Sarah in Simon's room, where he has lured her with candy. She's talking now, and she asks Eric to take her to her father, who she says is sick and needs her. Simon, on the other hand, asks his father to let her remain with them.

The next morning Annie remarks that she doesn't recall hearing Molly leave the night before. The two dismiss their concern, recalling that they were too entwined with each other to hear anybody leave.

Later Eric meets Sergeant Michaels for a visit to Joe and Sarah's trailer home, which is filthy and infested with rats. Sergeant Michaels has learned that Sarah's mother died of a drug overdose.

Back at the Camdens', Matt reads the paper at the kitchen table until Annie spots Molly in the living room. Matt admits she spent the night but says he slept downstairs on the couch. He tells Annie he needs to move out, to have "space," and she says they will discuss the situation later.

Upstairs, Mary is pounding on her door, which Lucy has locked from inside. Annie comes up to diffuse the argument,

and Lucy explains to Annie that she had to hide something. Mary reveals that the thing she was hiding is her diary, which is all about "sex." Annie, concerned by Mary's remark, sits them both down and gives them a fresh perspective on sex as a romantic expression, which calms them both down. As Annie leaves, she overhears Ruthie dancing to a song she has made up about the joy of having her own room.

Eric returns to the house after a futile search for Sarah's dad. With him is her grandmother, instead, whom Sarah doesn't recognize. The woman is upset that Sarah doesn't remember her, but Eric assures the grandmother that things will work out in time. To calm Sarah down, Ruthie and Annie take her and her grandmother into the kitchen to bake some cookies.

Eric encourages Matt to go with him on an errand so Matt can discuss his college plans. He takes Matt to the trailer and enlists him in the cleanup while they talk.

Later, Eric visits Joe at the hospital and gives him a ride home to the cleaned-up trailer. Joe is shocked to find that his trailer is not only spotless, but filled with people. All the Camdens are there to greet him—even Sergeant Michaels. Joe is stunned but still hostile when he discovers the plan they have for him: Sarah must live with her grandmother until Joe has straightened up his life, including enrollment in a treatment program for alcoholism. If he refuses, Sergeant Michaels warns, social services will be forced to intervene. Eric assures Joe that he and the church will help him in any way they can, and finally Joe relents.

That evening Eric and Annie are surprised to find all the kids making dinner. It's a Thanksgiving dinner, they explain, to express their thanks for having parents like Eric and Annie, who care so much.

My Kinda Guy

written by Greg Plageman;
directed by Joe Wallenstein

Season 2: Episode 40

Eric comes home to find Simon and Ruthie emptying cereal boxes, looking for the "surprise." Eric has a surprise for everyone—the Camdens will be hosting a French exchange student. Lucy and Mary are eager to know his age and marital status; Matt, on the other hand, worries that he will have another passenger to ferry around in his car.

When the kids leave, Eric explains to a frustrated Annie that the deed is an emergency favor for a friend. He hopes she'll get used to the idea eventually, especially since their unexpected guest is already at the front door.

The student, Guy, is totally charming. He apologizes for the intrusion, thanks Annie profusely for her hospitality, and gives her a box of chocolates. Eric gets a bottle of wine and a box of Cuban cigars. Mary and Lucy find him very attractive, but Ruthie voices her adamant distaste for the new stranger. Upstairs, Eric talks Simon into moving back in with Ruthie to give Guy a room temporarily.

Lucy and Mary go to their room and make a pact to treat Guy like a brother during his stay. Nevertheless, Mary decides to change into something more feminine. . . .

Meanwhile, Matt helps Simon move his things back into Ruthie's room. Guy appears and strikes up a conversation with Matt about a couple of flight attendants he met on the way over. He thought the two of them could join the women on a double date, and Matt agrees—although he has his own date for this evening. As for Simon, he's impressed with Guy's laptop computer. Everybody in the family is warming up to the new guest, fast.

Later Guy finds some privacy in the bathroom, where he can open a window, light up a cigarette, and laugh at how stupid the Americans are.

That night Eric and Matt meet on the way out—Eric thinks at first that Matt should stay home and entertain Guy, but Matt thinks that Eric should stay home and entertain him. Eric insists he needs to work on his sermon. Eventually

The Camdens welcome Guy, an exchange student from France, who flirts with both Lucy and Mary, then steals Matt's date. Annie and Eric discover e-mail and chat rooms on Guy's laptop computer. Ruthie and Simon get sick when they try some of Guy's cigarettes.

they agree that Guy will find something to do on his own, and they both leave.

Downstairs, Guy immediately chooses Lucy to flirt with, and soon they're leaving on a date to shoot some pool. Annie warns Lucy to be home by her curfew.

In Eric's office, Annie finds Simon tapping away on Guy's laptop. He's online with fellow fans of his favorite comic book character, The Tick. Together, they find a chat group about foreign exchange students and discover Eric online, too—not working on his sermon. Simon then helps Annie set up her own private chat room with Eric. Once alone, she enjoys exchanging some romantic e-mails with her husband.

Simon wanders into the hall and then discovers Ruthie in Guy's room, going through his suitcase. She finds cigarettes and persuades Simon to smoke one with her.

At the pool hall, Guy, Lucy, and Mary enjoy a game until Matt comes in with his date, Michelle, who studied in Paris for a summer. She and Guy hit it off right away—in French—and exclude everyone else. When it's time to go, Guy offers to catch a taxi for himself and Michelle, so that Matt and his sisters can go straight home.

At the Camden home, Simon and Ruthie send Happy to fetch Annie—they're in the upstairs bathroom, sick from smoking. Annie sends them both straight to bed.

Eric, meanwhile, is still online with a "chatter" he thinks is Annie. But the chatter is actually a couple of young hackers from the church who've been following the Camdens' chat. When they call him Spice Boy, Eric beams. After a minute Annie herself is back on, with a message to Eric to come home ASAP, they have a problem with Guy.

Eric stops at the pool hall and finds Guy. He snuffs out Guy's cigarette and tells him no smoking in the Camden house. Furthermore, he doesn't appreciate Guy's influence on Mary and Lucy. But Guy seems to have an excuse for everything.

The next day the whole family voices their dislike for Guy. Overhearing, Guy announces he's leaving and goes off to pack. Eric insists that everyone apologize, but Guy still says he plans to leave.

When Eric returns after taking Guy to the airport, Annie confesses she'll miss Guy's laptop. Eric says "So will Spice Boy," with a wink. Annie, of course, has no idea what he's talking about. He may as well have said it in a foreign language!

It was sex education. Even though the film showed monkeys engaging in sexual behavior, Kyle says he's looking at Simon's sisters in a whole new way.

At Eric's office, John Gannon stops in with a request—his daughter Connie needs a date to the prom, and he wonders if Matt would be interested in taking her. John's wife died, and he explains that he's having trouble being a good substitute mom. Eric is surprised by the request and by the fact that John knows that Matt doesn't have a date.

At home, and at Ruthie's insistent request, Annie tries repeatedly to phone for tickets to the Snappy the Stegosaurus show. Finally she gets through but learns that the show is sold out. Ruthie is terribly disappointed.

Eric comes home and repeats John Gannon's request to Annie. Matt overhears and tells them it's not a good idea. Eric guesses that Matt is rejecting the idea because the girl is not popular or pretty enough, and pressures him to take her. Matt bristles and says he'll take her out just to show them, but warns that they can't complain when they learn the reason for his hesitation.

In the hallway, Matt guesses what's bothering Simon. "Congratulations, you're a man," Matt kids. "I'd be better off if I was a monkey," Simon replies.

Like a Harlot

written by Sue Tenney; directed by Joel J. Feigenbaum

Matt does his dad a favor by dating the class harlot. Eric gets Snappy the Stegosaurus tickets from his ex-girlfriend, but after the show Ruthie no longer believes in Snappy, Santa, the Easter Bunny—or God. Mary and Lucy trick their way into a date with boys they don't know, but the joke's on them.

In the girls' bedroom, Mary gets a call from a guy who claims to be "a friend of your brother's." He asks Mary if she and Lucy want to double-date with him and his younger brother. Mary and Lucy accept the offer.

Meanwhile, Annie is so desperate for Snappy tickets, she's calling the radio station to see if she can win some. Eric mentions that he knows Snappy's creator, Debbie Miller, from high school and reveals that she's an old flame. Annie insists he find her number and call to see if she will give him tickets. To seal the deal, she calls Ruthie in and tells her all about it.

At school the next day, Matt asks Connie Gannon to the prom. She resists, knowing her dad is behind it. Plus, she adds, she doesn't have anything appropriate to wear. Matt says his mom and sisters will fix her up and assures her that everything's going to be fine. Across the hall Mary and Lucy are amazed that Matt is asking Connie out. "If Mom and Dad only knew . . ." Mary says. But their main focus is on their own "mystery dates." All they know is one of them is named Casey, and the other one is named Kyle.

Later, Simon runs into his friend Kyle and asks, "What are you so happy about?" Kyle explains that he and his brother have dates for that night.

At home, Eric gives Annie the happy news: he got two tickets from Debbie Miller. While a happy Ruthie's getting ready, Lucy and Mary tell Eric they're "hanging out" tonight, maybe getting a hamburger later, "no big deal." They don't mention their double date.

After Eric and Ruthie leave, Lucy and Mary ask Annie if it's okay to go out on a casual date with a couple of guys they just met. Annie's suspicious, but before they can talk more about it, Connie and Matt arrive. Annie takes her upstairs, and they go to work getting her ready.

A while later Eric and Ruthie return from the show. Ruthie's upset from their visit backstage—she saw the head come off the costume, and now she knows Snappy isn't real! She adds that she no longer believes in Santa Claus or the Easter Bunny, either!

Connie comes downstairs in the dress Annie made for her—she looks wonderful!—and she and Matt leave for the prom. When Eric wonders why Matt didn't want to take her out, Lucy, Mary, and Simon laugh. When Eric asks what's wrong, they answer that Connie is well known among the other students as, in polite terms, the "high school harlot." This news bothers Eric, but Annie has taken a liking to the girl.

Meanwhile, Debbie, in her Snappy costume, has come by to help smooth things out with Ruthie, but it only seems to make matters worse. Then the doorbell rings, and Mary and Lucy race

to the door. But they're shocked when they meet their dates: Kyle and Casey, who are friends of Simon's, not Matt's! Everyone—Annie and Eric, Mary and Lucy, Kyle and Casey, plus Ruthie and Snappy—head into the kitchen for ice cream.

At the school prom, outside the gym, Connie invites Matt to "fool around." To Connie's surprise, Matt politely refuses. Connie reveals that she can't talk to her father and that she wants to change her reputation for being promiscuous but that she doesn't know how. Matt tells her that she doesn't have to have sex with a boy to be liked. In fact, he adds, she should expect boys to do nice things for her without their expecting anything in return. Connie thanks Matt for being so nice to her. After a brief kiss, they go inside to dance.

Meanwhile, Debbie, as Snappy, tucks Ruthie in at the Camden home, and Ruthie says she's gotten over the shock. Debbie leaves, and Eric goes in to apologize, too. Along with losing her faith in Snappy, however, Ruthie has decided she doesn't believe in God, either. Eric doesn't argue, but he explains his faith to her, and the strength he gets from his belief.

At home, Eric is worrying, waiting for Matt to come home. Mary and Lucy beg Annie for help getting rid of their dates, but she refuses—it's just punishment for the girls for tricking their parents into letting them date boys they've never met.

When Matt drops Connie off at home, they wake up her father, who's asleep on the couch. As Matt says good night, Connie offers to tell her father all about the prom, and her father seems delighted.

When Matt finally gets home, he finds his own parents asleep on the couch. They wake up and ask him how his date went; he replies with a smile that it went well, then heads upstairs. Eric and Annie wait a moment, but then curiosity gets the best of them, and they follow Matt upstairs to get the details.

Meet the Actors

Stephen Collins

Catherine Hicks

Barry Watson

David Gallagher

Jessica Biel

Beverley Mitchell

Mackenzie Rosman

The Twins

Happy the Dog

Boyfriends

written by Brenda Hampton; directed by Burt Brinckerhoff

Ruthie is mad at Matt for going away to college. But Matt has a secret: he's actually leaving in a few days for a summer job. Simon is training Happy to win a dog-food contest. Eric is shadowed by Lucy's old boyfriends, Rod and Jimmy, for a career project. And Annie learns some shocking news about Mary.

Ruthie won't sit next to Matt in church. "She's angry that you're abandoning us," Simon says. "I'm not abandoning anyone," Matt protests. "I'm going to college." Simon perks up when Matt offers to help him train Happy to win a dog-food contest—if Simon will work on Ruthie. Lucy asks Matt when he's going to tell Mom and Dad about his summer job. He says he'll tell them when he's ready. Suddenly Lucy's ex-boyfriends, Rod and Jimmy, make a grand entrance. She slumps down in her seat. She's sure they're plotting something.

Later, in his office, Eric is flattered to discover that the boys have chosen him to research for their career-day class project—until he finds out why they picked him. "You only work an hour a week," Jimmy says. "It's not like you have a real job," Rod adds. They think it will be easy. Eric informs them that his job is twenty-four hours a day, seven days a week. He hands each boy a large Bible for their "research." "I don't suppose you have the Cliff notes to go with these babies?" Rod asks.

Matt and Simon begin training Happy to play dead when asked, "Would you rather have your Pow Chow taken away or be a dead dog?" Matt tries to get Ruthie to help, but she won't talk to him.

When Eric comes home, he and Annie discuss Mary and Wilson's relationship. Annie worries that they're acting as if they're a married couple and Billy is their baby. But she has a plan. Annie's dad has given Matt some money for graduation plus a little something for each kid. Annie wants to send them all to summer camp the same week that Matt will be at college orientation. A whole house empty for a whole week? Eric agrees it's an *excellent* idea.

Upstairs, Matt finds Billy wandering around—and Mary and Wilson asleep on her bed. "Have you two lost your minds!?" he shouts. Wilson says they must have fallen asleep after putting Billy down for his nap. Matt doesn't care what his excuse is.

"Haven't you learned anything from your mistake?" Wilson is stung. Mary tells Matt he can't talk to her boyfriend that way. "Boyfriend?" Matt shouts. "You're acting more like he's your husband!" Furious, Mary slaps her brother. Wilson and Billy leave.

That night Eric and

Annie have a talk with Mary about spending too much time with Wilson. Then they surprise her: they're sending her to basketball camp. Mary is thrilled! She wants to go call Wilson, but her parents challenge her to see if she can spend one evening away from him, to see if she's still independent and has a life of her own. Angry, Mary storms upstairs. But then she gets an idea. She can't call Wilson, but Lucy can. So she makes Lucy call him for her. Lucy relays all her messages. But then Lucy takes over the call when Wilson tells her he's found a guy for her.

Simon finally gets Happy to do his dead-dog trick! But when he tries to show Ruthie and Matt, Happy just lies there. When Matt and Ruthie leave, Happy does the trick perfectly! What's going on?

Meanwhile, Matt has been called into the office of his guidance counselor, who gives him some startling news. He encourages Matt to tell his parents—and tell them about his summer job, too. By tomorrow night, it'll be in the local paper.

After school Annie shows Lucy a brochure about Camp Catchurpride. She shows Simon a flyer about Space Camp. She tries to interest Ruthie in a trip to visit Grandpa in Phoenix. Nobody's taking the bait. "You'll never pull it off," Ruthie tells her.

Later Simon tells Ruthie that Happy does the trick, but not if anyone else is in the room. Ruthie says it's simple: she has stage fright. What'll he do? Simon wonders. The contest is the next day.

Wilson calls to apologize to Matt. Mary catches him and yells at Wilson over the phone: If *she's* not talking to her brother, *he's* not talking to her brother. Then she has to leave to go get her sports physical for basketball camp. Lucy takes the phone and learns from Wilson that the boy he's set her up with, Kenny, wants to meet her tomorrow after school.

Meanwhile, Eric has taken Rod and Jimmy on some rounds. Eric is apologizing for the depressing afternoon; unfortunately, it's part of a minister's job. But the boys are having fun: the homeless shelter makes better gravy than their moms; at the hospital, it was cool to see the guy who came in with a coat hanger in his eye. Minutes after arriving at the

nursing home, the boys have a huge crowd of seniors boogying to hip-hop.

On the way to the doctor's, Annie tries to talk to Mary about being angry at Matt. Mary blurts out that Matt has a summer job but isn't adult enough to tell his parents about it. Annie is stunned.

Later, at home, Annie tells Eric she's a little tired and the doctor roped her into getting a physical while she was there. And then . . . Matt walks in. He can tell his mom knows. "The good news is . . . I'm valedictorian." His parents are surprised and delighted. "The bad news is . . . I leave before I have a chance to make my speech. I got a job in a Washington, D.C. summer work program." He'll miss graduation. He'll be leaving in a couple of days. Sitting on the stairs, Ruthie hears everything. With tears in her eyes, she hugs her teddy bear and hurries to her room.

At the Pow Chow contest Simon and Happy are nervous as they wait for their turn. Eric tells them that when Ruthie is nervous at the Christmas pageant, they all take a deep breath and exhale slowly. Simon is doubtful but tries it. When it's their turn, Happy does the trick. The judges gasp and give them a standing ovation.

Back home, Lucy has changed her clothes a million times while getting ready to meet Kenny. Mary tells her he's here and drags her downstairs. But just then Simon rushes in shouting, "Turn on the TV!" Everyone gathers to watch—except Lucy and Kenny, who only have eyes for each other. A videotape of Happy doing her trick is on the news. Everyone cheers. But across town a bratty little redheaded girl screams: "Some blond creep stole my dog!" Her dog has been missing for two years, and she's sure that Happy is her dog Whitey. "We'll get her back for you, sweetie pie," her father promises.

Annie throws an instant ice-cream party to celebrate when the phone rings. It's Dr. Peterson. He wants her to come down to the office to talk, but she insists he give her his news on the phone. There's a pause, and then tears stream down her face. "Thank you for letting us know," she says softly, then hangs up.

As the kids dig into their ice cream, Eric asks what's wrong.

"Mary . . ." Annie whispers. "Mary is pregnant."

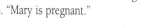

. . . And Girlfriends

**written by Catherine LePard;
directed by Burt Brinckerhoff**

In part two of the special
season finale, Matt reveals he's
class valedictorian, but he's
leaving for a summer job. A man
claims that Happy is really his
dog, Whitey. And Eric and Annie
confront Mary and Wilson about
Mary's possible pregnancy.

As the ice cream melts, Annie and Eric are frozen by the news that their fifteen-year-old "baby" is expecting a baby. Annie blames herself, but Eric is more interested in blaming Mary and Wilson. Annie realizes Mary has no idea, or she would never have agreed to the physical. They'll have to break the news to her.

Meanwhile, Matt and Mary are arguing as they head upstairs, and Ruthie hits Matt on the leg. "That's for the summer job." Simon is complaining that Happy should have won a medal or something. "Would you rather give up your Pow Chow or be a—"

Just then the doorbell rings. It's Eric's parents. "What time's graduation?" the Colonel asks.

"—dead dog," Simon finishes. Happy keels over—summing up how the rest of the Camden family is feeling. Annie and Eric reveal that Ruth and the Colonel may have made the trip for nothing. They just learned Matt's missing graduation. To their surprise, the Colonel sides with Matt. He thinks a job in D.C. is much more important than "walking across a stage in a muumuu and wearing a cardboard hat." Matt thanks the Colonel for taking his side.

With a house full of guests, Eric and Annie realize they'll have to postpone their talk with Mary.

On their double date at the pool hall, Wilson and Mary's smooching grosses out Lucy and Kenny. But Kenny wants to know all about Lucy. She's thinking he's definitely major league.

At home, Eric asks the Colonel not to interfere with the summer job issue and tells him Matt made valedictorian. The Colonel agrees that's important and says he'll make another phone call. Another? Matt arrives in time to hear his grandfather reveal that he made a phone call to help him get the summer job. Matt is upset to learn he didn't get it on his own and doesn't want to take it now. Nonsense, the Colonel says. Matt's qualifications won the job, but Matt won't listen. He says he'll see them at graduation.

The doorbell rings again, and Annie and Eric meet Jack Martin. He saw their dog on TV and he's sure it's his daughter's dog, Whitey. Simon and Ruthie are upset. Jack wants to take the dog then and there, but Eric says the family will have to get back to him. As Jack stomps out, he nearly runs into Annie's father, Charles, and his girlfriend, Ginger. "What time is graduation?"

Eric and Annie are overwhelmed. They sit out on the porch waiting for Mary. When the kids come home, Lucy and Kenny go inside as Eric and Annie go out to speak to Mary and Wilson. They blurt out the news: "Mary, you're pregnant."

Mary and Wilson look puzzled. "I don't think so," Mary says.

Annie is angry at Mary's attitude. "Why, because your birth control is infallible?" Mary nods. "It's called not having sex."

Now Eric and Annie are totally confused. Dr. Peterson must have made a mistake. Mary's angry at them for thinking she'd betray their trust. She drags a stunned Wilson into the house. Annie and Eric decide they believe the kids are telling the truth.

Rod and Jimmy grill Lucy about her date as the Colonel grills Kenny. She's worried, though. Kenny seems great—but she never gets great. What's wrong with him?

Upstairs Simon and Ruthie are upset about Happy. But then they get an idea. What if Happy doesn't look like Whitey? In the middle of the night Ruthie and Simon sneak into the bathroom and dye Happy's hair. And now . . . she's purple!

The next morning Annie and Eric are speechless when Jack Martin shows up with a lawyer. Even more so when Ruthie and Simon come down with their purple dog. "Food coloring?" Jack guesses. He sighs and admits he would've tried it, too. Then he takes out a leash and says, "Here, Whitey." The Camdens are dismayed to see "Happy" trot over to him. Eric hugs his sobbing kids.

Lucy decides her date with Kenny was too perfect. She calls Kenny to say she had a good time, but she doesn't think it's going to work out.

Matt catches Mary on the phone and chides her for being so wrapped up in Wilson that she doesn't realize Happy's been taken away, Ruthie and Simon are crying, and Lucy's upset over breaking up with Kenny. She needs to do better if she's going to take over his job as the oldest when he goes off to college.

Then Matt gets a phone call. His jaw drops as he listens, then manages to croak out, "Okay. Thank you." When he hangs up, he tells them it was Hillary Clinton congratulating him on being valedictorian and telling him to stay home, make his

speech, then come to D.C. Matt thanks his grandfather, who grunts "make us proud," then hassles him about his long hair.

Simon and Ruthie are still feeling depressed, but Rod and Jimmy have an idea. They enlist the Colonel's help. That night the Colonel and Ruth pretend to take the kids out for ice cream. But they're really on a mission.

Annie answers the doorbell and it's her father with Ginger, announcing, "Congratulate us! We're engaged!"

Just then the Colonel and Ruth return—totally disheveled, covered in mud. The Colonel makes a lame excuse that no one believes, then Annie demands to know where the kids are. At last the story comes out: They were trying to steal Happy back under cover of darkness, but failed.

The next day, however, Happy shows up at the Camden house on her own. Simon and Ruthie think it's proof that the dog knows her *real* family. Eric says it's not that easy. When Jack Martin shows up, Simon assures him they didn't steal her. Jack says he knows. She dug a hole under the fence. Eric says he doesn't want things to get ugly, but he can't let him take Happy. Jack admits he knows that, too. He was planning to bring her back this morning anyway. She cried all day yesterday. He realizes she wants to be here.

The next day at church, Kenny shows up and Lucy reconciles with him. Then Eric begins his sermon with Rod and Jimmy behind him. Eric begins by commenting that he wonders each week if anyone ever hears him, if he's said anything worth staying awake for. Then he introduces his two MITs. Rod and Jimmy present a mind-boggling speech about dog-paddling souls and the message of Ambidexterity—that God wants us to be good with both hands.

Eric is a bit confused, but after the service his parishioners congratulate him on an amazing service.

That afternoon the Camden family takes up a whole row at Matt's graduation. Eric and Annie are touched by Matt's speech, especially the part that includes praise for the times when they "illuminate the dark places, the doubt, the uncertainty," and help the kids find their way.

Annie leans over to Eric and whispers her news: "We're going to have a baby." *What!?* Annie nods. Dr. Peterson called. He got their tests mixed up.

Later, at home, Eric gathers the children around to make the announcement: He and Annie are going to have a baby. Ruthie's speechless. Jimmy and Rod exchange high fives. "You didn't do this just to get me to stay home and go to school, did you?" Matt asks. His parents assure him that's not the reason.

Then everyone congratulates Eric and Annie with hugs and kisses.

Season 3

Everybody's learning in Season Three. Annie finds out she's expecting twins, then learns her father is getting remarried. Mary gets a driver's permit, and Ruthie discovers Matt behind Santa's beard. Eric learns the value of life when he gets shot, while his parents, the Colonel and Ruth, adopt a young boy. Mary learns about herbal stimulants from a basketball teammate, and Matt discovers that Heather is getting married—and thinks he's losing Shana, too. Everybody has to learn how to live with twin babies in the house!

It Takes Two, Baby

written by Brenda Hampton;
directed by Burt Brinckerhoff

**Annie hates that she's so huge
so early in her pregnancy.
Matt moves into an apartment
with three cute college girls.
Mary and Lucy compete to see who
can rack up the most dates.**

Annie is three months pregnant, overweight, and miserable. Having a baby now is a lot harder than when she was twenty or thirty. Eric tries to reassure her. He even makes plans to cook dinner at home for their twentieth wedding anniversary, but she only takes that as proof that he doesn't want to be seen with his "fat" wife.

Meanwhile, the new school year has brought new changes to other members of the Camden household. Lucy is getting over her summer breakup with Kenny by deciding she needs to man-hunt by the book: the new best-selling book *The Rules*. She's convinced that she'll find not just a date, but the love of her life, the person she's meant to marry. Mary tells her that there are no rules, and bets that she can get more dates by breaking the rules. But Lucy replies, if she's such an expert, how come Wilson went off to college instead of finding a school in town? Mary retorts that she's looking forward to going out with lots of guys.

Ruthie has to deal with the prospect of no longer being the baby of the family. She claims she's having symptoms like her mommy: morning sickness, weight gain.

Matt has started attending a local college and has decided he wants to move out of the house. While studying notices on the school bulletin board, he's surprised to find that Connie, the girl he took to last year's prom, is auditing a few classes and is looking for a fourth roommate. Room with three girls? Matt agrees to come over that night to meet the others.

Back at the house, the phone rings twice, and both calls are for Mary. Not only does she have a date for Friday, but another guy is coming over tonight to shoot baskets. Two to nothing, she brags. "This is not a contest!" Lucy replies.

Matt tells his parents he may room with three girls, and he's all set to debate their arguments. So he's surprised when his mom says, "Hey, it's your life, and it's your money." When she leaves, Eric explains, "She can have your room painted like a nursery in twenty-four hours. Make sure you know what you're doing."

Meanwhile, Connie's roommates are skeptical about having a man in the house—till he shows up and they see how cute he is. "So . . . when can you move in?" Charlotte gushes. Connie then explains that they should set some ground rules: no one can have dates stay overnight, no parties without mutual consent, and no dating between the housemates. Everyone agrees.

Tall, handsome Jordan Johanson comes over to shoot baskets with Mary, and he tosses his jacket and his wallet on the kitchen table. A few minutes later, while Eric is looking for his keys and wallet, Simon comes in and talks him into giving him a ride to a classmate's house so she can borrow his textbook; Lucy and Ruthie tag along to get Annie a banana split from the Dairy Shack. In the rush, Simon finds Eric's keys in the fruit bowl, Eric tosses on Jordan's jacket, which he thinks is Matt's, and Ruthie picks up what she thinks is his wallet, but it's really Jordan's.

On their way out, they run into Mary, who has tumbled midgame on top of Jordan. She looks up at her family from the lawn and smiles, particularly at Lucy.

Matt comes by with Connie to pack some things—he's moving in tonight. Annie asks them to get rid of all the chicken in the freezer. Matt eagerly volunteers to donate it to his new apartment. As soon as she leaves, Connie gives Matt a kiss. "What about the rules?" he asks. "No dating." Right, Connie agrees. We'll be just like brother and sister. Matt gulps.

At the Dairy Shack, Eric goes to pay the bill and discovers he's got somebody else's wallet, which has a hundred-dollar bill in it. Eric asks if the boy would hold the hundred till he can get back with smaller bills. He explains he's got a pregnant wife who's having an ice cream attack and that he's a minister at Glenoak Community Church. "Sure you are, buddy," the clerk says when he holds up the picture that fell out of the wallet: a lewd picture of a naked woman.

When they return, Eric explains the mix-up to Mary's friend. Jordan explains that the hundred-dollar bill was money his dad makes him carry for car emergencies. Later, Eric tells Mary about the picture in Jordan's wallet. When he asks her what she thinks about it, she responds that he doesn't want to know what she thinks, he wants to tell her what *he* thinks. "Well, I don't like it," he says.

That night, as Matt arranges chicken in the freezer of his new apartment, Charlotte comes in and surprises him with a big kiss. They don't realize Amanda saw them.

At school the next day, Mary questions Jordan about the picture in his wallet. Embarrassed, Jordan says his brother put it there for a joke. Jim walks by and reminds Mary about their date. When both boys leave, Mary sees Brad and makes plans with him to go see *Star Trek* movie festival. Lucy is speechless, but she clings to her idea that *The Rules* works.

As Matt is sneaking out of the apartment to go to class, he's confronted by Amanda about last night's kiss with Charlotte. When he insists nothing is going on, she grins and says she wants to be next in line. Matt rushes out as Connie comes in. She gets the feeling that something's going on.

Meanwhile, Connie confronts Matt at school, calling him a rule-breaker. He insists Charlotte came on to him, the same way Connie did. She tells him he has to move out, but he

wants to know why Charlotte doesn't have to move out. Connie goes off in a huff.

While putting on lipstick at her locker, Lucy is surprised when Jordan asks her out for Saturday. In her head she hears the rule "Never accept a date after Wednesday." So she turns him down. "What about next Saturday?" he presses. Lucy is reluctant—isn't he dating her sister? But Jordan insists he's only interested in Mary as a friend, so Lucy agrees, with the condition that he tell Mary.

At home, Mary confronts Lucy about "stealing her boyfriend." Lucy counters that she only played basketball with Jordan, it wasn't a real date. But then Mary reveals she kissed him good night, which surprises Lucy, but she says she doesn't care, as Mary's the one who turned it into a popularity contest: "I win and you lose. Ha!" Mary yells back that the only reason she participated was that she didn't want Lucy to blame herself for losing Kenny, and she didn't want her to play by these dumb rules, which don't work. But then Mary realizes that sometimes, perhaps, they do work. The girls hug and make up.

Back at the girls' apartment, Matt shows up to find that Connie has packed his things. Even though he insists he did nothing wrong, he apologizes to Connie for upsetting everyone. She says she hopes they can still be friends, but he says he's very attracted to her. She says maybe they can go out once she's officially in school . . . in January 1999.

At home, Annie and Ruthie are napping when Eric sneaks in and wakes Annie up. He tells her he's taking her someplace special for their anniversary. He asks the girls to do him a favor and watch Ruthie, and Lucy quickly agrees, if he'll do her a favor and let her go out . . . with Jordan. Eric says he trusts Mary and Lucy, but not Jordan, then reluctantly agrees. Lucy screams for joy. "I've got a date!"

Annie has her eyes covered as Eric arrives at their secret destination. Annie laughs as they go in—it's the doctor's office. Dr. Lisa Landsberg does a sonogram so they can see their new baby. "This is the best anniversary we've ever had," Annie says, and Eric agrees. But a shock is in store for them when the doctor explains what they're seeing. . . .

After the doctor's visit, Eric takes Annie shopping to cheer her up. Then, dressed in a lovely new black maternity dress, she lets him escort her to one of her favorite restaurants: the Dairy Shack. They place their order, then find a seat and share a kiss. And when they look up, they're surrounded by all their kids holding their food. "Happy anniversary!" they all shout. Then Eric says, "Do you think we should tell them?" "Tell us what?" Mary asks. Eric smiles as Annie announces, "We're having twins!"

Drunk Like Me

written by
**Carol Evan McKeand
& Nigel McKeand;
directed by
Joel J. Feigenbaum**

Simon's worried the twins will be
girls and he'll be outnumbered,
especially with Matt gone. Eric is
the object of a divorcée's flirtations.
Matt considers joining a fraternity
with his new friend Kevin.

Season 3: Episode 45

Matt and his friend Kevin are getting a tour of the Rho Omega Frat House, which is a chaotic male slum. After making their way through the piles of empty pizza boxes and overflowing trash cans, they get to see their room. His reaction: "We're going to need shots." Kevin thinks the place is cool, but Matt is less than thrilled when the older frattybaggers peg him as "the minister's son" and warn him of an upcoming initiation.

Annie, meanwhile, goes down to breakfast and finds Mary, Lucy, and Ruthie eating cereal. From the same bowl. "We thought we'd save you some cleanup time," Lucy explains helpfully. The girls high-five one another when Annie says she feels that the new twins will be girls. Simon is horrified. Even more so when Annie announces that Matt's surprise gift—a car—is being delivered that afternoon for the group to work on. Quite a mechanic herself, Annie thinks if they all work hard on rebuilding the engine, they can have it up and running in a few days. Simon complains to his dad that they've turned the whole project into a "girl thing," but Eric doesn't want to be in on it because he doesn't know anything about cars. Later Annie suggests that Eric needs to do some "guy stuff" with Simon so he won't feel left out, especially now that Matt's not living at home.

Later that day Matt goes to see his father at work and finds him showing a very attractive and flirtatious divorcée, Nancy Randall, around the church. When she leaves, Matt tells his dad he's thinking of backing out of joining the fraternity, but he doesn't want to ruin his friendship with Kevin. He wants help with an excuse. Eric's excuse is simple: You don't want to. That's the best reason.

At home Annie and the girls meet Matt's new car: a faded '84 Chevy Camaro that backfires. Armed with the book *Auto Repair for Dummies*, Annie thinks they can do miracles. To keep it a surprise, she pulls some wires loose from the automatic garage opener. They can tell Matt it's broken. "You're going to lie?" Ruthie asks incredulously. "Fib," Annie corrects her. "It's different. We'll talk later."

Over pizza Matt tells Kevin he's reconsidering joining the frat. Kevin tells Matt he's just feeling insecure, but they'll feel great after initiation. When Matt says he's still not sure, Kevin responds angrily, "I thought we were in this together, pal, but evidently you're nobody's friend."

Coming home from the grocery store, Annie finds Lucy doing great things with the car; she's obviously inherited Annie's knack with cars. But Mary and Ruthie have disappeared. Simon's mad that they took "his" dog without asking.

While at the park Mary meets Jay Thompson, a boy from school. When he hears they're fixing up an old car, he's really interested, which gives Mary a great excuse to invite him home. Once there, she tries to pretend to know all about cars, and she's saved by Lucy's quick thinking.

Later, Matt gets permission to drive the family car to go to the fraternity party. Eric lectures him about drinking and driving, since he knows there's never been a frat party without beer. "Of course you'll do the right thing," Eric calls after him hopefully as Matt silently climbs the stairs to his attic room.

When Eric and Simon get to the pool hall, it's so crowded there's a half-hour wait for a table. Simon's not happy when Nancy Randall invites them to join her; it's supposed to be a guys' night out. He grills her and finds out that in addition to being good-looking, she's divorced and has no kids. "On the rebound, huh? I hear that can make people do crazy things." Embarrassed, Eric makes a joke, trying to apologize. Nancy takes the hint and leaves. Eric wants to know what Simon's problem is, and Simon replies, "Mentally, she was stuck all over you like a bunch of Post-its."

Meanwhile, Matt shows up at the fraternity party but decides not to go in. Instead, he winds up sitting in a booth at Madison's bar all by himself, and he meets the only other person in the bar who isn't drinking alcohol: a cute girl named Rita Chavez, a first-year med student on scholarship. He tells her he just bailed on a fraternity initiation. "Good for you," she says. Matt wonders why she's there if she doesn't drink. She explains it's because lots of college kids hang out there. "So what if I don't drink, right?" she asks. Matt smiles and makes a toast . . . just as Eric and Simon walk by and see him through the window.

Back at the Camden house, Lucy privately quizzes Mary from her car repair manual so she can impress Jay. Annie goes in to have a chat with Simon. He starts to tell her about Nancy, but Annie already knows all about it and tries to reassure him. Then they talk about the babies. "If the babies are girls, would it be so terrible?" she asks. Simon thinks it would throw the whole family out of whack. Annie nods sympathetically: If Matt is gone, "You'd be, what? Like King of the Universe, protector of the sisters, the watchful boyfriend eye?" Hmm, thinks Simon, maybe it won't be so bad after all.

When Matt comes home, he says, "I wasn't drinking" before anyone can even say hello. Eric assures him that he trusts him. Matt starts to go to bed when the phone rings. It's one of the fraternity brothers, who whispers that Kevin's in his car, drunk and in trouble. He tells him where, then hangs up.

When Matt arrives, he finds Kevin slumped over the wheel of his car, as if someone had dumped him there. He's drunk and also having trouble breathing. Matt shouts for help, but the other guys around are drunk and just laugh. Matt drags his friend into the station wagon and drives him to the hospital himself. As Matt waits in the waiting room, Eric shows up. The two are unable to reach Kevin's father or get the housekeeper to answer the phone. The doctor tells Matt that Kevin's blood alcohol level is five times the legal limit. There's a fifty-fifty chance it will kill him.

The next day Matt is still there waiting when Rita walks by. When she finds out he's waiting for Kevin, she tells him that Kevin's awake and that he's a very lucky kid to have no brain damage. He calls home to tell Eric, who's glad, but angry at the fraternity. Eric says they reached Kevin's dad on a business trip, but he won't decide whether to come home till he hears an update on his son's condition. When Eric hangs up, Simon comes in, suited up like a grease monkey, ready to go out and help the girls with the car. Obviously Annie's little talk has sunk in. When he meets Jay, he's totally awed to hear he has a Prowler; Jay's dad is a car dealer. As they walk over to take a look, Simon protectively asks, "So which of my sisters are you into?" Jay confesses neither, he's just broken up with a girl and he's interested only in the car. Simon smiles. "This could be the start of a beautiful friendship."

Meanwhile, Annie answers the front door to find Nancy Randall, looking more beautiful than ever. As Eric joins them, she confesses: she's on the rebound and has been flirting with him, and she wants to apologize. She's decided to go to another church. When she leaves, Annie and Eric laugh. Simon's radar was working perfectly!

At the hospital, Matt finally gets to talk to Kevin and is shocked that he's still going to pledge the fraternity. On the way out he runs into a fraternity brother named George. He hasn't brought flowers, he's brought a message: Kevin's out of the frat. The brothers don't think he can handle it and they don't want any more "situations." Matt is so angry—he can't believe they forced him to drink too much, then left him for dead, and now they're kicking him out. He leaves, disgusted.

But when he gets home, he gets a wonderful surprise: the "new" car his family has lovingly fixed up for him. He's delighted and jumps inside. Lucy asks if she can go, but Matt has somewhere to go. And he needs to go alone.

He goes to the Rho Omega Frat House and confronts the frat president about putting Kevin in his car and leaving him for dead. As he leaves, George catches up with him. "Hey," he says. "I could use a ride." Matt glares at him, till he explains: "I'm out. I won't do it anymore." Matt smiles and gives the guy a ride.

The Legacy

written by Catherine LePard; directed by Tony Mordente

Simon is forced to rat on a favorite teacher. Matt misreads a sexy professor's signals, Mary gets caught for skipping class and Annie takes up piano lessons with a handsome young hunk.

On the way to school, Ruthie is driving everyone crazy by practicing her trumpet: she gets spit in Mary's hair and causes Simon to stumble out of the car, spilling his stuff out of his backpack.

As his family drives off, Simon spots his science teacher, Mr. Lane, in the parking lot and waves. Mr. Lane waves back. But then the teacher hears some shouting and turns to look. One of his students, Mark Huff, has just been dropped off by his father. But the father jumps out of the car and chases after his son. "I said, 'You're welcome for the ride!'" he yells at the son. Mark turns around, a look of fear on his face. Mr. Lane senses trouble and steps in between them, asking if there's anything he can do to help. "Yeah, mind your own business!" Mr. Huff snaps. When the father charges forward, Mr. Lane shoves him back. "You just made a big mistake," Mr. Huff growls. Watching from a distance, unable really to see or hear what happened, Simon is shocked to see a favorite teacher behave with aggression.

At home, Annie's chewing up the shrubbery with electric hedge trimmers in her latest "pregnancy project": topiary. Eric points out that with every pregnancy, she becomes obsessed with mastering a new project. She proposes trading topiary work for piano lessons, and he offers to find her a piano teacher.

At school, Mary is trying to stay awake as her ancient English teacher, Mrs. McKee, reads aloud from *The Scarlet Letter* in a monotonous drone. After class Mary complains with her friends Cheryl and Corey. Cheryl says they should bag the class tomorrow.

At the junior high school, Simon's been called into the principal's office. When he sees Mark, his dad, and Mr. Lane waiting, he shudders. Principal Howard asks Simon to explain what he witnessed that morning. Simon's confused and doesn't want to say anything to get Mr. Lane in trouble. He tells what he saw, adding, "But I was far away and I couldn't hear what was going on, and I probably didn't see anything." He's upset when he leaves, but Mr. Lane tells him he did great. When he leaves, Mr. Huff insists the principal call the police.

Matt's studying with his friend Scott at the pool hall when their beautiful forty-something English lit teacher, Dr. Alison LaRoe, comes in and smiles at them. "Dr. LaRoe's stalking you," he says. When she invites them to play pool, Scott jumps at the chance. Matt feels weird about it.

Simon comes home to find Ruthie lying on the floor. She got rid of the trumpet, she explains, and switched to the flute because it has a cute case; but blowing it makes her dizzy. Simon tells her all the instruments have cute cases, and she should try something else. In the meantime, Annie's new piano teacher arrives: Mrs. Hinkle's twenty-something nephew, Josh. Annie and Lucy gawk. Who wouldn't be interested?

Back at the pool hall, Matt walks Dr. LaRoe back to her car and . . . kisses her. "What are you doing?" she asks, startled, and he realizes he's completely misread her signals. The next morning Matt tells his dad what happened when Annie walks in, dressed up and wearing more makeup than usual. She gets mad when Eric looks surprised and says she looks great—as if that means she usually doesn't. Then she hurries into the living room as the doorbell rings. Time for her first piano lesson with the handsome Josh Hinkle. Matt laughs as his father sighs.

At school, at least some of the Camden kids are having a great day. Mary and her friends cut class to play like children on the playground. Ruthie's hip music teacher, Mr. Kelly, tells her to "find what makes you happy and get down with it." Ruthie picks the tuba. But Simon is miserable when he finds out Mr. Lane got suspended.

Matt's life is even worse. He skips Dr. LaRoe's class but then Scott hands him his graded test. He got a big fat C minus. Scott is outraged; he thinks it's retaliation for the kiss. He tells Matt he's got to confront her. Matt does, but she insists that last night wasn't the first time a student has made a pass at her and assures him it didn't affect his grade. His essay deserved a C. "I'm an adult," she says. "And up until today, I thought you were, too." What a train wreck, Matt mutters to himself.

At home, Eric is stunned when Simon rushes into his arms in tears, even though he's supposed to be at school. But Simon says he couldn't help running home: Mr. Lane got suspended, and it's all his fault. Eric tries to reassure him and tells him he'll talk to Mr. Lane.

Later Eric meets with Robert Lane at the pool hall to hear his side of the story. Mr. Lane clarifies that he's not mad at Simon, who did the right thing. Robert knows he shouldn't have pushed Carl Huff, but when he saw him come after his son, a switch flipped. "I was twelve years old again, and my dad was coming at me," he says, and shakes his head. Until this incident, Robert had thought he was over all that. Eric suggests he might like to talk to a professional about it. Robert then says he'll have lots of time—he's been fired.

Eric comes in to find Annie happily practicing piano, swaying to the click, click of the metronome. When he suggests that he wouldn't blame her if she indulged in a little flirting with her handsome teacher, she storms out. Eric then finds Simon in the bathtub, completely dressed, wearing earmuffs and a football helmet—to drown out the sound of Ruthie's saxophone—and doing his homework. Eric tells him about his talk

with Mr. Lane and assures him the teacher's not mad at Simon.

When Matt comes home, he tells his dad he's misread the situation with Dr. LaRoe again. Eric suggests that maybe Scott's the one misreading the signals and he should stop taking his advice. Matt goes back to school and apologizes. Dr. LaRoe is impressed. And they go off to play a *friendly* game of pool.

Annie then has a talk with Mary about skipping class. But what Annie's even more upset about is that Mary's not getting anything valid out of a great classic novel about societal shame, scorn, and ostracism. Mary admits she hasn't read the book.

Meanwhile, Eric has gone to the Huff house and finds Mark nervously hiding in the bushes. The child claims to be looking for something just as the door opens and Carl Huff hurls an opened suitcase out into the darkness. Women's clothes spill out into the yard. Carl yells for his son to get into the house, but Eric tells the boy to stand behind him. Mrs. Huff comes outside, crying, and is even more humiliated to see the minister watching. Carl threatens to call the police, but Eric stands his ground. Mrs. Huff has silently picked up all her clothes and now stands with Eric and Mark. Carl slams the door, and Eric takes Mark and his mother away.

At the next basketball game, Mary, Cheryl, and Corey spread out behind the concession stand instead of on the basketball court—wearing cards with red A's for Absentee. Instead of getting sympathy from friends, they're getting hassled for doing something so stupid and selfish that it kept them out of the game. "Why don't they just stone us?" Corey complains. "Now I know what Hester Prynne must've felt like," Mary adds. The girls look at one another. Suddenly they understand *The Scarlet Letter.*

At the end of Annie's piano lesson, Josh tells her she's smart, beautiful, and dedicated, and he hopes he meets someone like her one day, then kisses her on the cheek. Annie is speechless, flattered . . . and embarrassed. She goes to Eric and apologizes for unconsciously encouraging the flirtation. But Eric knows sometimes it takes an outsider to make a pregnant woman believe she's beautiful.

That night Matt walks through the house to see how all his siblings are dealing with Annie's off-key playing. Mary's reading *The Scarlet Letter* with her Walkman on. Simon has on his earmuffs and helmet. Happy is wearing a bathing cap. Ruthie's accompanying her mom with her latest instrument—her voice.

At school the next day, Mr. Lane is back, with some help from Eric. He talks to the kids about the cycle of abuse, and his own experience. Then he tells them, "If someone's hurting you, you have to tell someone who can help. A teacher, a counselor, someone you can trust."

Cutters

written by Sue Tenney; directed by Anson Williams

Mary blames Lucy's new friend Nicole for her sister's bad biology grades, then discovers Nicole has a horrible secret. Worried about the twins coming, Ruthie flunks her math test on purpose to get her mother's attention. Meanwhile, Matt suffers from a rare experience: a girl rejects him.

Mary is trying to read *Hamlet*, but Lucy and her new friend Nicole are gossiping about a guy named Danny Johnson. When Mary goes down to complain, her parents tell her she shouldn't have saved her reading until the last night. Mary can't believe she's getting in trouble for trying to study. She tells her parents she thinks Nicole is bad news.

Across the hall, Simon can't study because Ruthie's dancing around the room. She says she doesn't have to study because she's naturally smart. Simon tells her it's great that she can take care of herself, but it's the squeaky wheel, like Lucy, that gets all the attention. Just wait till the twins come.

At the Crawford University library, Matt strikes up a conversation with a pretty girl named Becky from his psychology class. When he finds out she made a C on the last test—he made an A—he tries to set up a study date with her. But she shakes her head no and leaves. Matt feels as if he's losing his touch.

At the high school Lucy is having a midday makeup break, then hurries to meet up with Nicole. Her new friend is a little upset and complains that she doesn't have any other friends to talk to. "I'm really glad you're my best friend," she says to Lucy, who responds with her new big news: Danny Johnson just broke up with his girlfriend. When Danny walks by, followed by an entourage of friends, Lucy urges Nicole to say hello to him. "Hi!" Nicole blurts out. Danny stops, whispers something to his friends, and they all laugh as they walk off. Nicole is crushed.

But things only get worse when their biology teacher, Mr. Jackson, announces a pop quiz. The kids moan, but the teacher claims it should be no problem if they did their homework. Lucy and Nicole trade horrified glances. They didn't. Mr. Jackson asks to see them after school. When they show up, he tells them they'll fail biology if they don't improve. Then he hands back their graded quizzes: Lucy got a D-minus, and Nicole got an F. Not only do they need their parents to sign the quizzes, Mary has heard everything.

That afternoon Eric is making lunch when Matt comes down. In his pajamas. For breakfast. Eric instantly sizes up the problem: "Who's the woman?" "What woman?" Matt asks innocently. "The woman who rejected you."

Meanwhile, Annie invites Nicole to dinner that night, and when Eric asks them how school was, Lucy says great and changes the subject. As they're carrying their dishes into the kitchen, Ruthie shows her mom a note from her teacher to sign. Lucy and Nicole squirm when they hear Ruthie failed a math test, even though math is her best subject. Annie learns from the note that Ruthie answered "51" to every question. Annie realizes something's up and agrees to sit down and help Ruthie with her homework. Ruthie gives Simon a thumbs-up sign. When they're alone, she tells him, "You told me that if I did bad in school, I'd squeak and Mom and Dad would have to oil me even after the twins get here." Simon groans.

Mary catches up with Lucy and accuses her of lying to their dad. Lucy says she didn't exactly lie, she just didn't tell him about the test yet. Mary blames her friendship with Nicole for her problems. "There is something weird about your friend!" she insists. The girls don't know it, but Nicole has heard every word.

Angry, Mary goes and tells her parents that Lucy lied, and reveals her problems in biology. "I told you Nicole was a bad influence on her," she says. Biology is the only class Lucy is failing, and it's the only class the two girls share. Mary is upset that her parents aren't going to yell at Lucy; they're going to give her a chance to explain. And they say it's unlike Mary to squeal on her sister. Mary is shocked.

When Mary goes back upstairs, Matt drags her to his room and tells her about Becky's rejection. He begs her to tell him what's wrong with him. Mary doesn't want to do this, but finally she says that *maybe* it's his long hair. Or that he's always so sure of himself. Or that little whisker thing under his lip. Or . . . Matt curtly thanks her and shoves her out the door, where Simon's outside listening. "Maybe Becky doesn't like the way you dress," he suggests. Matt slams the door.

Annie comes upstairs to study with Ruthie and is soon confused by her weird answers. Ruthie proudly says, "I need a lot of help, huh? I guess we'll have to study together every night, even after you have the babies. I hope that's okay with you two," she tells Annie's tummy. Annie smiles. Now she understands.

Later Eric confronts Lucy about her biology grades. Lucy is angry that Mary told and defensive about her friendship with Nicole. Eric agrees to tutor them both, if Nicole's parents agree.

Meanwhile, Mary opens the upstairs bathroom door and nearly screams. Nicole is in there, and Mary is stunned by what she sees. "Don't say anything. Please," Nicole begs.

The next day Mary tries to get her father to forbid Lucy to see Nicole, but she won't explain why. When her father won't agree, she decides to talk to Lucy herself. She tries to catch her at school, but Lucy blows her off. Lucy's concerned, though, when Nicole doesn't show up for biology class.

Meanwhile, Matt's decided to try again with Becky—this time with his hair groomed and wearing a sports jacket. He suggests they get together "just to study." At last she agrees, as she really needs the help. She tells him he can come by her apartment that evening. Matt's on top of the world.

That afternoon when Eric brings the kids home from school, Ruthie races home with her news. She answered everything right on her math test. The teacher even let her take yesterday's test over! Annie's delighted, but she has no idea that Simon said he'd pay her fifty cents for each right answer.

Mary and Lucy come in fighting. Mary wants to talk to her, but Lucy won't listen. She accuses Mary of being jealous of her friendship with Nicole. Exasperated, Mary finally reveals that she saw Nicole in the bathroom last night: "She was cutting herself with a razor." Lucy won't believe her at first, but Eric and Annie do. Nicole, it seems, is what psychologists refer to as a "cutter." Eric explains to Lucy that after eating disorders, self-mutilation may be the fastest-growing problem among teen girls. Lucy is worried about her friend, but Eric tells her Nicole's dad is coming over and that they'll talk about it then.

In the meantime, Ruthie uses Happy to hunt down Simon and make him pay up. Things only get better for Ruthie when her mom says they can study together every day, even when she makes good grades.

When Ted Jacob comes by, Eric tries to gently break the news to him about his daughter's problem. Ted is shocked, but not because he didn't know. He's shocked because she's doing it again. He explains that they moved to Glenoak to give Nicole a fresh start after she had therapy. Now he doesn't know what to do. Eric gives him the number of a friend who runs a treatment program at McNeal Hospital in Chicago.

When Matt meets Becky for their study date, things are going well till he decides to make a romantic move—just as her extremely good-looking boyfriend comes in the door. Matt accuses her of using him to make her boyfriend jealous, but Becky just laughs. She told him it was just to study, and Jeff knew he'd be here. Miserable, Matt grabs his coat and leaves.

At the Camden house, life goes on. Lucy apologizes to Mary and thanks her for being her big sister. Annie gives Simon his twenty dollars back. When Matt comes home, she asks him how his date went. In answer, he takes off the sports jacket, throws it on the floor, and stomps on it.

The doorbell rings, and it's Nicole and her father, Ted. Lucy runs to give her a hug. Though she's sad to learn Nicole is going away to Chicago, she's glad Nicole's going to get help. As Mary turns to leave, Nicole thanks her for telling her family about her problem.

Later Eric studies biology with Lucy, who apologizes for being stupid about biology and about Nicole. "I never want to hear you call yourself stupid again," he says. "Biology's tough, and no one knew about Nicole, not even her parents." He knows Lucy misses her and promises that he'll always be there.

. . . And a Nice Chianti

written by Greg Plageman; directed by Harvey Laidman

Lucy, Simon, and Ruthie want to ride the bus rather than ride with Mary, who has just received her learner's permit. Matt gets arrested for stealing a car. The family helps a runaway girl who's expecting, and Eric helps a church member come to terms with the death of her son.

Season 3: Episode 48

The Camden kids announce they've decided to ride the bus to school from now on. Simon says it's "to meet new people, make new friends." But Annie knows the real reason. They hear a horrible screech of tires outside, and they all cross their fingers. Eric comes in and sadly nods. "I got it!" Mary shouts as she runs in. "I got my learner's permit! I am an official licensed driver!" Matt pats her on the back. "Chauffeur," he corrects her. One by one her horrified siblings file out of the kitchen.

The next morning everyone's racing to catch the bus, except Ruthie, who's not allowed. She comes out wearing a football helmet. "That's not funny!" Mary snaps.

Taking a deep breath, Simon climbs on the junior high bus. The front's full of geeks, the back's full of tough guys. He tries to sit next to a girl, but she puts her book bag in the seat. The bus driver hassles him to sit down, and he manages to find a spot right smack in the middle. Simon sighs. So far, riding the bus stinks. But it's better than the alternative.

Lucy boards the high school bus to find something even more horrifying: "Oh, no. Freshmen." The boys are checking her out. The girls are freezing her out. A kid named Stevie hits

on her, even though his "part-time" girlfriend is sitting right there giving Lucy evil looks. Lucy sighs. So far, riding the bus stinks. But at least it's safer than riding with Mary.

When they get to school, Simon saves a geek from being beaten up by a bully who's demanding he hand over his homework. Simon very politely suggests that if the bully lets go, he's sure the geek would be glad to help him with his homework. The bully obliges and introduces himself to Simon, leaving the other students in awe. As Lucy gets off her bus, she's threatened by Stevie's girlfriend.

Eric goes by to visit with Elizabeth Brown, a church member who's just gone through a divorce. Surrounding her are photos of her son, who was killed in an accident three years ago. Despite group therapy, she still can't get over his death. Eric suggests that instead of trying not to think about him, she might try picking a short period every day to really think about him, to cry, to let all her feelings out. Then put an end to her grieving for the day and leave herself open to help from others. She's doubtful but agrees to try.

On the way to school in his own car, Matt spots a young pregnant girl standing beside her car on the side of the road. Matt pulls over to help her, but as he puts his head under the hood of her car, she zooms off in his Camaro! At first Matt's relieved when two police officers stop and get out. He tries to explain about the pregnant girl who stole his car, but the police don't believe him. Instead, they arrest him for stealing this car.

When Elizabeth Brown goes to the beauty parlor, she sees a vivacious woman named Carolyn Fulton, who's "happy to be alive." She learns that the woman had a heart transplant that saved her life about three years ago. The heart came from a young man. Elizabeth can't help but wonder. . . .

After school Annie pulls up and gets out of the car so Mary can drive. A lot of the kids who know her wave, and Annie proudly pats her giant tummy. When she sees her middle child, she waves, but an embarrassed Lucy pretends not to see her and rushes onto the bus. Mary's annoyed to find that Annie has changed all the radio stations to classical music, because it's good for the babies. And that Ruthie is still wearing her helmet.

Simon discovers on the way home that he's become a hero. Now all the tough guys want him to get the geeks to help them with their homework.

Elizabeth rushes into Eric's office with her news. She's sure she's found the recipient of her son's heart. She wants Eric to call her. Eric reminds her that organ recipients usually want to remain anonymous and that they're supposed to go through the hospital. But Elizabeth believes this woman is different. Reluctantly Eric agrees to do what he can.

When he gets home, he and Annie are shocked to see Matt come home late—with Sergeant Michaels of the police department. He explains what happened and that they're checking out Matt's story. But until they find the girl, Matt's an official suspect.

The next day Eric meets with Carolyn Fulton and talks to her about her heart transplant. But when she reveals the donor died in Oregon, he realizes it wasn't Elizabeth's son. But maybe she is the person he's been looking for after all. . . .

At school, Lucy gets threatened again by Sheila, so she goes to Mary for help. No way, Mary says, after they all insulted her driving. But Lucy insists she's not riding the bus to get away from Mary's driving; it's to get away from Mom. She's embarrassed to be seen with her so pregnant. It shows that her parents can't control themselves. Mary is disgusted. "I hope Shelia beats the snot out of you," she says.

Meanwhile, Simon gets some surprising news from Marvin. Tough guy Nick's going to be mad—he made an F on his essay. Simon can't believe it; didn't Marvin help him? Yeah, Marvin says, but admits, "I'm just a C student." Simon learns too late that all the kids at the front aren't necessarily smart geeks. They just bury their noses in their books because they're scared of getting beaten up.

Meanwhile, Eric and Sergeant Michaels have found the missing girl at a community medical clinic, and Eric brings her home. Her name is Theresa, and Annie tries to make her feel welcome by smiling and saying they have something in common, but that only makes Theresa stare at the floor, ashamed. Eric has called her parents, but they find out her parents don't know about her pregnancy. While folding laundry with Annie and Matt, Theresa apologizes to Matt and explains her situation: Her parents always told her they'd throw her out if she did anything like this, so when she found out she was pregnant, she stole the car and ran away. Theresa says she knows she should put the baby up for adoption, but she keeps hoping there's another way. Matt reassures her that parents can talk tough, but he's sure they'll let her come home.

That afternoon, when it's time to get on the bus, Lucy sees Sheila coming and races to jump in the car. A few minutes later, faced with angry tough guys, Simon joins them.

When they get home, Annie and Eric have a meeting with Dan and Cheryl, Theresa's parents. Dan and Cheryl say they suspected she was behind the car theft. Then when Theresa stands up and reveals her condition, her parents shake their heads. Instead of being glad to see her, they yell at her for embarrassing them and making the biggest mistake ever. That's when Annie stands up and makes a speech about how she and all her children are human, they all make lots of mistakes. But

Dan protests, "There are some mistakes you just don't forgive, and this is one of them." They tell Theresa that she made the mistake by herself, and that she can fix it herself. Then they leave. The Camdens are stunned by their lack of love for their own daughter. At the top of the stairs, the Camden kids hear all this and they're ashamed that they've been embarrassed by their mother—a mother who's so full of love.

That night Eric goes by to see Elizabeth Brown and to tell her that Carolyn Fulton isn't the heart recipient she's been looking for. But he suggests maybe she still wants to meet her. Elizabeth says she could use a friend, but what she really needs is someone who needs her. A lightbulb goes off in Eric's head.

Two weeks later Elizabeth, Carolyn, and Theresa stop by his office following a shopping spree and explain that Elizabeth is letting Theresa stay with her. Then Eric tells Elizabeth he's had some responses to his inquiries about organ recipients. She's confused when he uses the plural. Just then a man walks in the door. He was the recipient of Elizabeth's son's heart. As they hug joyfully, another woman comes in. And another man carrying his son. The woman says she's alive because she received a kidney from Elizabeth's son. And the man, well, his eyesight was saved thanks to her son, and now he can see his own son. Elizabeth cries tears of joy as she realizes that in some small way her son still lives . . . through these people he saved.

And the Home of the Brave

written by Brenda Hampton; directed by Harry Harris

Annie struggles to accept her father's marriage to Ginger. Lucy tries to clarify her relationship with Jordan. Matt and Mary get lost on a road trip. Annie adds new meaning to Veterans Day by bringing home a homeless vet, who repays the Camdens' kindness in a very special way.

Season 3: Episode 49

It's Grandpa and Ginger's wedding day, and all the Camden children have a list of chores to do. Mary and Matt are looking after the bride and groom. Lucy and Jordan are babysitting the younger kids.

There's only one thing Eric left out: the reception. Annie's handling that. Sort of. With only five hours to spare, she's still in her bathrobe thinking about what she'll do. "Unless they call it off," she says, perhaps with a glint of hope in her eyes. While Annie's accepted Ginger as her father's new girlfriend, she hasn't accepted her as his new wife. Eric's worried about her attitude, and she admits she's in a rotten mood. But she promises to behave at the wedding. If there is one.

A little later Jordan's in the kitchen cooking hot dogs. Ruthie is impressed when he makes one for her imaginary friend, Hoowie, just the way he likes it. When she says he's better than Lucy's old boyfriends Jimmy Moon and Rod, Lucy scolds her that it's rude to talk about your old boyfriends in front of your new boyfriend. "Boyfriend?" Jordan says. This is news to him.

Matt and Mary meet up with Grandpa and Ginger in the hotel restaurant. Grandpa suggests that the girls go shopping, while he and Matt spend some time together. But Ginger's suspicious of this idea; she asks Grandpa if he's planning a trip to the cemetery, where his first wife is buried. He says he always takes flowers by when he's in town. Ginger argues that they agreed to leave the past behind them—especially on their wedding day. Before Matt and Mary can stop them, the bride and groom are arguing so much, they're even talking about calling off the wedding. Grandpa tells his grandkids to go for a ride while he and Ginger settle things, but he warns them not to go home, as they will surely tell their parents. Mary pulls a map out of the glove compartment, closes her eyes, and points to a random spot. Matt agrees to go there, and they take off on a short trip to "Turtle Mound."

Back at the house, Jordan finds Lucy hiding in the closet from embarrassment. He says he wasn't sure how she defined their relationship because she has never openly talked about it. He assumed she saw other guys. While this thought doesn't make him happy, he does like the mystery.

Meanwhile, Annie reluctantly goes to the supermarket to get food for the wedding reception that she hopes never happens. At the door she sees a young security guard kicking an old man and calling him a bum. Annie stops him and tells him he should be ashamed. The guard says the manager says these people are ruining business. But the vagrant says he's not a bum, he's a veteran; doesn't anyone remember that today is Veterans Day? He tells Annie his name is Sergeant Millard Holmes and that he fought in the army in World War II.

Annie drives back to the house and explains that instead of groceries, she's brought home a dirty, hungry old veteran. While the old guy is in the shower, Eric throws out his clothes and wonders whether he's really a veteran or not. Millard comes out in a towel and shows Eric his military dog tags to prove it. Eric wonders why Millard doesn't take advantage of some of the services for veterans. Millard avoids answering and promises to be out soon.

At the hotel, Grandpa and Ginger argue in their rooms and decide to call off the wedding after all.

Downstairs, Jordan confesses to Lucy that he's seeing someone he thinks she knows. Fine, she says, as long as it isn't this girl, Ashley, who stole Jimmy Moon from her. Jordan nods. She's the one. Lucy groans.

Meanwhile, Matt and Mary have been driving the whole time, but suddenly they have a flat tire. Neither one knows how to change a flat, but it doesn't really matter. Matt left the spare at a gas station when the car was being repaired. Matt checks the map to find out how close they are to Turtle Mound—and yells! Mary's been giving him directions to a town that's on a Florida roadmap from 1969! The last owner must have left it in the glove compartment.

Eric has gone to the Veterans Administration Building to try to find help for Millard and is frustrated to find it closed. One woman is there catching up on paperwork, and when she hears the name Sergeant Millard Holmes, she invites Reverend Camden in.

Jordan apologizes to Lucy and says he has no feelings for Ashley. The question is: Does she still have feelings for Jimmy Moon? She insists she never thinks of him.

In the middle of it all, Annie lies down for a nap.

In the desert, a tow truck stops to help Matt and Mary, but they have to call Grandpa on the man's cell phone to get a credit card number. Grandpa picks up the phone, but just then Ginger comes to Grandpa's room to apologize to him, and he leaves the phone receiver dangling.

At home, Eric is trying to convince Millard to get help from the Veterans Administration, but the proud man insists he doesn't need a handout from Uncle Sam. But when he hears about Eric's problem with Annie and the reception, Millard insists on helping out. He explains that he was a short-order cook for forty years. He promises Eric that if he'll give him some cash, the keys to the car, and the house, he'll have a feast waiting for them after the wedding. Eric is skeptical, but an apathetic Annie tells him to do it.

At the hotel, Grandpa is dressed for his wedding and waiting for Ginger in the bar. He meets another widower who got remarried. Grandpa asks how it worked out. "Lasted eleven months," the man says, adding that she took half of what he and his wife had saved over the years and went to Vegas; his kids still aren't speaking to him. Grandpa gulps.

Just before the wedding Annie has a talk with Ginger. She tells her she knows she should be grateful that her dad found someone to love him, but . . . she's not there yet. Ginger understands. She tells Annie she lost her mother when she was five, and she's still not over it. She'll never try to take Annie's mother's place. Lucy interrupts to ask, "Has anyone seen Matt and Mary?"

A state patrolman has. He's just given them a ticket for driving ten miles over the speed limit. There's no way they'll make it to the wedding now.

At last the wedding takes place. Eric says, "You may kiss the bride." Grandpa kisses Ginger. Eric kisses Annie. Jordan and Lucy kiss. "I said the *bride*," Eric points out. Ruthie looks at Happy and says, "So forget it."

When they get back to the house, the family is stunned. Millard has left a fabulous feast including a small rose-covered wedding cake. And a note. He tells them thanks for the greatest gift of all—a chance to do something for somebody else. Happy Veterans Day. The family is so touched, they head out into the night to try to find him.

Matt and Mary rush to the church and find it empty. Then they rush to the house, where they discover the untouched feast. They wonder if the wedding took place. But their concern isn't enough to destroy their appetites. They voraciously dig into the food, but they promise not to touch the cake.

Out in the night a lone figure walks along the dark road until a van stops and picks him up. It's Millard, who climbs into the already packed Camden van. The van turns around and heads back to the house, where an amazing feast is waiting to begin.

Johnny Get Your Gun

written by Brenda Hampton; directed by Kevin Inch

Eric and Annie feel as if they're surrounded by violence and kids. A boy at school threatens to blow Simon away with a gun. Eric gets shot.

Season 3: Episode 50

Matt comes in complaining that Mary hit him in the face with a basketball. Mary's version is that "he ran into the ball" because he was too busy thinking about Shana. "Shana?" Annie doesn't know any Shana. Eric comes home, but before he can say a word, Annie says, "I don't want to know. Nothing. Not a word." He's been to the Golden Gloves Tournament. He starts to tell Simon about it, who cuts the conversation short when his new girlfriend Deena calls. She's crying and says that her old boyfriend, Johnny, is "going to come after you."

"When you say 'come after me' what exactly do you mean by that?" Simon asks nervously.

At school the next day, Simon spots Johnny cornering Deena by the lockers. Heart pounding, Simon goes up and puts his arm around her and introduces himself. He says Deena is his girlfriend now. "We'll see about that, buddy," Johnny snaps.

Trying to hide his black eye, Matt walks to class with Shana. He wants her to tell him something about herself. She says she'll tell him about her life when he can handle it.

After school Johnny starts hassling Deena again. When Simon says she's riding home with him, Johnny points his index finger at him like a gun and says, "Just when you least expect it, you're going to turn around and find a .38 special

pointed right at you." He laughs and walks away. Some kids who saw the incident warn them not to tell as it will only make Johnny madder. Then Eric arrives, and he's happy to give Deena a ride. But when he asks them what's wrong, they say, "Nothing."

Later that night the phone keeps ringing, but there's no one there. When Eric questions Simon, he finally confesses that Deena's ex-boyfriend threatened to shoot him.

Meanwhile, Matt and Mary go to a quick mart where Shana is working. Her big brother George is hassling her while trying to buy beer, but he behaves when he meets the Camdens. When they leave, George twists Shana's arm until she gives him Mary's phone number. But she begs him to leave Mary alone.

Later that night Eric and Annie discuss Johnny's threat. They've called Deena's parents, and they've decided to keep both kids home the next day. They tried to call the assistant principal, but his home number is unlisted.

Finally, Simon's assistant principal, Mr. Blackstone, calls. But all he will do is call the parents to come in for a meeting and ask them to send their son to a counselor. Eric is outraged. When he leaves, Annie tries to reach Sergeant Michaels, but he's not in.

Then George calls and asks Mary out. She's delighted but can't go out on a school night. George tells her to say she's going to a friend's house, and adds that she shouldn't tell Matt. Just as she hangs up, Matt warns her that George might ask her out, and that he might be dangerous.

Eric goes to Johnny's house and tries to talk to his father, John Sr. The man is polite, but he won't invite a stranger in. Eric tells him Johnny threatened to shoot Simon. Johnny just laughs and says he was joking around, everybody does that. Eric then asks the father if Johnny has ever been in trouble before, and if the family owns a gun. John Sr. tries to shut the door, but Eric can see the answers in the man's eyes.

At home Lucy has just watched *Gone With the Wind* with Jordan, which makes her want to slap him—just like Scarlett slapped Rhett. She thinks it's romantic. Jordan disagrees.

When Eric gets home, Sergeant Michaels comes over and confirms that Johnny has a record, and that the family has a registered gun. A .38 special.

At the junior high school, Eric, Sergeant Michaels, and Mr. Blackstone have a meeting with Johnny's father. But as Sergeant Michaels goes over Johnny's record, John Sr. has an excuse for everything. He refuses to remove his gun from his home, insisting it's for protection. He and Eric get into an argument, and John Sr. threatens to go to the school board and the chief of police and complain about harassment. He shouts that he's going to put Johnny in private school. Then he storms out. Eric

and Sergeant Michaels exchange a look. Could their problems really be over that easily? The policeman warns Mr. Blackstone to alert the rest of the staff that Johnny shouldn't be allowed back on school property.

At the high school, Mary asks Lucy to tell their mom she went to her friend Cheryl's house to study. She admits it's a cover so she can go to the pool hall with George. But Lucy refuses to lie for her. Just then Jordan comes by and says she can slap him. But that's all wrong, Lucy says. It's supposed to be dramatic, romantic. They're supposed to be arguing and he's supposed to try to kiss her and then she's supposed to slap. But we *are* arguing, Jordan insists. Then he kisses her, and she slaps him—right in front of a teacher. Mary comes to her rescue and explains they're rehearsing a scene from *Gone With the Wind*.

When Matt sees Shana at school, he notices she has a bruise on her arm. She tries to explain it away, but when Matt persists, she admits her brother has a problem. Matt wants to talk about it, and Shana blurts out the ugly truth. She studied her brains out to get a scholarship, works a crummy job to make a better life for her and her brother; her dad left when George was born, and their mother smacked him around because she blamed him

for their dad's leaving. Shana glares at him, resenting that he's pressured the information out of her, then walks away.

Eric goes home to check on the kids, but he has to go by the church to cancel an appointment. Annie tells him that Matt called and he'll pick up the kids at school. Eric says he'll be back soon.

When Matt picks up the kids, he asks Lucy where Mary is. "She went to someone's house to study." Matt knows Lucy, and he can tell she's lying. Matt, frightened now, shouts, "Is she out with Shana's brother?" Lucy nods, trying to make it sound like a study date. She says she thinks Mary mentioned the pool hall. Matt quickly drives away.

Meanwhile, Annie's worried . . . worried that Johnny might come by their house, worried about Eric. She calls Eric.

At the church office, Eric gets the page and reaches for the phone . . . just as he senses someone else's presence. He looks up. Lurking in the shadows is Johnny. He's holding a gun.

Eric slowly raises his hand. "Easy now, son . . ."

Johnny pulls the trigger, then runs away as a stunned Eric clutches his shoulder. He's been shot.

By now Matt has dropped off the kids and tells Annie he's going to pick up Mary. But she wants Matt to stay with the kids. Eric hasn't answered his page, and she wants to go to the church to check on him. If there's trouble, Matt doesn't want his pregnant mother going. The phone rings, interrupting them. Matt answers. When he hangs up, he tells them Johnny's been arrested for possession of a weapon, and Eric is with Sergeant Michaels. He adds that Eric will be home in a couple of hours. Worried, Annie asks if Eric's okay. Matt confirms that he is, but Annie is suspicious. Matt hurries out before she can question him further.

At the pool hall, Mary and George are having fun playing pinball. But when Mary starts to beat George, he gets angry. "You've got a problem," Mary tells him. Matt arrives and tells the apologetic George that he'll get Eric to counsel him in a couple of weeks. Mary's instantly alarmed. "Why a couple of weeks?"

By now Annie's figured things out and shows up at the hospital, where Eric's being treated for his gunshot wound. "Did you actually think you'd be able to hide this from me?" she asks.

A week later Eric and Sergeant Michaels watch as a judge sentences twelve-year-old Johnny to the State Youth Authority until he's twenty-five, the maximum sentence allowed. As the guard takes him away, Johnny cries, "I want to go home!" As his stricken parents leave the courtroom, John Sr. stops and apologizes to Eric for not listening to him. "Thank God, he didn't kill anyone." "Believe me," Eric says, "I do."

No Sex, Some Drugs, and a Little Rock & Roll

written by Sue Tenney;
directed by David Plenn

Season 3: Episode 51

It's an hour before Simon's bedtime, and he's trying coffee for the first time! He's copying Matt, who's drinking it to pull an "all-nighter" for a college exam. Lucy's on the phone with Jordan, as usual, while Annie's trying not to get annoyed by Ruthie's gum-smacking habit. Eric arrives to tell Annie that his old college band is playing a local gig. Eric asks Annie if they can stay overnight in the Camden's driveway; they travel in an RV. Mary gets home from basketball practice. She's wowed by the energy her teammate Diane is showing lately. Her intensity is tournament-level, even at practices. What's her secret?

The next morning Simon is exhausted; the coffee kept him awake, of course. Matt warns him about caffeine addiction. Speaking of addiction, Lucy's on the phone again, right up until the second it's time for everybody to leave for school. And Ruthie's chewing gum again. Everybody's got a habit!

An exhausted Matt runs into a pal on campus who shares a secret study aid—a bottle of pills called Body Petrol Plus.

Uncertain about its safety, Matt pockets the unopened bottle. At basketball practice, Mary discovers Diane's energy source: Body Petrol Plus.

An RV pulls up at the Camdens', and Eric's pleased to see Donny, Ray, and Chris looking pretty much the way he remembers them from the seventies. Even their clothing style's the same. After some masterful guilt-tripping by the band, Annie decides it's okay for them to camp in the driveway. Meanwhile, Simon's in the kitchen sneaking coffee, which he's starting to crave, and Lucy's telephone addiction is getting harder to hide; Annie decides she can't use the phone all weekend, to help her break the habit. Upstairs, Mary notices a bottle of Body Petrol Plus in Matt's desk. Just like what Diane uses, she thinks.

The next day at practice, Mary tries Body Petrol Plus. "Two pills work better than one, and four work even better," Diane assures Mary, who finds out one is plenty. Diane's right, they really pep you up!

Meanwhile, the band enjoys home life with the Camdens and confesses that life on the road doesn't afford them an opportunity to have families. Later Eric takes some fresh towels out to the RV and smells incense burning—are the guys

There's a web of potential addiction in the Camden house. Simon picks up the coffee habit. Ruthie chews gum all the time. Eric's old band-mates smoke in their RV. Mary tries an herbal stimulant called Body Petrol Plus, which she gets from her teammate Diane. Diane overdoes it and suffers serious side effects.

covering up marijuana? They don't answer his question but smile mischievously. Eric tells them, in a diplomatic way, that they have a "zero-tolerance" drug rule in their house. He adds that his best friend is an officer who often shows up unannounced. The men nod and grin but admit nothing. Later, Annie notices their affection for Jimi Hendrix, Keith Moon, and other rock musicians who died from overdoses.

When Eric discovers a bottle of Body Petrol Plus beside Matt, who's fallen asleep at his desk, he hits the roof. Matt defends himself by saying he hasn't taken any. Eric explains that the pills are dangerous. They contain ephedrine, from which people have died. Mary overhears the conversation and tells Eric that she has taken the same pills, which she got from Diane, who got them from her father.

Meanwhile, Eric's old band buddies invite Annie to play along with them at their gig. They also let her know that they're aware Eric doesn't want to hang out with them anymore.

Eric goes to Diane's dad, Bill, to warn him about ephedrine's side affects. Bill sees only the short-term energy boost it seems to provide. Eric can't convince him that the risk Diane is taking far outweighs the little kick she gets.

Later Matt rights some wrongs. He returns the pills to his classmate with a warning. He pours Simon a cup of cold coffee without the usual sugar and chocolate-powder flavorings—to show him what it really tastes like. And he turns Ruthie off from chewing gum by letting her know the main ingredient is tree sap. Eric's proud of Matt for taking responsibility.

Eric apologizes to the band for avoiding them and finds out they're smoking cigarettes, not marijuana. Eric apologizes for thinking they were doing something illegal. Back inside the house Annie tells Lucy the Camdens are getting another phone line, to Lucy's delight.

The band, The Flower and Vegetable Show, invite both Annie and Eric to their gig as guest musicians. The whole family's going, except Mary, who has gone to shoot baskets with Diane. As usual, Diane is overly energetic from her pills. But as the two girls begin to play, something horrible happens. . . .

The Camdens notice a commotion on their way home—police cars and an ambulance at the park's basketball courts. It's Diane. She has had a heart attack and is lucky to be alive.

Let's Talk About Sex

**written by Brenda Hampton;
directed by Tony Mordente**

Mary goes to a co-ed sleepover,
and Lucy goes parking with Jordan.
Matt turns their experiences into a
class project on human sexuality.
Simon takes a baby-sitting class.

Season 3: Episode 52

Jordan gives Lucy a ride, over his shoulder in a fireman's carry, to the Camdens' front door. Then he gives her a surprise when he says, "See you tomorrow night"—to Mary. After Jordan leaves, Mary explains. He meant after the basketball team party. The boys' and girls' teams are getting together for a sleepover.

"A co-ed sleepover?" Lucy gasps. Won't there be *sex*?

Matt appears. "If either of you is thinking about having sex, forget it," he says. Mary responds that just because he needs a project for his human sexuality class, the whole world isn't thinking about sex.

Across town, Annie and Eric are at the Glenoak Community Center for a class on alternative birthing. Unfortunately, it's the My First Baby class night. Annie explains to the teacher that they can't leave because Simon's there for a class in babysitting; the teacher invites the pros to attend, even though they already have five kids. Eric suddenly feels old.

Back at the house, Jordan calls Lucy and says he's going to skip the sleepover. He wants to take Lucy out instead. But Lucy wants to know: Does this mean he's giving up all co-ed sleepovers, or just this one? Jordan says "all," and adds that his parents have banned him from going. While they're on the subject, Lucy asks if he's ever had sex. Jordan pauses, then confirms that he has, and adds that he doesn't want to talk any more about it.

Annie, Eric, and Simon get home. Annie tells Eric she's invited two of their First Baby classmates, Barbara and Cassandra, over tomorrow night. She adds that it would be nice if Eric spoke to Cassandra's boyfriend about attending the class. Maybe Eric could even speak to Barbara's boyfriend, Sam. And maybe he could also land Sam a job, even though Sam has no skills and a criminal record. Eric agrees to meet these young men at the pool hall.

Upstairs, Simon tells Ruthie he can't baby-sit her dolls. He's a professional now, he adds, and Ruthie can't afford him.

The next day Matt worries that he still has no idea for his human sexuality project, and Lucy worries that she has none of the details about Jordan's sexual experience. Annoyed at all of her questions, Jordan demands that she stop asking them. Later, she asks Mary why he hasn't tried anything with her, and Mary says that maybe it's because he really likes her and respects her. Unconvinced, Lucy tells an irate Mary that she's going to find out if he's really attracted to her—maybe even by having sex with him.

Simon worries about not having a baby-sitting job. He can baby-sit Ruthie tonight, Annie says, when she, Cassandra, and Barbara go out to meet Eric and the boyfriends. Matt will be home if there's a problem. But Ruthie says no. She won't let Simon baby-sit her unless, she tells him privately, he "lets her do anything she wants." Simon says, "No fire, sharp objects, or playing in the car."

Ruthie extends her hand: "Done!"

Upstairs, Lucy gets back to Jordan on the phone and says she'll go out with him tonight, but she wants it to be someplace where they can be *alone*. Mary also wants Jordan to give her a ride to the co-ed sleepover, and neither girl wants Eric and Annie to know what's up.

The sound of loud music lures the girls downstairs, where they meet Annie's new friends Barbara and Cassandra. Both unwed mothers-to-be are only sixteen, Mary's age. Mary and Lucy exchange nervous glances, then run back upstairs.

Barbara explains her dilemma to Annie: she told her boyfriend, Sam, she wouldn't marry him unless he got a job, but the truth is she never wanted to marry him. Cassandra's problem with her boyfriend, Roger, is that he's mad she dated his brother, and doesn't even know she's pregnant.

At the pool hall, Eric helps Barbara's boyfriend, Sam, fill out a job application for a restaurant job. Then they meet Cassandra's boyfriend, Roger. Sam congratulates him on Cassandra's baby, and that's how Eric discovers that Roger didn't even know about it! Soon Annie arrives with Cassandra and Barbara, and the teenage couples attempt to talk through their problems. Annie and Eric, meanwhile, agree that no matter how one looks at teen pregnancy, it's never a good thing.

Back at the house, Simon has his hands full with Ruthie, while Matt has left to pursue a project idea that Lucy gave him when she left with Jordan. He knows he has to catch up with them before they do anything!

He drives to the Dairy Shack, where Arnold, the waiter, tells him Lucy mentioned MacArthur's Point, the local "lovers' lane." Matt finds Jordan's parked car and angrily orders Lucy out. They leave Jordan and drive to pick up Mary, too.

Jordan returns to the Camden's house and bravely tells Annie and Eric everything that happened. After Jordan leaves, Annie and Eric sit Mary and Lucy down for a discussion about everything from premarital sex to teen pregnancy to personal responsibility and romance. Matt videotapes the dialogue and it becomes his human sexuality project.

Here Comes Santa Claus

written by Chris Olsen
& Jeff Olsen;
directed by Joel J. Feigenbaum

Ruthie finds Matt behind Santa's
beard. Eric and Annie give and
receive. The spirit of Christmas
arrives in the form of a pawnbroker.

Season 3: Episode 53

Simon puts on a show for Annie and Ruthie in his beloved, but outgrown, Christmas pajamas. Out in the garage, Eric gives the older kids Christmas assignments—volunteer projects for Mary and Lucy, and a job for Matt as Santa Claus at the mall! Although Matt's far from excited, Eric adds that Matt will make a hundred dollars a day; with this money he can rent a tux and buy tickets to the charity ball that his new girlfriend, Jenny, wants to attend.

In the living room, everyone gathers for the annual Camden Christmas drawing. Each year they draw names for a gift exchange. For the person whose name is drawn, a gift must be made, a service must be done, or a personal belonging must be given up. The actual exchange takes place on Christmas Eve.

In the foyer, Lucy's boyfriend, Jordan, arrives with a present for her, and explains that he and his family will be out of town for the holidays, visiting his uncle Ray and his pet monkey. Lucy lies and says that his gift isn't wrapped yet, but Ruthie knows better. Lucy confirms he will receive his present when he returns.

Mary goes with Eric to serve meals at the soup kitchen, where she meets another volunteer, Carlos, who is homeless. He's tall, dark, and handsome, and Mary's smitten. By the time Eric gets back to see how she's doing, she's already invited Carlos, in the spirit of the season, to stay at the Camdens' house over Christmas. When Eric asks what Mary thinks of his gift idea for Annie—a nice chain for Annie's inherited gold cross—Mary responds that he doesn't have the money for it.

Back home, Lucy gives Annie a gift idea for the person she picked, Eric. Because Eric has been looking at his old 45 records and reminiscing lately, Lucy suggests Annie fix up an old record player for him. Annie loves the idea. In the garage, Simon untangles strings of Christmas lights and explains his decorating plan to Ruthie. This year, he'll string the house lights indoors; it'll look just as pretty and it'll be much safer than climbing ladders outside. Especially if Annie decides to help, since she's expecting and not as sure-footed as normal. Upstairs, Mary persuades Lucy to open Jordan's present by allowing Mary to sneak a peek. They get a big surprise: it's a shoe-shine kit. What kind of gift is that from a boyfriend?

Later Jenny stops by and discovers that Matt's at work. She explains that she was going out to buy some mistletoe and decided to drop in. Ruthie wants to join her, and Annie says okay. Annie doesn't mention where Matt's working; he's made it clear he doesn't want everyone to know.

Meanwhile, Matt's partner at the Santa station is an "elf" named Joe, who bemoans the fact that he's never been promoted to the Santa job. Never mind the fact that he's small and thin, and impatient with children.

When Jenny and Ruthie show up at the mall, Ruthie asks Jenny to take her picture with Santa! As soon as Ruthie climbs onto Santa's lap she recognizes Matt—but just to be sure she yanks his beard down, which ignites a big scene with the other kids waiting in line.

Meanwhile, Carlos has arrived at the Camdens'. He elects to stay in the garage, where he'll be out of the way. Talkative Simon gets him to help with the lights and learns that Carlos left his family two years before, after some kind of disagreement; he's been backpacking across the country ever since. Although he reveals no more, Simon warns him that Eric and Annie will get his story in short order. Which is exactly what they do.

Lucy tries to get going on her volunteer project and calls everyone in the church directory to invite them to audition for a live Nativity scene at the church. She can't imagine anyone would do such a thing voluntarily, but she's in for a surprise the next day. When Eric takes her to the audition, a hundred people are waiting to try out! Even a rebellious-looking teen with blue hair steps forward to audition for the part of baby Jesus.

Lucy's got her work cut out for her.

Eric goes to Rocky's Pawn Shop with his old collection of 45s. Rocky's surprised he wants to sell, but Eric explains it's for something special. According to the gift exchange rules, he's giving up something he owns. He plans to buy Annie a chain for the cross pendant she inherited from her mother.

Back at the house, Matt arrives with Ruthie in tow. Thanks to the disaster at the mall, he got fired, and Ruthie's faith in Santa Claus got dashed. Mary's upstairs, struggling with a telephone operator, trying to track down Jordan's Uncle Sal to clarify the meaning of Lucy's gift. Even though Mary doesn't know Sal's last name, the operator manages to find a number. Carlos sticks his head in momentarily; he's looking for a place to hide from overly talkative Simon.

Downstairs, Carlos finds refuge in a game of Go Fish with Eric and Mary. When Mary gets up, Eric tells Carlos some good news: Someone who wishes to remain anonymous has provided a plane ticket so Carlos can visit his family for Christmas.

Jenny and Matt drive to a deserted street and dance to the music on Jenny's boom box. Because Matt lost his job and he's in Santa pants instead of a tux, it's not exactly the charity ball. Jenny's sorry she took Ruthie to the mall and accidentally caused Matt to lose his job, but she's given herself a Christmas present this year. She's not going to feel guilty. Suddenly, Matt has an idea. The two rush back to the mall and discover that Joe the "elf" has been promoted to Santa; there's an opening for his old job. Jenny grabs it and becomes a part-time Christmas elf.

The next day Mary is sad that Carlos is gone, but she thanks the person who gave him the ticket anyway—it was Joyce, who runs the soup kitchen. After talking to Eric, she decided that reuniting Carlos with his family was the best thing she could do this Christmas.

Finally, it's Christmas Eve, and Simon is still fretting about what to give his gift-exchange pick, Ruthie. Eric suggests Simon pray for guidance, which he does. He wants Ruthie's faith in Santa Claus restored while she's still young.

That night the family exchanges presents. Simon's prayer hasn't been answered yet, so he gives Ruthie his very own Christmas p.j.s, just to "hold her" until it happens. Lucy thanks Mary for getting a number for Jordan and telling him to call; it turns out the shoe-shine kit was for the monkey, and Jordan told Lucy he loves her. Mary gets a promise from Lucy that she'll volunteer three months at the soup kitchen. Matt gets fuzzy dice to hang from his car's rearview mirror, made by Ruthie from one of her stuffed animals, and a picture of her on "Santa's" lap. Then Eric gives Annie her present—a beautiful chain for her mother's cross, which he bought by selling his records. Annie's speechless. Ironically, she sold the cross to buy Eric a jukebox for his records.

The next morning Simon and Ruthie hear someone outside. When they answer the door, they find the pawnbroker in a Santa suit. He has a gift for Eric and Annie—a box of records and a cross. Ruthie's amazed. She doesn't know Rocky, so she's sure it's really Santa. "Thank you, God," Simon prays.

There's just one hitch—everyone who volunteered for the living Nativity backs out at the last minute. The Camdens have the right spirit, though. They fill in for all the parts, and it's Christmas after all.

Season 3: Episode 54

Nobody Knows . . .

**written by Brenda Hampton
& Catherine LePard;
directed by Harry Harris**

Mary doesn't want the DMV to
know she can't parallel park.
Aunt Julie doesn't want Eric
to know she's moved into town.
Deena doesn't want Simon
to know she has leukemia.
But they all find out eventually.

Mary, Lucy, and Annie wait outside a Division of Motor Vehicles examination office for Mary's turn to be tested for a driver's license. What the DMV officer doesn't know is Mary can't parallel park—not even a little bit. She's praying the officer won't ask. If he does, Lucy knows an effective ploy. "Cry."

Annie steps away and calls Eric at work. She's feeling amorous. Can he get away? Eric hasn't known her to be this way; he wonders if it has to do with her pregnancy.

Across town, Matt pulls up at a stoplight and notices a familiar-looking figure crossing the street, headed for a run-down residence hotel. It looks like his Aunt Julie, Eric's sister. Matt calls to her, but she doesn't respond before the light changes and he has to go on.

At the pool room, Eric is shooting a game with Simon's girl-friend, Deena. She confides that she wants to tell Simon a secret that Eric knows about, but she's scared. Eric suggests she can trust Simon.

Back at the DMV, Mary is asked to parallel park, and she pulls out her best trick: she cries! The officer decides that nobody has to know. Mary feels guilty for "cheating," and she cries in the car. When Matt congratulates her at home, she bursts into tears.

Downstairs, Simon, Ruthie, and Happy share the couch in front of the TV. Simon tells Ruthie he's concerned about Deena. "She seems cold, distant." Ruthie asks if they're breaking up, and Simon is unsure of what to do.

Ruthie knows. She thinks they should call a sidekick! "You mean *psychic*?" Simon says. He's against it, but Ruthie gets a number from the operator anyway. It's a local number, and the elderly woman who answers is not a psychic at all, just a woman named Mabel who happens to be a good listener. Wanting the little girl caller not to worry, she tells Ruthie that Simon and Deena will be together for fifty years at least.

Eric comes home. He and Annie sit by a romantic fire. He's amazed Mary passed the driver's exam; is she really ready to drive? But Annie's pleased and sends Mary and the other kids out for pizza. The house now silent, Eric and Annie get to spend some time alone. . . .

In another part of town, Matt drives to the residence hotel and finds Aunt Julie living there. He visits her and learns that she's still recovering from the alcoholism that caused her to lose her job as a school principal. She's starting over with a new job in a local school, but she's not ready to make contact with her family yet. She also reveals that the Camdens make her feel pressured about being sober, and that she needs some space.

Matt promises not to reveal her situation, but he's concerned about seeing Julie with a half-full bottle of whiskey.

Back at the house, Mary's still upset about passing her test by crying for sympathy. Lucy suggests Mary learn to parallel park and take the exam again.

Later, Deena comes over and tells Simon her secret—she has leukemia. It's in remission, but every year she has to be tested because it may come back. The time for her yearly test has come. Simon tries to be understanding, but he soon storms off to his room.

The next day Annie's amorous mood has turned 180 degrees. Eric's in the doghouse with Simon for "hiding" Deena's secret. "Not telling what people tell me is part of my job," Eric explains. He adds that Deena's condition doesn't have to change things between them.

At breakfast, Matt shares with Eric and Annie a dream he says he had. In it, Aunt Julie was back. She was teaching again. When he leaves, Annie says, "Our kids are terrible liars." They're pretty sure Matt's saying that Julie *is* back.

Meanwhile, Ruthie calls her "psychic" again and inquires about Deena's health. What's going to happen to Deena? Mabel hears the worry in Ruthie's voice. She tells Ruthie to tell Simon everything is going to be all right.

And it is. Simon waits for Deena at her gym class, and they talk. She informs him that her tests went well. When Deena's gym teacher, Mr. Fischer, discovers them talking, he sends Deena on to class. Mr. Fischer confides that he isn't too worried about Deena—his own leukemia has been in remission for twenty years now. They agree it would help Deena to hear this news.

Meanwhile, Aunt Julie has contacted Annie, who has gone to visit her at the school where she works. Julie tells Annie she's on the road to recovery but needs to do it her way. Annie's pleased, but Julie says she's not ready to face Eric yet.

What Annie and Julie don't know is that Eric's already tracked down Julie's hotel. He confronts her there, and she insists she doesn't need help; but Eric can't help noticing a half bottle of whiskey on the table.

Meanwhile Mary is getting all the help she needs, as Lucy and Matt together try to teach her to parallel park between a pair of empty trash cans. It's a noisy process, but she'll learn eventually.

Eric and Annie discuss their separate meetings with Julie. Annie tells Eric he should apologize to Julie when she's ready to talk. Soon the doorbell rings, and it's Julie. When Eric brings up the bottle, Julie explains that it belonged to a friend who died of alcoholism. She keeps it as a reminder not to make the same mistake. She thanks them for their concern, asks them to keep the bottle for her, and leaves.

All That Jazz

written by Sue Tenney; directed by Harvey Laidman

Annie faces a doctor who almost killed Matt. Matt learns that Heather is engaged. Rod's mother dies. Simon gives his girlfriend a gift.

Simon's pal Nigel is spending the night, but he's having no fun. All Simon can think about is Deena. "It's our three-month anniversary," Simon says. "The big one." He needs to think of the perfect gift.

In another room, Mary watches Lucy get dressed for a date, envious. Mary says when she was going steady with Wilson, guys asked her out. Now he's gone, and she never gets asked. That gives Lucy an idea. What if there was a rumor that Mary and Wilson were together again. . . .

Matt wanders in and gets some important news: his sisters saw Matt's old girlfriend Heather at the mall—she's back in town!

Across town, Annie and Eric preregister at the hospital where Annie expects to deliver. Suddenly, Annie spots someone and says, "Please tell me I'm seeing things." Eric looks shocked, too.

The doorbell rings at the Camdens. Lucy answers, and it's her ex-boyfriend Rod. She chides him for dropping in when he knows she has another boyfriend. "I didn't know where else to go," he says. "My mom just died." He says he wants to hide from everybody. Lucy and Mary let him hide in their closet.

Eric and Annie get home, and Annie hugs Matt and cries. The person she saw at the hospital was the doctor who delivered Matt—and almost killed him. Dr. Hastings. They thought he left after that, but there he was working at their hospital again! Annie doesn't want him anywhere near her.

The next morning Matt leaves with Simon and Nigel for the mall so Simon can get a present for Deena. Matt also wants some new pants as he's thinking about visiting Heather. Upstairs, Mary and Lucy keep a lookout so Rod can run to the bathroom. "Everybody deals with death in their own way," Lucy tells Mary. Minutes later, Rod runs back out, and Ruthie sees.

Nigel frowns in the backseat of Matt's car because they didn't go straight to the mall. They're stopped in front of Heather's house, where Matt's thinking about going inside. Nigel's out with two lovesick losers. "Aren't we having some fun now?" Nigel gripes. Matt decides to go on to the mall. They get pants for Matt and hair combs for Deena and head back to the house.

Eric enters the house through the back door. He just heard about Rod's mother and asks Annie if Lucy knows. Annie is certain she doesn't, and suddenly asks Eric to call the hospital. "Something's wrong," she says.

At the emergency room, Dr. Warren tells Annie she's okay, except for slightly elevated blood pressure. But Annie claims she's not okay as long as Dr. Hastings is on staff, and she makes

Dr. Warren promise the man won't deliver her child. Concerned about her stress level, Eric suggests they go talk to Dr. Hastings, but Annie refuses.

Back at the house, Lucy serves Rod a sandwich and tries to be understanding about his loss. Mary gets a phone call from Michael Towner, the guy who ran her over, who says a rumor's going around that she and Wilson are getting back together. He would like to see her.

Ruthie comes to the closet to comfort Rod. She lost her hamster once. . . . Then Eric and Annie come in, expecting to tell Lucy the news about Rod's mother, and find them. Ruthie blurts out, "Rod spent the night, and his mother died!"

That afternoon Matt goes to Heather's house, and she walks out to his car. "How are you," he says at the door. "Engaged," she replies, barely able to face him.

Mary's in the pool hall with Michael. He says he'd like to go out with Mary, but there's a lot of water under the bridge. One time he accidentally ran over her with his car and fled the scene in fear. She once flushed his head in the toilet after he wrote crude things about her on a bathroom wall. He asks if she would consider going out with him if she and Wilson break up.

Meanwhile, Eric's in his study with Rod, who's laying it on the line. When his mother had cancer, he went everywhere with her. When she died, he was at her side. But not Rod's dad. He kept busy remodeling the house. When she died, he was laying linoleum. Eric finally understands why Rod's mad. He tells him to stay at the house as long as he wants.

In the hallway, Simon and Ruthie pass. She's wearing the hair combs Simon bought for Deena. Ruthie runs, and Simon takes off after her.

At Heather's house, Heather tells Matt she wants Eric to perform her wedding. Angry and upset, he stalks off. Meanwhile, at the Camdens', Rod tells Lucy he's not going to his mother's funeral; she advises him to go.

Matt arrives home and sees Mary and Michael Towner in a

major lip lock on the front porch. When Mary sees Matt, she shoves Michael to the ground. "And that's for running me over," she says, and runs inside, where everything's happening at once. Simon and Ruthie are fighting over hair combs. Annie's mad at Dr. Hastings. Lucy and Rod are hashing out Rod's feelings. Nigel just wants to go home. Then the phone rings. Dr. Hastings wants to meet with Annie and Eric.

At the hospital, Annie and Eric hear the explanation that has been twenty years in coming. Annie was right—he was too inexperienced for her complicated delivery. When Matt lived, he knew that there was a God and that he was not ready to be delivering children. He went back to medical school for another three-year residency. Then he spent six years at a teaching hospital, working with high-risk babies. He's devoted his life to this field, and when he was invited to return to Glenoak and head up the neo-natal division, he almost didn't take it for fear of seeing them. His story heals Annie's anger.

Back at the house, Lucy reveals that Wilson called to ask if Lucy heard the false rumor that he and Mary were back together. He says he'll call Mary later, but Mary can't forget Michael Towner's kiss. She picks up the phone and calls him. In another room, Simon decides to let Ruthie keep the hair combs. They make him think of what a jerk he was to Nigel. He'll make Deena a card.

Heather arrives to clear things up with Matt and tells him he has to get used to the idea of her getting married. He says he'll try, and they share a warm hug.

Rod asks Annie about his choice regarding his mother's funeral; she says his father needs him, and she and Eric will go with him, if that will help.

Later, at church, Eric delivers a sermon about forgiveness and reconciliation. Rod hears the sermon and decides to go to the funeral. His father apologizes for his behavior, and Rod tells him that they now need each other. The two hug as the Camdens look on. A new relationship is about to bloom.

The Tribes That Bind

written by Catherine LePard; directed by Bradley Gross

Season 3: Episode 56

Bobby Tripp, who lives next door, makes fun of seeing Ruthie's underwear while out on the playground. "I told him I have a big brother and he does, too, so you might have to beat him up," Ruthie tells Simon after school. Simon shakes his head.

Later that afternoon the Camdens have a family meeting. All are present except Annie, who's out grocery shopping. They discuss what needs to be done when the twins arrive: cooking, laundry, watering plants. . . . The only one without any duties is Lucy, who's going to Camp All By Myself, an overnight camp stressing self-reliance. Annie arrives, tired and swollen-looking. "Get the groceries," Eric reminds them.

Annie's not happy. She ran into Mrs. Beeker at the store, who said the ladies in the church have been planning her baby shower—in the Camden house! She calls her friend Patricia, "So I have at least one person I like at my baby shower." Then she lies down for a nap.

Matt tells the others he's expecting lots of changes when the twins arrive. It's not going to be the same old routine, the same old family anymore. This throws a scare into the other kids, especially Simon. "Once those babies ride into town, it's over," he tells Eric.

Eric asks Matt to be more upbeat in front of the others. Matt says it's just weird—at nineteen, he could be the twins' father. Eric thinks, *If he could be their father, then I'm old enough to be their* . . . and now he's depressed.

Mary comes out of Eric and Annie's room carrying a very small luggage bag in preparation for Annie's delivery. It doesn't seem large enough to Eric, but Annie reminds him they've done this before.

Lucy calls from Camp All By Myself. She's miserable. Nobody talks to anybody there. The camp's name says it all. Eric tells her to hang in there—if Annie can handle the baby shower, Lucy can handle some time alone.

Later Nigel comes over and delivers a coffeepot for the shower. Lucy calls again and talks to Mary and Matt; she wants out. The kitchen door opens, and there stands the hated Bobby Tripp. Ruthie, Simon, Nigel, and Happy go into the yard where his brother Darryl and their dog, Sid Vicious, await them. They talk, and come close to blows, until Simon says, "I'll get back to you."

Lucy's on the phone again, with Annie this time, who says of course they'll come get her, if she can't "hack it." That does it for Lucy; she's staying.

Mrs. Hinkle arrives for the party. She doesn't like showers, and she's depressed to hear that she's early. She thought she was late.

Stephen Collins

Multitalented Stephen Collins stars as *7th Heaven's* Eric Camden, and he has directed two of the show's highest-rated episodes. As an actor, he has starred in many television movies, numerous feature films including *Star Trek: The Motion Picture* and *The First Wives Club*, and four Broadway plays. He has had starring roles in New York Shakespeare Festival productions and directed a successful regional production of the play he starred in on Broadway, *The Old Boy*. He played JFK in *A Woman Named Jackie*, which won an Emmy for Best Miniseries. And he was nominated for an Emmy for his performance in *The Two Mrs. Grenvilles* with Ann-Margret. Mr. Collins has also written two published novels. Born in Des Moines, Iowa, he lives in L.A. with his wife, actress Faye Grant, and their young daughter, Kate. Beside Mr. Collins's computer at home is a note from Kate: "My dad is nice, brave, funny, and number one."

Catherine Hicks

Catherine Hicks portrays Annie Camden in her fourth television series regular role. Before *7th Heaven*, she starred in the series *Winnetka Road*, *Tucker's Witch*, and the popular daytime drama *Ryan's Hope*. She earned a 1980 Emmy nomination for Best Actress for her starring role in the TV movie *Marilyn: The Untold Story*. Her feature film credits include *Star Trek IV: The Voyage Home*, while her onstage credits include starring with Jack Lemmon on Broadway in the play *Tribute*. Ms. Hicks double-majored in theology and English literature at Notre Dame University and attended Cornell University where she earned a master of fine arts degree in acting. From Scottsdale, Arizona, she now lives in L.A. with her husband and her daughter, Catie.

Barry Watson

Prior to landing the role of Matt Camden on *7th Heaven*, Barry Watson appeared on the series *Malibu Shores* and guest-starred on many other popular shows, including *Baywatch*, where he was one of the first characters to actually drown! He was in the HBO original sci-fi movie *Attack of the 50-Foot Woman* with Darryl Hannah, and he starred in the feature film *Teaching Mrs.* *Tingle* with *Dawson's Creek* star Katie Holmes. His first acting job was on the daytime drama *Days of Our Lives*, but while his career was first getting started, he also waited tables, worked as a cashier, and even parked cars. Mr. Watson grew up in Michigan and Texas, and moved to L.A. on his own at the age of fifteen.

David Gallagher

Before David Gallagher became *7th Heaven*'s Simon Camden, he was in two hit films: *Phenomenon*, with John Travolta, and *Look Who's Talking Now*, with Mr. Travolta and Kirstie Alley. He also headlined the direct-to-video sequel to *Richie Rich* and starred in the Disney made-for-TV movie *The New Adventures of Spin and Marty*. Also on TV he guest-starred in *Walker, Texas Ranger* and had a recurring role on the daytime drama *Loving*. On stage, he originated the role of young Scrooge in the Broadway seasonal play *A Christmas Carol*. In his spare time Mr. Gallagher enjoys basketball and video games. He is the oldest of five children and lives with his family in L.A.

Jessica Biel

The role of Mary Camden is Jessica Biel's television acting debut. Since then she has costarred with Peter Fonda in the feature film *Ulee's Gold* and played Jonathan Taylor Thomas's love interest in the Disney movie *All I Want for Christmas*. She began her performing career at age nine in singing roles in regional musical theater—in *Beauty and the Beast*, *Anything Goes*, *The Invisible People*, *Annie*, and *The Sound of Music*. After that, she worked as a professional model in several television commercials and in national and international print advertising campaigns for companies including Limited Too. She was named one of *People Magazine's* "50 Most Beautiful People." Ms. Biel enjoys many sports, including Rollerblading, mountain biking, snowboarding, gymnastics, soccer, basketball, and football. She was born in Ely, Minnesota, grew up in Colorado, and now lives with her parents and younger brother, Justin, in L.A. and Colorado.

Beverley Mitchell

Beverley Mitchell plays *7th Heaven's* Lucy Camden. Before that, she had a recurring role on the comedy series *Phenom* and guest-starred on *Melrose Place*, *Baywatch*, and *Quantum Leap*. She starred in the TV movies *White Dwarf*, *Mother of the Bride*, *Baby of the Bride*, and *Children of the Bride*, and she also starred in the mini-series *Sinatra*. Her first feature film role was in *A Killing Obsession*, and she costarred in the film *The Crow: City of Angels*. She is an honor student and is active and outspoken in the fight against drunk driving and drug abuse. She participates in the Kmart Kids Race Against Drugs and Y-Cart racing around the country. Her hobbies include cardio kickboxing and singing. She lives with her mother in Southern California.

Mackenzie Rosman

Mackenzie Rosman plays Ruthie Camden on *7th Heaven*, and it is her television debut as a series regular. She has been in a number of television commercials for products ranging from Nike shoes to Tuffs diapers—her first job as an actress. She loves all animals, especially horses, and works with several charities benefiting animals. Off the set of *7th Heaven*, she enjoys reading, dancing, biking, skating, swimming, skiing, and horseback riding. She lives in L.A. with her younger brother, Chandler; mother, Donna; and lots of pets, including a rat named Lucy!

7

The Twins

The Camden twins are played by six infants. Quadruplets Nikolas, Lorenzo, Zachary, and Myrinda Brino are the main "performers." They're backed up by twins Bryce and James Braxmeyer.

The Brinos were just five and a half months old when they made their prime-time debut as Annie's babies in February of 2000. At first, the babies didn't have to do much. But as they get older, they'll get more direction—to smile, cry, or walk according to the script!

When the Brinos are not busy working, they enjoy being toddlers at home with their mom and dad, Shawna and Tony.

Happy the Dog

Happy is Happy's real name. She is a terrier mix, weighs about thirty pounds, and *7th Heaven* is her first acting job. She has been a guest on *Access Hollywood* and *The KTLA Morning News* in L.A. She lives at Boones' Animals for Hollywood in Castaic Lake, California.

the ladies of the church. At a
local restaurant, Eric and Morgan
step into a racial battlefield.

Next door at the Tripps', Ruthie, Simon, and Nigel take a stand in the front yard along with three more friends: Keesha, Lynn, and Mary. Bobby and Darryl come out with their older brother, Mark. He and Mary are instantly smitten. The fight's off again.

That afternoon a gaggle of women arrive at the Camdens and take over the kitchen.

At a diner, Matt plays pinball with his friend John. Their dads, Eric and Morgan, are seated at a table. The waiter brings both Eric's and Matt's orders. Morgan's, and John's, however, are slower coming. Because Morgan and John are black, the foursome exchange uneasy glances: Could racism be the reason for the poor service?

The kids catch some of the shower guests snooping around the cupboards. When Mary confronts them, Mrs. Beeker says the parish house is church property, which gives them the right. It happens again upstairs—the ladies go through drawers and the medicine cabinet. Then, downstairs, one of the women asks Patricia, who is black, to fill her teacup.

Meanwhile, at the diner, Morgan confronts the waiter, who tells him to take his business elsewhere. Then Eric confronts the owner, who calls the police. Two officers arrive in a patrol car. They warn the owner about the cost of trying to run a racist business. Morgan and Eric joke about what they'd buy with a legal settlement. Because Morgan's also a minister, he says his church could use a new organ. The owner apologizes, and the policemen join the ministers.

Back at the house, the kids continue discussing the pros and cons of the expected twins. In the living room, the woman who continues to request Patricia's assistance explains that she is now older and feebler, and appreciates all of Patricia's help at the shower. The woman tells her that she was married to a black man; it becomes clear that her requests were not motivated by any racist intent.

Later Patricia answers the front door and finds Mrs. Tripp, for Annie. She wants the Camden kids to stop threatening her kids. Annie suggests the Tripp boys stop teasing. The conversation gets uglier by the minute. Finally, Patricia closes the door on the woman. She turns and finds the church ladies eyeing her with disapproval. Annie ends the baby shower and shoos them away by faking labor pains.

Matt arrives and finds the younger Camdens waiting for him to join the clan war. Outside, they have an opponent lined up for Matt, an eighteen-year-old Tripp named Steve. Matt remembers him from his economics class, and the two agree that the youngsters should stop fighting. But the kids can't wait any longer; they dive into each other, and Matt and Steve break it up. Everybody's about to go home when the Tripps crack a few jokes comparing the overly productive Camdens to their dog's litter, and the fight is on.

Later Eric and Annie sit quietly together. Eric shares his anxiety about the twins and the Camdens' future in a world with so many problems. But Annie is optimistic: no matter what, she thinks the Camdens can hack it. Even Lucy, in a yoga position at Camp All By Myself, murmuring a mantra.

In Praise of Women

written by
**Brenda Hampton
& Sue Tenney;**
directed by
Burt Brinckerhoff

Annie experiences complications in the birthing room. The rest of the family has complications in the waiting room. David and Samuel are born.

Season 3: Episode 57

The Camdens have checked into the hospital and are waiting for Annie to deliver the twins. Emotional, Annie glares at Eric and says, "I'm giving birth to twins, and you took a snack break?" Eric blushes, thinking of the vending machine just down the hall from their birthing room. Eric says he's worried they forgot something at the house, and Annie chastises him for not concentrating on her and her contractions. The rest of the family sits nervously in the waiting room.

In the meantime, Happy's at home, eating out of the refrigerator, which someone left wide open during the family's hasty evacuation. The door to the house is open, too.

Back at the hospital, Dr. Allison says Annie needs a c-section, but Annie says no, even though she originally requested it. Annie yells at Eric, "Find Dr. Hastings. He owes me, he'll listen."

Eric leaves to find him, but first he finds Matt in the hallway, fidgety. Eric suggests he donate some blood, since Matt's blood type matches Annie's. But Matt doesn't like the thought of going under the needle.

Throughout the hospital, the other Camden children are dealing with the situation in their own ways. Ruthie wanders away from Simon and enters the birthing room and says hi to Annie. Lucy and Matt share a moment at the nursery. Simon prays alone in the chapel—for brothers, not more sisters. . . .

When Dr. Hastings enters Annie's birthing room, he says he'll try to help her deliver without a c-section. He gives her an epidural for the pain. Minutes later she's relaxed, even singing. The drugs have taken effect.

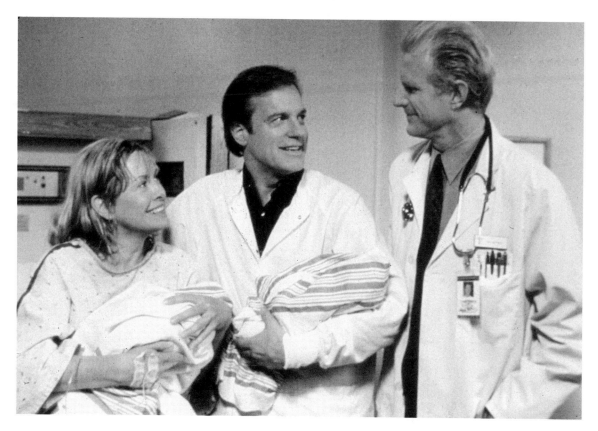

At the blood bank, Eric spots Matt nervously waiting for the needle. "You don't have to do this," Eric says, and together they leave.

After Simon prays for boy babies, he tells Matt he wants to be a big brother to them the way Matt was to him. The compliment is enough to make Matt cry, and go back to give blood.

As Annie's pain medication begins to wear off, she asks for Eric's hand. Simon abruptly enters and asks if he can have his ear pierced. Eric says they'll talk about that later.

Dr. Hastings tells Annie the first baby is fine, but the second is a breech, meaning it's not in a head-first position. After the first baby is born, he'll have to manually turn this baby around before she can deliver.

Annie points out this is the first time her mom hasn't been present for a delivery.

Suddenly, Matt bursts in to announce that he gave blood, and he meets Dr. Hastings for the first time.

Outside, Lucy tells Mary she wants to break up with Jordan, right now. She heads for the nearest public phone.

Back at the house, a number of animals have entered through the open back door, attracted by the smell of food. Joining Happy in the kitchen are a squirrel, a skunk, a pair of rabbits, and three birds. Happy gets up on her hind legs and goes shopping on the top shelf.

Excited about the approaching delivery, Matt gets Simon from the chapel, where he's been praying for an earring.

Finally, it's time for Annie to start pushing, and all the kids are back in the waiting room except Lucy, who's still on the phone with Jordan. A long line of anxious people are waiting behind her.

In the birthing room, Annie delivers the first baby. The second baby's heart rate drops, and Dr. Hastings rotates the baby in Annie's womb. Finally, she delivers that one, to the relief of an angst-ridden Eric. The twins are both boys.

Later, in the Camden family tradition, the kids all sing the theme song to the *Mary Tyler Moore Show*, all the way down to the inspirational refrain, "You're going to make it after all." It's the song they've sung for the birth of every child in the family—ever since Matt, as a toddler, told Grandma Jenny he wanted to sing it when Annie delivered Mary.

Each family member does a line in turn, finishing with Ruthie. And then Annie tosses an exultant, imaginary beret in the air.

It Happened
One Night

written by
Brenda Hampton
and Greg Plageman;
directed by
Tony Mordente

**The Camden family is shell-shocked
with brand-new twins in the house.
Ruthie is feeling neglected and tries
to run away. Matt tries out a new
delivery job at the Dairy Shack. And
Mary faces some tough questions
when she meets Jordan and Wilson
at the pool hall.**

Season 3: Episode 58

The twins seem to cry *all* the time. The Camdens take turns feeding them, changing them, *singing* to them, but nothing helps.

Ruthie's feeling neglected. But singing "Sometimes I feel like a motherless child" doesn't help her case with Annie. Annie tells her she's a big sister now, and more important than ever, she could *really* use her help. But Ruthie is totally grossed out watching her mother breast-feed the twins. "I don't want to see you feed either one of them again until they're eating with knives and forks." Annie smiles. "You know I fed you this way." Ruthie makes a face and runs out.

Eric is trying to catch a quick nap, but first he tries to wrangle Matt into some evening baby-sitting. But Matt informs him he's got an important new delivery job at the Dairy Shack using his own car. Do they pay gas or mileage? Eric scoffs. Do they pay car insurance or depreciation? No, Matt admits. Eric bets him twenty bucks the job doesn't last the night.

Meanwhile, Simon's reading stacks of parenting books and offering his mom and dad advice. Eric shakes his head and starts to go take his nap, then remembers to tell Lucy and Mary to make dinner. When he gets to his room, he finds Ruthie sitting in the cradle she slept in as a baby, and when he tries to get her out so she won't break it, she screams "Mommy!" and pretends that Daddy hurt her . . . foot. Annie takes her to put a Band-Aid on her boo-boo, then informs Eric she's taking a nap. Eric sighs. Just how long can a man go without sleep, anyway?

During cleanup duty after supper that night, Simon complains about the weird casserole Mary and Lucy made. No wonder—Mary realizes they were supposed to *add* tuna to the Tuna Helper! But Mary's been preoccupied all evening, planning an escape from "jail." Lucy reluctantly agrees to cover for her. "When someone says 'Where's Mary?,' you say, 'You just missed her.'" Lucy rolls her eyes. Mary finally slips out.

But the Camden Parent Radar is working 100 percent. When Eric sees Mary backing out of the driveway, they know what's going on: "A guy." And they know Lucy's covering. So they give her more and more chores: mop the kitchen floor. Scrub the tub upstairs. After all, she's got Mary there to help, right?

Ruthie packs to run away. Eric reacts casually, but he tells Simon not to let Ruthie out of his sight. To bug Matt, Simon orders from the Dairy Shack while Lucy mops the floor by dancing around with rags on her feet.

Across town, Matt's job-training at the Dairy Shack is like boot camp, under the leadership of the owner's pompous son, Roger. The fact that the three other new high school guys look and act like Curly, Larry, and Moe of the Three Stooges doesn't help.

When Matt arrives with the Dairy Shack delivery, Simon is shocked to learn that it's $17.35. Annie admits she added on to the order. Simon makes fun of Matt's paper hat, but he forks over the money. As he takes the food to the kitchen, though, he sees the back door open. Ruthie! Simon races outside and finds Ruthie hiding in Matt's car, trying to run away. They finally lure her out only to discover that Happy has jumped into Matt's car and eaten his next delivery. "That'll be $7.50," Matt informs Simon.

At the pool hall, Jordan—Lucy's ex-boyfriend—sits down with Mary while she waits for her date. They have a great time together. They're about to leave when Mary's old boyfriend Wilson rushes in with his son, Billy. He explains that he's late because he couldn't get a sitter. They try to talk, but it's tough: Billy is misbehaving, and Jordan is playing pool nearby. Wilson confesses that he wishes he'd never gone away to college. He lives in a tiny apartment. Billy's in day care and is sick all the time. "I'm miserable. I'm lonely. And I can't stop thinking about you." He kisses her, but she doesn't kiss back. She can't stop looking at Jordan. Wilson wants to move back so they can be a couple again. Mary resents the pressure and realizes she doesn't want them to be a couple. She tells him not to base his decision on her.

When Matt gets back to the Dairy Shack to pick up his replacement order, Roger fires him. He's been gone so long, he lost one of their biggest customers. But Matt won't give up. He delivers the order anyway. He's delighted to find Shana open the door of her new apartment. "What time do you get off?" she asks. Matt rips his dorky little paper hat in two. "I just got fired. Isn't that great?" While they're making out, Roger calls, frantically looking for his delivery boy. Shana says it's a shame Matt got fired—he gave her the most friendly service ever. Roger begs Matt to come back, but he refuses. He'd rather spend the evening with Shana and lose the twenty bucks to his dad than go back to working for Roger with the Three Stooges.

When Mary gets home later than she planned, Lucy is livid. Especially when Mary asks, "What happened to you?" She's a mess from scrubbing and cleaning times two all night. *Especially* when she finds out Mary spent much of the evening with Jordan. "And you had me lie to Mom and Dad! I lied and lied and lied. I wove a twisted web of lies and deceit and walked a tightrope on it all night long." Mary gives her a look. "Are they standing right behind me?" Lucy squeaks. Mary nods. Mary confesses she went out, and both girls get grounded for a couple of centuries.

Annie takes a very special book in to show Ruthie. It's her "baby book"—the book Annie made of all the special moments of the first years of Ruthie's life. She wants Ruthie to have it. Ruthie's delighted and hugs her mom, agreeing not to run away.

When Annie gets back to her room, Lucy comes out wearing the double baby carrier with two crying babies. She paces the house, singing. Around the house all the Camdens listen to Lucy's beautiful voice, some joining in, and soon realize . . . the babies are fast asleep.

Paranoia

written by Ron Darian; directed by Stephen Collins

Everyone's paranoid. Eric is convinced his deacons are plotting against him. Sergeant Michaels won't return his calls about Jimmy Moon, who seems to be involved with drug dealing. Trying to help him, Lucy goes against her parents' wishes. And Matt doesn't understand why.

Fred and Norma Moon come to Eric's office to talk to him about their son, Jimmy. A deacon named Lou barges into the office and seems surprised to find Eric there. Embarrassed, he hurries out. Then the Moons confess, "We think Jimmy is doing drugs."

At home, Lucy confides to Mary that she saw Jimmy come out of the counselor's office. She's worried he might be doing drugs. Mary warns her to stay away from him. But Lucy thinks maybe it's her fault. Maybe Jimmy turned to drugs when she broke up with him.

Meanwhile, Matt has had an argument with Shana, and he's trying to call her to apologize. But her answering machine isn't working, so he can't leave a message. While he's on the phone, Shana calls from a phone booth and tries to leave a message with Ruthie. She wants to apologize for their fight. She makes Ruthie promise to give Matt the message, but when Matt runs up and tells Ruthie he's expecting an important call from Shana, Ruthie only responds with "How come?"

Eric is in his study struggling to write his Sunday sermon. He tells Annie he's worried about taking time off for the twins—worried he might get fired. After twenty years of dedicated service! Just then Lou calls. He and another deacon, Sid, are going to help out by doing the church bulletin all by themselves. When they hang up, Sid asks, "When are we going to tell him?" "Not until Sunday," Lou replies. Then adds, "He has no idea." Eric hangs up and tells Annie, "I'm telling you, honey. There's something going on."

The next day after school Mary and Lucy think they see Jimmy smoking pot in a car with some friends. Lucy tries to go over, but Mary grabs her. Seconds later two police cars screech into the parking lot. The cops arrest Jimmy and his friends.

Eric is working on his sermon on his church office computer when Lou and Sid barge in. Everyone acts nervous. The men make excuses and then hurry out. Seconds later, Eric gets a phone call—someone wants to talk to Lou. He needs an address to deliver the desk. The desk that was ordered by Reverend Bergen. Eric hangs up, shaken. A new minister? But before he can think about it, Lucy barges in to tell her dad that Jimmy's just been busted. When he doesn't "spring into action," like usual, she gets very upset.

Meanwhile, Simon is trying out for the junior high school baseball team. He's going out for catcher, but a kid tells him the coach's son is going out for catcher, too. Simon's heart sinks. But then Mary shows up. Simon thinks it'll help him get on the team if the coach knows he's related to Mary, a local high school basketball star. But after practice, he confides in Mary that he's worried about making the team. Her advice: Show the coach he's got more team spirit than anybody. Simon decides that's a great plan.

Later that night Lucy checks with her dad about Jimmy. Eric tells her that he's okay, the charges have been dropped, but feels he can't reveal any additional information. It's confidential. Lucy can't believe it. "If you don't want to help him, I will," she says and storms out. She's even more frustrated that her mother counsels her to let Jimmy's family take care of him and "let Lucy take care of Lucy."

Meanwhile, Ruthie keeps taking phone calls from Shana but doesn't give Matt any of the messages.

The next day Lucy tries to talk to Jimmy at school. She knows his drug problems are her fault, she says, and she wants to help. Jimmy notices a couple of tough kids waiting for him. He tells Lucy, "I don't need your help. Just stay the hell away from me." He joins the other guys, leaving Lucy in tears.

Eric comes home upset. The deacons were having a secret meeting at the office. Then he went to see Sergeant Michaels at police headquarters, but the man totally avoided him. Plus he hasn't returned any of the twenty messages Eric left the past two days. On top of it all, Lucy's still mad at him for not helping Jimmy.

Mary stops by baseball practice and tells the coach what Simon told her: that it didn't matter where he played. The important thing was being part of the team. He'd even be thrilled just being the equipment manager. The coach seems impressed.

Shana finally shows up at the Camden house, and she and Matt realize they've both been trying to apologize. Matt's shocked that Ruthie hasn't given him any of Shana's messages. But then he finds out why: Mom and Dad have each other, Ruthie says. Mary and Lucy have each other. Simon has the twins. That just leaves her and Matt. But he's always busy. She thought if Matt and Shana didn't get together, he'd have more time for her. Matt's not angry. He makes a date with Shana for Saturday night, and another date for the afternoon—with Ruthie.

Results for baseball tryouts are posted, and Simon is on the list. As equipment manager. He freaks out and calls Mary at school, demanding that she talk to the coach.

At the church, Eric meets with the Moons, who at first are simply relieved that Jimmy got off, regardless of what he was doing. Eric tells them he thinks the police may have made a deal with him to be a police informant on other drug dealers. His parents are shocked that such a thing could be legal with-

out their permission. Eric urges them to talk to their son. Eric has to leave because Mary has asked him to pick up Lucy at school so she can talk to the baseball coach. He arrives in time to see Lucy walking up to Jimmy Moon and some other guys. Suddenly, detectives jump out with guns and bust them, shouting at the kids, including Lucy, to go down on their knees. Lucy is terrified.

Meanwhile, Mary has a talk with Simon at home. Simon thinks he would have made the team, if not for Mary's big mouth. She finally admits that he didn't make the cut. But the coach says he can work out with the team. And Mary promises to help him improve enough to make the team next year.

At home, Lucy's parents start to lecture her, but she speaks first. She's found out that Jimmy's been an informant for months, ever since he got caught with his first joint. She knows now that her parents were right. To make it up to them, she'll baby-sit the twins so Mom can go to church. Her parents are impressed.

On Sunday Eric preaches on "our need to control things" when we are in the dark. About our "paranoia that something unexpected is about to happen." He's confused when his sermon is punctuated by giggles from the audience. Suddenly, the back door opens and an elderly man in clerical robes bursts down the aisle. He introduces himself as Reverend Bergen. And he cheerfully confirms Eric's belief that the whole church has been plotting and scheming behind his back all week. They've been planning a celebration picnic for his twentieth anniversary. The beautiful old desk is a present from him; it was his desk when he was the minister of the church many years ago. The biggest surprise of all? All the other Camdens knew about the surprise, and they didn't blow the secret!

Sometimes That's Just the Way It Is

written by Linda Ptolemy; directed by Kevin Inch

Simon thinks a broken chain letter has brought him bad luck. Ruthie can't get any attention around the babies. Eric has to counsel a couple considering divorce. Matt joins the Army.

Season 3: Episode 60

The Camdens wake up in the middle of the night to drawers and doors slamming. But it's not a burglar. It's Simon, searching for his old Red Lightning ring to protect him against the curse of now being the middle kid in the family.

The next day a church couple, Emily and Ted, come by to see Eric at his home office. Ruthie is turning cartwheels, but as long as the twins are in the room, nobody even notices her. In Eric's study, Emily is stunned to hear Ted quietly announce that after fifteen years, "I want a divorce." He's felt this way for years, but his mind's made up. He can't be married another second.

Upstairs, Simon's wearing garlic on a string around his neck and tries to put up a lucky horseshoe, but it falls. He asks Ruthie if she answered that chain letter he sent her. She hands him three envelopes—addressed to Simon Camden, Master Simon Camden, and Señor Simon Camden. No wonder! The letters have to go to *different* people. He tells her she has to keep the chain going or bad luck will befall her. She says, "Bad luck already befalled on me the day the babies were born." Simon throws salt over his shoulder.

Mary and Lucy are plotting how to escape the house. It's impossible these days; their parents need so much help with the twins. Simon comes in and posts a flyer on the fridge: "Lost: Red Lightning Ring. Reward." He asks his sisters if they continued the chain letter he gave them. Mary didn't; she thinks they're dumb. Lucy's thinking about it; she doesn't want to jinx the relatively good luck she's been having lately. Simon begs them to do it.

Emily goes into the kitchen and makes tea while she has a good chat with Annie. Later Eric comes in and tries to talk to her some more, but she wants only Annie's advice.

Eric is frustrated that his whole family butts in on his counseling: Simon talks to Emily about bad luck. Lucy advises her to have a child on her own or adopt. At last Emily goes home, and Mary is ecstatic to see that she's left her purse. Hurray! An excuse to leave the house!

Mary and Lucy are enjoying their freedom driving in the car with the radio on, the windows down—especially when two handsome hunks flirt with them at a stoplight and beg them to meet them at Landsburgers. They know they shouldn't, but after their errand they stop for a milkshake.

Meanwhile, Eric stops by Ted's apartment, but the man's enjoying his freedom too much—playing loud rock 'n roll, drinking a beer while wearing only his socks and underwear, watching TV whenever he wants. Emily was a control freak, he says, with too many rules. He's happy to be free.

At Landsburgers, Mary and Lucy sip shakes with the guys, who say they're twenty-one and go to Yale. Mary and Lucy give them fake names, and say they're nineteen and go to Brown. In France. The boys ask for their number, but the girls say no and ask for the guys' number.

Meanwhile, Matt comes home and tells Annie he's joined the Army to help pay college costs. Annie can't believe he'd do something so crazy! She starts to yell at him about how serious it is, and how dangerous. When Eric comes home, she's upset that his reaction is, "How much would he get?" Then they try to talk Matt out of it. They think he hasn't thought it through. Matt's angry. "I'm a grown man. I've considered all the options. I'm in."

Mary and Lucy leave the burger place, but the boys follow them. At a stoplight, the guys show the girls how to play fire drill. They jump out and run around the car before the light changes. Laughing, Mary and Lucy copy them. Horns blare, and they drive on. At the next stoplight, they try it again. But while they're out, a car suddenly squeals around a turn. It's Ted. He's driving drunk on his way to get more beer. With a sickening crunch, he smashes into the Camdens' station wagon and totals it. Terrified, Mary and Lucy cling to each other in the middle of the street.

The next morning Annie and Eric talk about the accident with the girls. Ted only has a few broken bones. But it's a miracle that the girls are alive. Lucy starts to cry, and Mary explains. "We're not alive because of some big miracle. We're alive because we're bad." She explains about the boys and the fire drill game.

Just then Ted and Emily come by. He's on crutches, with a neck brace and a broken arm. He apologizes to the girls, and they accept it. But Annie doesn't. She tells the girls to go, then delivers a blistering speech about how stupid he was to drink and drive. He could have killed her daughters. He could have killed himself or someone else. It's selfish, and she doesn't forgive him. She leaves the room, and Eric follows. That's not how he usually works, he says . . . but sometimes shoving the truth in someone's face is the best thing to do. They decide to try it with the girls, too. They tell them they understand how they want more freedom. But they almost got themselves killed. If they want more freedom, they have to earn it by being more responsible.

Left alone, Ted apologizes to Emily and says he guesses he'll come home with her, at least until the bandages come off. But Emily shocks him by saying she won't take care of him just so he can then leave her again. Suddenly, she notices Ruthie tap-dancing with sparklers, trying to get their attention. She races over and tells her she should never play with fire, even to get attention. She smiles then and says she was going to get the twins a present, but they have so much. Is there anything Ruthie wants? "Just don't tell my parents about the sparklers!" Then Ruthie tells Emily she'd make a good mom, and adds, "Take the twins. Please." Emily claps at Ruthie's joke.

Later, in the kitchen, Simon stuffs his chain letters down the garbage disposal because he found out they were illegal. Ruthie tells him he didn't get in trouble "only because you're lucky." Simon's delighted to think he might be lucky. His mother comes in and tells him lucky rings, chain letters, spells, and garlic have nothing to do with luck, good or bad. Eric smells smoke, and Ruthie confesses about the sparklers. Then Matt comes home, and they lay down the law: he's not going to join the Army. They're surprised when Matt simply says, "Okay," then leaves the room. That was easy. A little too easy. They go upstairs and question him. Why isn't he joining? "Failed the test!" he reveals.

Upstairs, Simon and Ruthie can't believe they didn't get in trouble. They're lucky Matt came in the door and distracted their parents. "I've got my luck back!" Simon says. "So I guess you won't be needing your Red Lightning ring anymore," Ruthie says, and pulls the missing ring out of her shirt. She's been wearing it on a chain the whole time. "My luck keeps getting better and better."

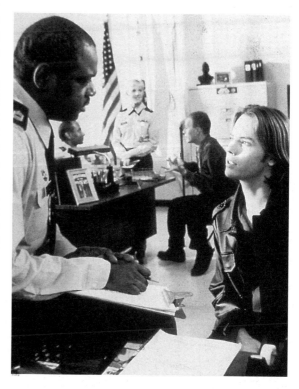

Eric meets with his friend Jack Brenner, president of Crawford University. The headline on the latest edition of *The Crawford Courier*, the school's newspaper, reads: CRAWFORD PRESIDENT IN ALLEGED EXTRACURRICULAR ACTIVITIES WITH CO-ED. "You know what the worst part of it is?" Jack says. "It's not alleged." He confesses to Eric that he had a brief relationship with a grad student, but that it's been over for a while. "I never meant for anyone to get hurt."

Matt and Shana are studying at the pool hall, where a group of students plan a demonstration to get Brenner fired. Matt admits the man's behavior is despicable, but he thinks it's his private business.

Meanwhile, Simon can't get Mr. Malone, one of his customers on his newspaper route, to pay his bill. But Mr. Daniels, his boss, says he'll have to fire Simon if he can't collect. As his unofficial assistant, Ruthie is outraged. The next day when they deliver papers, they see Mr. Malone get out of his car. They chase him all the way to the front door, asking him to pay up. But he simply rushes into his house and slams the door. Ruthie says Mom can squeeze the money out of him, but Simon doesn't want his mother to think he can't handle the job. When they stop by Mrs. Hinkle's house, they tell her they're about to be fired. The elderly woman storms off to have a talk with her neighbor.

In the school parking lot, Mary hits a car and leaves a message offering to pay for any damage. She doesn't want her parents to find out. "They'll find out," Lucy says. "They always do. No secret, no lie, no stupid thing we're about to do escapes them."

When Eric comes home, he tells Annie that Jack Brenner hasn't resigned, so the board will vote on it. Annie's upset, but Eric points out that he broke no laws, since the student was an adult and agreed to the relationship. "Do you think he's fit to lead the university?" Annie asks. "The university our son attends?" Eric admits he's disappointed in Jack. But should he be fired for that?

Upstairs, Mary gets a phone call from the person whose car she hit: Miles Olsen. Mary tries to flirt her way out of the situation, but Miles bluntly tells her, "You're not my type." But he was wondering if Lucy would go out with her. "I think she's a goddess." Mary agrees to set up a date—anything to butter him up. When she hangs up, she searches the yearbook for Miles's picture. There he is. A junior, and a total nerd! She tells Lucy she's made a date for her with him. "He thinks you're a god-

We the People

written by Catherine LePard; directed by Harry Harris

Eric, Annie, and Matt deal with the fallout when family friend and college president Jack Brenner's personal mistake sparks campus debate. Mary tries trickery to avoid paying for a car she hit, and forces Lucy to go on a date. Simon may get fired from his newspaper route because a customer refuses to pay.

dess." Lucy's excited till she checks the year-book, then she wants to gag. But Mary insists she has to go through with it so he'll go easy on her about the dent in his car. Lucy reluctantly agrees. "You owe me for the rest of time."

At the university, Doug Lightner is leading a mob of protesters inside the administration building. Matt says Doug doesn't speak for everybody. Just because he's the loudest voice doesn't mean he's the only one who should be heard. A shoving match follows.

At home, Mrs. Hinkle calls Simon with a plan. Simon asks his mom where the fishing stuff is. Annie's suspicious, but before she can investigate, Matt and Shana come in and try to sneak upstairs. When Eric and Annie call them back, they see what Matt was trying to hide: a black eye! Matt explains that a fight broke out at the demonstration. He got a two-hundred-dollar ticket for disturbing the peace. But he insists he had to speak up against the self-righteous minority. He doesn't respect Jack Brenner, but he thinks it's an issue of privacy. He knows what it's like living in a fishbowl and having people judge what he does because he's a minister's son.

When Miles comes over, he tells Annie and Eric his grade point average, his career plans, then gives them a card with his phone number, car model, license plate number, and a copy of his valid driver's license. Lucy's due home at seven; he says he'll have her home at six forty-five. "Doesn't seem like Lucy's type, does he?" Eric remarks.

At school, Matt apologizes to Doug. Doug agrees things got out of hand. Matt doesn't understand why people care so much about the issue. Doug says he doesn't understand why people care so little.

Simon, Ruthie, and Mrs. Hinkle put their plan into action. When Dan Malone peeks out his door and tries to snatch his newspaper, it seems to inch out of his reach, and he has to step outside. Behind some bushes, Mrs. Hinkle and Ruthie reel in the newspaper with the fishing rod, while Simon runs up and blocks the door. Mr. Malone tries to flee, but his feet are stuck. "No Pest Strips," Mrs. Hinkle cackles. He's forced to pay up.

Lucy's dinner date with Miles is embarrassing. His conversation is obnoxious. He knocks over a waitress's drinks with a pool

cue. Lucy endures it, for Mary's sake. But when she comes home and Mary asks her to go out with him again, Lucy refuses. She says Mary loves driving more than she loves her own sister.

Annie goes to visit Jack's wife, Gillian. She's doing okay, but she's upset that people have forgotten all the good things her husband has done for the college. She doesn't like that she's the "wronged victim" and more popular than ever on campus. And she can't believe that in 1999 girls are getting the message that it's okay to sleep with a married man. "What are we teaching our daughters?"

Eric stops by to see Jack, who's considering resigning. Jack admits that he doesn't know what Gillian thinks—he's afraid to ask. "I don't think you should resign," she says, walking in. "I think you should fight. We both should." Jack's eyes fill with tears as he hugs his wife. Eric smiles, knowing they'll be able to work things out.

When Miles shows up for a date the next night, Mary confesses everything. Miles can't believe it. On top of everything, he says she didn't hurt his car. "You didn't happen to notice that your 'ding' already had rust on it?" When Mary goes back inside, Annie gets the whole story out of her. Mary says she didn't mean for anyone to get hurt. Annie thinks it's no small thing: she lied, cheated, and used her sister and an innocent boy to avoid taking responsibility for her own actions. "A family is like a pond," she says, "and what one member does is like dropping a stone in a pond. It makes ripples and affects other people." She sends Mary to help Simon and Ruthie with their paper route. She has a talk with Lucy and sends her to help, too.

Eric, meanwhile, has gone to the board of trustees meeting. The place is packed. Someone calls out that they can all guess what the minister is going to say. But Eric surprises him. "I was going to say that Jack Brenner's a friend of mine. And I don't like what he did. Should he be punished?" Some people yell yes. "How?" Eric asks. "And how much? By whom? And who gets to decide?" The university is a family, he says. Like a stone dropped in a pond, what happens makes ripples that affect us all. He hopes Jack Brenner has learned that. And he hopes the board remembers it as well.

The Voice

written by Ron Darian; directed by David Plenn

Matt thinks his girlfriend, Shana, is dating another man. Annie slips out for a much-needed girls' night out. Ruthie tries to convince her family that the monkey she sees is real. Eric and Simon try to help the school's elderly custodian, who says God told him not to retire.

Rudy Steineger, the elderly custodian at Simon's school, comes to see Eric and asks him many questions: How do you know there's a God? Do you talk to God? Does God ever talk to you? "Why?" Eric asks warily. "Does God ever talk to you . . . out loud?" Rudy says yes. "He told me to talk to you."

Mary and Lucy have a one-night job working at a country club party. But they're worried their parents won't let them take it, because there'll be alcohol and the party will run so late. They decide to act very responsibly for a day or two, then ask permission.

When Eric comes home, he asks Simon if he told Rudy to come see him. Simon says no but adds that he talks to Rudy a lot; Rudy tells neat stories about the old days. "Do you find it odd that God talked to him and told him to come see me?" "No," Simon replies. "You do a pretty good job most of the time. Why wouldn't God recommend you?"

While Annie makes dinner, Eric shoos Ruthie outside to play. She bounces her ball hard, then waits . . . but it doesn't come back down. She looks up. A monkey in a tree has it! She tells everybody about the monkey, but they think it's just imaginary.

Matt's at the library studying when he sees Shana come in, hug the man behind the desk, and leave with him. What's going on?

Back at the house, Annie gets a call from her friend Patricia. She knows Annie needs a break from the twins. Her idea: Friday, at seven, a meeting of the Women's Interdenominational Church Council. Annie smiles. Not that scam again! She can't possibly get away. But Eric overhears and insists that she go, even though he doesn't understand what the WICC does. Then Eric gets a call. It's the vice principal at Simon's school. Rudy the custodian is in trouble. Eric agrees to meet him in the morning.

The next day Vice Principal Blackstone tells Eric that Rudy had agreed to retire. They'd given him a nice early-retirement package. But now he won't go, and he's doing weird things. Yesterday he took all of the money in petty cash and bought twenty-five gallons of shellac. But they don't need any shellac! Eric assures him he didn't talk Rudy out of retiring. Blackstone says he's down in the basement thinking he's talking to God. They can't have that! If he doesn't accept retirement by the board meeting tonight, they'll have to fire him. Then he'll have to kiss his pension good-bye.

Matt stops by Shana's apartment on the way to school but freezes when he sees the same man from the library come out of her apartment. Did he stay there all night? Matt's devastated.

Mary and Lucy agree to baby-sit the twins to butter up their mom. Eric tells Annie he has to go to the school board meeting. He doesn't think it's fair to fire Rudy. Simon overhears and begs to go along.

At the library, Matt tries to summon the courage to speak to the man he's seen with Shana. Suddenly, the guy says, "Matt? Matt Camden? Don't you remember me?" It turns out he's Tucker Berelson, Matt's best friend from fifth grade who moved away. He gives Matt a huge hug and asks if that was Matt outside his apartment building that morning. Relieved, Matt realizes Tucker lives there. Another friend walks by, and Tucker starts to give him a hug, but the other guy backs off. "What can I say?" Tucker laughs. "Some people are huggers, some aren't." Matt realizes he's made a huge mistake.

At the pool hall, Annie is having a great time with her good friends at their "meeting." Patricia calls the meeting to order, then they have a huge gripe session about all the things their families do to drive them crazy. They all toast one another with Diet Coke.

At the school board meeting, the gym is packed. Rudy says he knows it sounds crazy, but God told him he still had work to do. Eric argues that many people in the room talk to God every day; maybe we just don't get as clear an answer as Rudy does. He convinces the board to wait a few more days.

Minutes after Eric and Simon get home, the doorbell rings. It's their neighbor Curtis, who recently lost an arm in an accident. "Sorry to be bothering you this late," he says. "But it's about my chimp. He's missing." Eric is stunned. "Your . . . chimp?" Curtis explains that he volunteered to be in a new program to see if chimps can be trained to help out handicapped folks. Eric leads the man upstairs to Ruthie's room. Lying on the bottom bunk, she points above her. The chimp, wearing some of Ruthie's pajamas, pokes its head out from under the covers. Eric is amazed; Ruthie's "monkey" is real! Curtis takes the chimp, and the chimp finally gives Ruthie the ball back.

Matt shows up at Shana's apartment with flowers. He apologizes to her about jumping to conclusions about Tucker. She shrugs and says, "What if I am seeing Tucker?" Matt freaks out and says he thinks they should only date each other. "Is that what you really want?" she asks. He says definitely. Then she laughs and reassures him she's *not* dating Tucker. They seal the deal with a kiss.

Mary and Lucy are feeding the babies when Annie comes home. She's so proud of them, she says. So proud that she's going to let them both work at the country club tomorrow and then send Matt to pick them up so they won't have to drive home late. Then she leaves. Mary and Lucy look at each other, stunned. "You asked her," Mary accuses her sister. "I did not," Lucy insists. Annie sticks her head back in. "I ran into Corey's

mother at the, um . . . place where I was. She told me all about it." The girls just shake their heads.

Soon after Eric and Simon come home, the phone rings. There's been an accident. It's Rudy. Eric and Simon rush over to the school. Police headlights cut through the darkness, illuminating the school's football bleachers—collapsed into a pile of wood and twisted metal. Vice Principal Blackstone explains that security called when they found Rudy shellacking the bleachers at eleven o'clock at night. "And you know why?" Blackstone complains. "Because God told him to!" When the police went up after him, the bleachers collapsed. "I'm holding you responsible, Reverend!" Blackstone says. The school is pressing charges.

Eric goes over to the police car and asks Rudy what happened. Rudy apologizes. God said he had to shellac those bleachers. "I guess God wanted me to get them ready for the marching band competition tomorrow. I mean, the kids deserve nice smooth bleachers, don't they?" Then one of the policemen says if this had happened eight hours from now, when those bleachers were filled with students, who knows what would have happened? Lots of kids would have been hurt. Someone might have been killed.

"Thank God this happened now," Vice Principal Blackstone says. Eric gives him a look. "What did you say?" "I said, 'Thank . . .'" Blackstone falls silent, realizing that Rudy has saved his students from a disaster. He walks over to the police car and shakes hands with Rudy. "Whatever you want, Rudy, just name it." Rudy smiles and says he thinks his work is done here. He thinks he would like to retire. "I think I'd like to go fishing!" he tells Simon with a grin. "Come on, Rudy," Eric says. "We'll take you home."

All Dogs Go to Heaven

written by Chris Olsen & Jeff Olsen; directed by Paul Snider

Simon freaks when his birthday date with Deena is spoiled by their siblings. Matt spends the evening riding with Sergeant Michaels for a class. And Eric helps out with some church members' unusual mom, who's dying.

Season 3: Episode 63

Lucy is helping Annie clean the kitchen—on a Friday night! "Once again everyone has something to do but me," she complains. Annie points out that her father doesn't have anything to do, either, which doesn't exactly help matters. But, in fact, Eric says he does. Burt and Cheryl Carberry asked him to visit with their dying mom. Annie's a little suspicious. Whose mother is it? Eric doesn't know. Annie wonders why in all these years of going to the church, they never knew they had one of their mothers living there? It seems strange. Eric insists he's not making it up just to get out of the house and away from helping with the twins.

Just then Matt and Mary come downstairs arguing. Michael Towner has invited Mary to come over to watch movies, and Matt says she can't. Annie agrees when she learns he's older, rents a house with five other guys, and is throwing a party. But she can go to the movie theater with him.

The rest of the Camden kids, except for Lucy, have evening plans as well. Matt says he's going to ride along with Sergeant Michaels tonight for his social sciences class. Annie's worried, but Matt promises he'll be fine. Simon's taking Deena to a fancy restaurant for her birthday. Even Ruthie comes down all dressed up. "I've got a date," she says. Lucy can't take it!

At the Carberrys' house Eric finds out that their "Mom" is a scruffy-looking old dog. They explain that she came to them a stray on a cold night, and the next morning she'd had a litter of puppies. But she's old now and in a lot of pain from a broken foot that the vet says won't heal. She needs to be taken to the vet to be put down, but they can't bear to. Will Eric do it?

When Michael Towner shows up, he realizes he's left his cash card at home. Annie totally embarrasses Mary by suggesting that it's a ploy to get Mary back to his apartment. She finally lets them go, but says, "Don't make me ask to see the ticket stubs."

As they leave, Deena arrives with her older brother, Jack, a cool-looking seventeen-year-old musician, who's driving Deena and Simon on their date. Sparks instantly fly between Jack and Lucy. Simon is horrified when Jack invites her along to help chaperone and Lucy jumps at the invitation.

When Mary and Michael get to his apartment, they find that his roommates are throwing a party. "Ever kissed good night at the beginning of a date?" Michael asks flirtatiously. They start making out just as Michael's roommate Pat opens the door and drags them inside to the party. But soon they leave. She says she wouldn't be comfortable with everyone older and drinking. Michael says he wouldn't be comfortable lying to her mom. "Ever made out at a cash machine?" Michael asks. They stroll off to try it.

Meanwhile, Eric has arrived at the animal hospital. He gets out, looks at Mom, then gets back in and starts the car. "I can't do it." Instead he takes her to the Dairy Shack. He buys himself a shake and Mom a burger. But she won't eat it. Eric tells her he doesn't know what to do other than "pray that God takes you home, but I can tell you this—no one goes one millisecond sooner than the universe is ready to embrace them." He can't take her home. But he *can't* take her to the vet, either. So he takes her to the park. When they get there, Eric's a little spooked sitting in the dark with no one else around. And he almost has a heart attack when Sergeant Michaels shows up—after a ranger called about a homeless man hanging out in the park with a dog he knows belongs to someone else. Michaels says he'll let the ranger know everything's okay. Then he gets a call for a public disturbance. A party near the campus. Michaels tells Matt it's okay if he wants to sit in the backseat so nobody will see him.

Simon breaks out into a cold sweat at the fancy French restaurant he picked out. He can't read the French, and the prices aren't even listed. The waiter looks down his nose at him. But Lucy saves the day by saying in French, "I don't want to ruin your beautiful language with my terrible accent. I am afraid you will weep and that will spoil our evening." The waiter laughs and becomes much more friendly. He offers to make suggestions, and Lucy thanks him, but says that since Simon is treating, they would all be embarrassed if our tastes were too extravagant. The waiter winks at her, and Simon is truly amazed. He never knew his sister could be so cool.

Meanwhile, Sergeant Michaels has shown up at the party at Michael Towner's apartment, and Matt sees lots of people he knows. With a grin, Sergeant Michaels tells him he'd be glad to pick him up down the block in about fifteen minutes. Matt gratefully sneaks out of the car. Soon Michael and Mary walk back by. They spot the police car with the back door open. "Ever made out in a police car?" Michael says. Giggling, they jump in for a two-second experience. Matt hears a familiar giggle and backs nonchalantly toward the car. When he turns around, all three teenagers scream. Moments later a crowd gathers to watch Michael hold Mary back from trying to clobber Matt for interfering with her life one more humiliating time. Sergeant Michaels hates to spoil the date but decides he better take the two Camdens home—Mary in the front seat, Matt in the back.

When he gets back to the police station, he lets them fight a bit, then takes Matt out to talk. He tells him that he's an older brother, too. He used to go crazy watching after his sister, telling her who to date. In college, she dated a real creep who drank too much, smoked pot, cheated on her, and treated her badly. He forbade her to go out with him. "So what happened?" Matt asks. "She married him," Sergeant Michaels said. And he treated her the same way. Later they divorced, but he always regretted that he wasn't more of a friend to his sister and that he hadn't treated her like a grown woman. He tells Matt Mary's got two parents already; he should try being her friend.

At the park a mean-looking stray growls at Eric. He figures out it's Huck, a stray the Carberrys told him was a friend of Mom's. A dog who ran away because he was mistreated. Eric talks soothingly to the dog and calms him down. Huck lies down beside Mom. And then Huck sits up and howls. Eric looks at Mom. She's quietly passed away.

The next morning Annie wakes up to find Eric asleep beside her. Groggily, he apologizes for getting in late and adds, "I finally talked the park ranger into burying Mom in the park." Annie's eyes pop open. Then Eric remembers she doesn't know. "Mom was the family dog," he explains. He's got another surprise, in the bed with him. Huck the stray. Annie says no, they absolutely cannot keep him! Eric rushes out to tell the Carberrys what happened, but not before commenting on another big surprise: the twins are still asleep after seven hours. They've finally slept through the night! On the way out Eric passes Matt and Mary, who've been up all night talking.

When Eric arrives at the Carberrys, they say they talked to the vet and the park ranger. They know what's happened, and they thank Eric for all he's done. One more thing, Eric says. He knows it's hard to replace a dog, but could they find it in their hearts to take in Huck? "It's a miracle!" the Carberrys say. Huck has never let a person come near him. At first they say it's too soon, but then they think that maybe it's a gift from Mom, and they say yes. "Do you think dogs go to heaven?" they ask. Eric smiles and says he knows they do.

There Goes the Bride, Part One

teleplay by Brenda Hampton & Sue Tenney; story by Sue Tenney; directed by Tony Mordente

Matt's ex-girlfriend Heather is getting married, and his current girlfriend, Shana, is upset that he's so involved. Mary lies about dating Jordan, while Lucy tries to fix up her two friends Joe and Shelby. Eric learns some unsettling news about his sister, Julie. And Ruthie, mad that she can't be the flower girl, puts a hex on the wedding.

Eric and Annie are worried about how Matt is going to handle his ex-girlfriend Heather's wedding. After all, he was once in love with her enough to follow her across the country. Matt overhears them and says he's fine. Heather has Mason, and he has Shana. And Shana's fine going to his ex-girlfriend's wedding. She loves weddings.

Ruthie comes in in a bride's outfit. Brides are beautiful, she says. Everyone pays attention to you. And people give you lots of free stuff. "Don't you need a groom?" Annie asks playfully. Ruthie asks the first unmarried boy she sees, Lucy's good-looking friend Joe, who comes in with Lucy and their friend Shelby. When Joe and Shelby go into the living room, Eric asks: Is Joe Lucy's or Shelby's? Neither, Lucy insists. They're like the Three Musketeers. Eric wonders how long that will last.

When Lucy leaves, Annie tells Eric some unsettling news. The day before, she saw his sister, Julie, come out of Dr. Hastings's office. "Dr. Hastings, the baby doctor?" Eric asks. Annie nods.

When Matt calls Shana, he finds out she's actually upset about the wedding. So she's not pleased when Matt says he has to go meet Heather at the church. On his way out Ruthie begs to be a flower girl in the wedding. He says he'll ask Heather.

Mary's bopping around with a basketball constantly in her hand, humming as if she's the happiest girl in the world. She denies it, but Eric and Annie suspect she's got a new boy in her life.

The doorbell rings, and Lucy answers it. It's Joe, and he just has to share a big secret with her. Lucy loves secrets, but this one floors her. Joe gives her a big kiss and admits he's in love with her. Startled, Lucy says he can't be—they're Musketeers. Embarrassed, Joe leaves in a hurry. Lucy doesn't know what to think.

Matt meets Heather and Mason at the church, and they ask him to be an usher. When he calls Shana to tell her, she asks, "Anything else? You're not going on their honeymoon, are you?"

Across town, Eric stops by Dr. Hastings's office and says he needs to ask him something about Sam and David. "Why was their Aunt Julie in your office yesterday?" Hastings just smiles. Eric will have to ask her.

Lucy calls Shelby and tells her about Joe. Shelby says she would love to be in Lucy's shoes. Lucy hangs up. "How could I be so stupid?" she says. "Shelby likes Joe." Mary says she knew the "guys as friends" thing wouldn't last. But Lucy gives

Mary a hard time. She's been playing basketball for two hours, huh? How come she's not sweaty and she smells like aftershave? She's dating somebody Mom and Dad don't approve of, isn't she? Mary confesses: it's Michael Towner. Lucy won't tell. She thinks secret love affairs are romantic.

Meanwhile, Deena and her cousin Cindy come over, and Cindy's a real pain. She won't shake hands because of germs, and she criticizes everything. Simon is afraid she hates him, and afraid she'll make Deena hate him, too! But when Deena goes to the bathroom, she gives Simon a big kiss, seconds before Deena comes back in. "What did I miss?" Deena asks.

Eric goes home and admits to Annie that he went by Dr. Hastings's office. Just then the phone rings. Guess who's coming to dinner? His sister, Julie. And she has something she wants to tell them.

Meanwhile, Matt goes to pick up Heather at the bridal shop. He's bowled over by how beautiful she looks in her wedding gown.

At the Camden house, Eric and Annie are surprised when Julie comes in with a guest. Dr. Hastings. "Hank," she reveals, is her new boyfriend. They sit down to a very uncomfortable dinner. Finally, Annie drags Eric into the kitchen to help with coffee and tea. He can't help it, he explains. Hank Hastings is the doctor who almost killed Matt. Annie reminds him that he helped them when Sam and David were born. Eric doesn't care. He doesn't trust him. When they go back in, they hear the babies crying on the monitor. Annie sends Hank and Eric up to check on them. When Annie steps into the kitchen, she spots Mary in the backyard kissing *Jordan*. She'll have to talk to her later.

Upstairs the men joke about changing the babies' diapers, but when Hank asks, "So it's okay if I date your sister?" Eric flatly says no. He says Julie is a recovering alcoholic, which Hank already knew. Eric doesn't want her to get hurt. Suddenly, they hear Julie yelling that she wants to leave. Downstairs, a furious Julie throws the baby monitor at Eric. She's heard every word. She says he's never going to let her forget she's an alcoholic.

Matt goes to Mason's bachelor party, and things are getting wild when Shana shows up. Matt cringes—he forgot he was supposed to go by and see her before the party. Does he still love Heather? Matt insists it's over. "Don't break my heart," she warns. A tipsy Mason comes over and makes a pass at Shana. Later, Matt is stunned to see Mason smooching with a good-looking girl. Some of the other guys tell Matt she's Mason's *other* girlfriend. He's invited her to the wedding, and he's plan-

ning on keeping her as a girlfriend *after* the wedding. Matt heads over to have a talk with him.

A short while later Matt rings Heather's doorbell. When she answers, he tells her, "You can't marry Mason." She thinks he's been drinking, but he's totally sober. He won't tell her why, but she has to stop the wedding. Heather is angry. She says Mason called to warn her that Matt had been acting crazy at the party and that he would try to break up the wedding. She tells Matt not to come to the wedding, and to stay away from her for the rest of her life. Matt suddenly kisses her. She's moved, but she pulls away and slams the door in his face.

The next day Annie confronts Mary about Jordan. Mary says it all happened accidentally. What about Michael? Annie asks. Mary says his parents think she's trouble because she's a minister's daughter. Annie warns her that she's risking her relationship with her sister.

The next morning there's a lot going on in the Camden family. Ruthie tells Simon not to bother getting ready for the wedding. Since she didn't get to be flower girl, she put a hex on it. It's not gonna happen. Matt tells his parents he's not going but won't explain why not. Mary calls Jordan to say she can't go out with him, but he won't accept it. Across town, Aunt Julie and Hank decide to elope.

Soon everyone, including Shana, is at the wedding. Heather's mother, Donna, apologizes to Ruthie about not being a flower girl; they already promised Mason's nieces. Ruthie says, "I'm sorry, too." "For what?" Donna asks. "You'll see," Ruthie replies ominously.

Lucy has given Shelby a makeover to try to get Joe to like her, and when Joe sees her, he's dazzled. But when they all sit down together, Joe whispers that Shelby looks great, but not as great as Lucy. Lucy gulps. Just then the wedding begins. The bride comes down the aisle, and all goes well till Eric says, "If there is any person present who believes these two should not be wedded in holy matrimony, speak now or forever hold your peace. . . ."

"Don't do it!" Matt yells from the back of the church. Heather, deaf, doesn't hear him. She turns to see what everyone is looking at. Matt signs to her, "Don't do it!"

Heather tells Mason, "I'm sorry." She runs down the aisle into Matt's arms, and they kiss. The church is in an uproar. Shana looks as if she's been hit by a truck. Mason runs after Heather, but she and Matt run down the church steps, jump into his car, and squeal off down the road.

"Wow!" Ruthie says. She can't believe it—her hex worked!

There Goes the Bride, Part Two

written by Brenda Hampton
& Sue Tenney;
story by Sue Tenney;
directed by Burt Brinckerhoff

Matt returns to the church with Heather, who's learned the truth about her fiancé after leaving him at the altar. But Matt realizes he may have lost Shana forever. Lucy tries to mend her friendships with Joe and Shelby, while Mary reveals her relationship with Jordan. Julie and Hank decide to get married. And Ruthie finally gets to be a flower girl.

It's fifty years in the future. Matt is married to both Shana and Heather. What a lucky man! he thinks. Then both women say they're leaving unless he chooses. He says he can't! They insist.

A car door slams. Matt looks up. He's been daydreaming! "Do you want a doughnut?" Heather asks. "I don't know about you, but I'm starved." Suddenly the reality of what he's done, breaking up Heather's wedding and running away with her, sinks in. "What are you thinking about?" she asks sweetly. "Nothing!" he says too quickly.

Back at the wedding, no one leaves. They all want to see what happens next. Mason angrily says that Heather will come to her senses and return. Donna begs Eric to find them, and he goes to make some calls. Annie tries to comfort Heather's mother. Then she notices a very attractive girl with Mason. "Who's that?" she asks. Donna distractedly says it's Suzy, a friend of Mason's family. "She does look friendly," Annie says as she watches the girl stroke Mason's face. "A little too friendly," she mutters under her breath.

Deena tracks down Simon, and he tells her about Cindy kissing him. But Deena's not mad—she already knew. It was Cindy's idea, a test of their relationship. Simon can't believe it.

Mary is worried when Jordan comes in the church and sits with her. What if Lucy sees? But Jordan is tired of hiding. And when Lucy, Shelby, and Joe come over, Jordan takes Mary's hand and tells Lucy that he and Mary want to date. They both say they didn't want to hurt her, but Lucy runs out. Joe runs after Lucy, and Mary leaves with Jordan. Shelby suddenly feels all alone.

Meanwhile, Julie and Hank have gotten a marriage license. But Julie suddenly makes a U-turn. She doesn't want to lie or sneak. That's what she did all her life as an alcoholic. She wants to go to the church and tell Eric they're getting married.

Matt decides he and Heather should call and let people know they're okay. He calls his dad at the church office. He tells his dad he knows he has a million questions, but for the time being they're just going to have to trust him. "Are you and Heather married?" Eric asks abruptly. Matt says they're coming back to the church as soon as he talks to Heather. Then he'll explain everything. But first he calls Shana. He tries to explain. She says she's not mad. She just hates and despises him. "No need to explain," she says sweetly. "Just drop dead."

At the church Julie and Hank show up in the middle of everything and tell Eric they're getting married. His reaction? He just starts laughing. "I can't wait for Hank to meet the Colonel. Welcome to the family, and good luck." Julie and

Hank take the kids home while Eric and Annie wait with Mason and Donna for Matt and Heather.

Back at the house, Mary has finally had it with Lucy being so upset about her "stealing" Jordan, even though Lucy is the one who dumped him. So she tells Lucy she's going to stop sneaking around. She's going to date him, and there's nothing she can do about it. Lucy is steamed! She calls Joe and asks him to come over—now. As soon as Joe arrives, the girls are in a cuddling contest on the couch. Lucy puts her arm around Joe. Mary snuggles up to Jordan. Jordan is a little freaked out, but Joe is delighted that Lucy is finally showing him some affection. But then Julie comes in and breaks up the party. After the boys leave, she tells Hank she's not sure she wants to get married anymore. Hank is stunned and decides he should leave. Julie watches him go, then starts to cry.

At the church, almost all the guests have gone when Matt and Heather arrive. Heather looks as if she's been crying, and she runs off, followed by her mother. Mason tells Matt to stay away from them. Annie and Eric ask Matt for an explanation, but he says he has to go. He has to go see Shana. He's sure he loves her, and he can't lose her. He leaves, and his parents are more confused than ever. There must be some other reason that Matt broke up the wedding. But what?

When Matt gets to Shana's apartment, she says she's glad he came by—so she can throw a glass of water in his face. She slams the door. Opens it, throws out a towel, then slams the door again.

At the church, the groomsman, Zack, and Suzy tell Annie they need to talk to her. Suzy says, "I need to tell someone the truth about Mason."

At the Camden house, Julie has a big talk with the girls. She tells Lucy she should admit she's upset about Mary and Jordan because she's jealous. And Mary should admit that that scene in the living room wasn't about liking someone; it was about making Lucy jealous. She also gives Lucy a hard time for using Joe. There's no excuse for using people, she scolds them. Then she leaves them alone to work things out. Instead, Lucy calls Shelby to tell her what happened. She called because she could use a best friend. Shelby says, "So could I. Do you know where I could find one?" Then adds, "Today you made me feel lonelier than I've ever felt before." Lucy feels terrible.

When Shana takes out the trash, she finds Matt still sitting there. She tells him she's mad at him because she's been hurt by men all her life: her father, her brother, her other boyfriends. Matt made her trust again, made her feel safe. Now he's broken her heart. She slams the door again. This time Matt sadly walks away.

At the church, Annie, Suzy, and Zack go in to see Heather. Suzy insists that Heather hear what she has to say about Mason.

Matt calls Shana's answering machine. She doesn't answer but listens to his message. He says that he loves Heather like a sister and that he knew Mason was no good. He just couldn't let her marry him. But he needs to tell her, "I love you. Funny, it's the first time I've told you that, and I guess it's also the last." When Shana hears this, she begins to cry.

Back at the church, Heather has now changed out of her wedding dress. Mason goes to her and tries to kiss her, but she stops him. She says Matt told her everything. Mason says she can't believe Matt, but she counters with, "What about your girlfriend, Suzy? Can I believe what she says?"

At home, Lucy hears Mary telling Jordan that she has to pick Lucy over him. He says he still cares about Lucy, too, and doesn't want to hurt her. Lucy comes in and the girls make up. Later Lucy, Joe, and Shelby decide to go back to being just friends.

Suddenly, the Camden household is in a flurry preparing for another wedding. . . .

At the church the day of Julie and Hank's ceremony, Shana comes in and gives Matt a kiss. "I love you, too," she says. A "friend" explained everything: Heather. Matt feels lucky to have both girls in his life.

At last Julie and Hank get married, and Ruthie finally gets to be a flower girl. Simon gives the bride away as Eric presides over the service. When he gets to the part when he has to ask if anyone objects, everyone turns and stares at Matt. "Very funny," he says.

That night in bed, the excitement continues as Annie and Eric discuss the latest surprise that Julie and Hank have sprung upon them: They're having a baby!

Season 4

It's a season of crises. Eric has a heart attack. Mary's world spins out of control when she gets arrested for vandalizing the school gym. Simon gets busted for having cigarettes, and Lucy rejects the in-crowd. Eric's sister, Julie, decides to leave her husband on the same day she delivers their baby. Matt's girlfriend gets accepted to NYU, 3,000 miles away. Annie's dad is diagnosed with Alzheimer's. When times are dark, the Camdens know they can count on one thing—one another.

The Tattle Tale Heart

written by Brenda Hampton; directed by Burt Brinckerhoff

Eric's parents discover their daughter has gotten married, and is having a baby. Matt and John find an apartment. Eric has a heart attack.

Eric and Annie are spending the evening in the living room with Eric's visiting parents, the Colonel and Ruth. The Colonel has plenty to gripe about, as usual. One, neither Eric nor his sister Julie named a child after him. Two, Julie is late to arrive with her new boyfriend. Three, Simon's wearing his cap in the house. Simon removes it to reveal a new close-shaved haircut. It's extreme, and totally different from the look his adopted "uncle" George is wearing—Rastafarian dreadlocks.

Upstairs, Lucy and Ruthie whisper about something the Colonel and Ruth don't know yet: their daughter Julie is married, and she's going to have a baby!

The next morning, Eric comes downstairs to find his dad making breakfast in the kitchen. The Colonel asks Eric why Julie hasn't come by to see them and wonders if there's something wrong. Eric plays dumb, shakes his head, and rushes out of the room.

Upstairs, Lucy and Ruthie discuss ways to remodel the room they now share. Ideally, they say in front of Matt, their big brother will move out, freeing up a room. Mary tells Matt she thinks it's time for him to go, too.

Across the hall, Eric's annoyed at Julie for not visiting as promised the night before. To add to his frustration, his counseling work is piled up on account of a company layoff that's affected some of the church membership. Annie reminds him they're also scheduled to look for a new car, replacing the one Mary wrecked. Finally, Eric's concerned about keeping the kids from telling the Colonel and Ruth about Julie. . . .

As soon as everyone's in the kitchen, the Colonel makes a few remarks about Julie and her boyfriend. Eric and Annie say nothing except to express surprise that the Colonel's allowed Ruthie to watch cartoons on TV, which he usually forbids. Annie starts to ask her about it when Matt enters and tells Annie he's looking for an apartment.

At Eric's office, Eric juggles phone calls and visiting parishioners. He sits down to counsel a couple when Julie calls. She promises to be at Eric and Annie's that night.

Matt arrives at the address of an apartment for rent and is surprised to find that John Hamilton's there, too.

Back at the house, Mary and Lucy tell Annie how they'd rearrange their living spaces if Matt moved out. Simon and Ruthie have another plan as well. Annie nixes them both, since Matt has already refused the garage and nobody thinks he's going to get a job to pay for an apartment. Suddenly, Ruth shows up and loudly proposes a shopping trip for her, the kids, and maybe even Julie. Annie hurriedly derails the idea with the excuse that the children are moving their rooms around—she just decided.

Off in the living room, Simon and George trade a few insults about each other's new hairstyles. Then Simon says, "You didn't tell them, did you?" George smiles. Simon knows he had better be nice to George or George will tell what he knows. "I never should have told you about Julie," Simon moans.

Just then Eric enters the room with a handful of bills. The Colonel comes in, too, with an invitation for Simon to tag along with him to the hardware store. Simon backs out because they're moving their beds around upstairs. Then Annie comes in with a message for an exhausted Eric from Sergeant Michaels—Eric's needed to help deliver a sensitive message to the wife of a man who was stabbed during a drug bust. Through it all Eric remembers to tell the Colonel the news: Julie and Hank are coming over later.

Meanwhile Mary and Lucy cook up a plan to get Matt a job. They're going to get Hank, a doctor, to find him something at the hospital.

Matt and John have concluded that they will take the apartment together, since John has a job and Matt has a car; if John can get a car, and Matt can get a job, then everything will be perfect.

All this time Eric's running around town, making the call with Sergeant Michaels, trying to return a call from Lou, picking up blood pressure medicine for Mrs. Hinkle, grabbing some extra hamburger for Annie's supper menu. Annie tells him to eat something because she's worried about him.

Matt does get a job through Hank, to Mary and Lucy's joy. The girls start packing for the move immediately. Matt breaks the news to Annie, who can't believe it. He'll be gone the next day. Simon's not pleased either, until Matt says he can come over to the apartment Saturday, with Nigel.

When Matt enters Ruthie's room to tell her about his move, he learns that Ruthie slipped and told the Colonel and Ruth about Julie's marriage and pregnancy. Then Simon defends Ruthie, saying he told George, who certainly told them. Then Mary and Lucy defend Simon, saying they spilled the beans, too.

Outside, the grown-ups get the grill ready. Eric arrives with groceries. Julie presents Hank, and her big stomach, to the Colonel and Ruth. To Annie and Eric's amazement, they seem perfectly pleased. Suddenly, Hank looks at Eric, who's clutch-ing his arm in pain. They call an ambulance; Eric is having a heart attack.

At the Glenoak Hospital, Eric learns his attack was mild, and treatable with a diet change and more relaxation. His parents' positive reaction to Julie's marriage and pregnancy helps a lot.

At home, everybody reacts differently. Matt wishes he'd moved out sooner, to take some of the pressure off his dad. Mary and Lucy feel guilty about being selfish over Matt's room. Ruthie worries about having bugged him for new tennis shoes.

That night Annie gathers all of the kids into her room, then calls Eric at the hospital. All at once, the group yells good night to Eric. "See you tomorrow," Annie whispers. "Tomorrow," Eric says. And then he looks up and says, "Thank you. Thank you for tomorrow."

Life Is Too Beautiful

**written by Brenda Hampton;
directed by Tony Mordente**

After a heart attack,
Eric gets a second chance at life,
and finds every moment beautiful.
Annie is exhausted trying to
shield Eric from stress.
Everyone learns a lesson
about helping others.

The kids file through the kitchen with their dirty dishes, passing them off to Annie, who loads the dishwasher. Eric comes in last and kisses Annie, then heads for the front porch to relax.

The next morning, Eric squeezes orange juice in the kitchen, singing loudly, waking everyone up. Then he calls Matt and John's apartment and hangs up after a couple of rings. It's a good thing; Matt barely has time to throw on a shirt and run out the door, almost late for work. Eric tells Annie he calls every morning, wanting to make sure Matt keeps his job. Annie warns him to take it easy—to remember he's still recovering from a heart attack.

Simon enters the kitchen and posts a newspaper article about healthy eating on the fridge, then reminds Eric to do his anti-stress meditation. Eric dutifully heads for the bedroom and gets into the lotus position.

Mary and Lucy knock at the door and enter. Mary has a trigonometry test that needs a parent's signature. She shrugs off the bad grade she got, figuring she'll never need trig in "real life." The comment launches Eric into a speech about problem solving, real-life challenges, good grades, and sound thinking. Lucy escapes into the hall.

In the kitchen, Ruthie runs into Simon, who asks her if she's done her homework. He's trying to be the man of the house while his dad recovers. He's even taken up shaving, which Matt finds amusing.

Annie heads upstairs to relieve Eric, who says he doesn't mind Mary's request for help. In fact, he wants everyone in the family to ask for help from someone they've alienated. He believes this exercise will help restore broken friendships. Downstairs, he goes on and on about the wonder of bread, changed by heat to become toast. Annie shakes her head at Eric's newfound fascination for life, and rolls her eyes.

At school, Mary asks Lucy to participate in Eric's exercise by helping her with a little basketball practice. Lucy says she doesn't think that's the kind of help Eric had in mind. Matt spots John on campus and shares Eric's assignment with him. John likes the idea. He says he'll try it on Shana, Matt's girlfriend. Simon gets some help from Jim, a big kid at school, with an armload of books, even though the big kid kind of laughs at him.

At the house, Mrs. Beeker shows up wanting to be helpful, but Annie turns the gossip away. Mary comes home, and Annie detours her around Eric so he can rest. Simon then steps in to help Annie, and sends Ruthie off to take a bath. Then Lucy approaches him and asks for career advice. Simon can't think of a vocation that suits her interests—unless it's boys. Matt suggests a technical school, since there are a lot of boys there! Lucy flares at the insinuation that she has no other interests.

Outside, Eric lies on the picnic table, singing to the stars above.

At the apartment, Matt discovers John and Shana in the middle of a big cleanup. Matt finds their new friendship unsettling. They're having a great time, thanks to Eric's plan.

At the kitchen table, Mary's math homework has her and Annie both in tears, but Annie refuses to bother Eric with it.

The next day, Annie tries to turn Mrs. Beeker away again, then relents when the woman admits that she snoops in other people's lives because she's lonely. It immediately becomes apparent that Mrs. Beeker wants to be a help around the house.

At the high school, Lucy befriends a group of girls she calls "the weird group." Then a popular girl tells her she would have made the cool group's "A-list" if it weren't for her new friends. Lucy decides this is okay with her.

At the apartment, Shana and Matt have a fight about the time she's been spending with her new buddy, John. She responds by asking John for a ride to work, instead of Matt.

Then later, in the car, Simon scolds Matt for undermining Simon's authority as man of the house at home and for laughing at him for shaving. Matt apologizes and they even hug, which makes Ruthie wonder when things are ever going back to normal.

At the house, Mrs. Beeker turns out to be an excellent trigonometry tutor for Mary. Lucy comes home with the news that she's working for Habitat for Humanity. She thanks Mary for giving her the needed push, and they hug. At the apartment, Matt and Shana make up with a hug.

Eric tells Annie about the mental pictures he saw when he had his heart attack—moments in time when his father, the Colonel, his grandfather, and even his great-grandfather and others were extending helping hands to others. It made him think that the best thing he can do is be a good father.

Eric's heart attack has given him a new appreciation for life, which is what gave him the idea for the exercise in helping others. It really paid off, too. It's how Lucy got a new, better group of friends. It's what reaffirmed her commitment to Habitat for Humanity. It's how Shana and John became better friends. In a way, it's even what caused Annie to allow Mrs. Beeker to help out.

For the Camdens, things are on the way back to normal.

Yak Sada (One Voice)

written by
Elizabeth Orange;
directed by
Bradley Gross

Season 4: Episode 68

Annie gets up, showers, and heads downstairs and puts breakfast out for everyone, including Happy. Then she heads back upstairs. When she comes back down, she's dressed and the kids are eating. Mary asks to drive, but Annie says she will—there are lots and lots of family errands to do. Simon comes down last, complaining about having to take home ec. He did it to be with Deena, and now he feels like "one of the girls." Lucy tells Simon she thinks Mary and Ruthie have something going on.

Eric comes downstairs last, upbeat and ready to get back to work. "Don't work too hard," Annie says, concerned because Eric is recovering from a mild heart attack. Then she accompanies the kids to the car.

Matt stops her, though, and says he promised Annie would hem a skirt for his girlfriend, Shana. Even though Shana needs it by lunchtime for an interview, Annie gives in. After she delivers the kids to school, she sews—and completely forgets to meet Eric for his newlywed counseling session. She calls, and he says it's okay.

Eric has the twins with him while in the middle of a counseling session. One of the young men at the session, Ryan, is surprised Eric has the babies. Ryan comes from a "traditional" background, and it's clear he's probably going to apply the rules he learned at home to his new marriage. Eric laughs it off: the Camden philosophy is to do whatever's necessary, whenever.

At the junior high school, Simon and Deena talk about home ec. Simon's very uncomfortable with being the only guy in the class, so she suggests he switch to woodshop. Simon loves the idea—it sounds so manly.

Back at the newlywed session, Eric and Ryan go head to head over Ryan's attitude. Annie shows up just as the session's over and asks Eric to control his anger, since he's still recovering.

Matt shows up at Shana's house, and she wishes he hadn't. He discovers her "interview" is with a man she hasn't seen in twenty years, her dad. Later, Matt learns she's asking him for help with school costs.

Back at the house, Lucy anguishes for losing Mary, who's been allowed to pick up Ruthie from soccer practice. But she won't tell Annie why she wanted so badly to go. Mary arrives at the school and asks Ruthie why she didn't leave her uniform in her locker. "I wanted you to see it," Ruthie says proudly. It's a football uniform.

At home, Annie and Eric discuss human rights violations in Afghanistan, where women are severely persecuted. Annie hands Eric a pamphlet that she got at a street demonstration outside the high school. It claims that gender persecution is being committed in the name of religion.

Later, on the porch, Annie does some painting, and Eric tells her he's considering not performing the marriage ceremony for Ryan and Jessica because of Ryan's attitude.

Meanwhile, Lucy tries to console Simon's qualms about home ec by pointing out that she spent the summer working construction. "That doesn't make me a guy," she says. Simon's interrupted with a call from a classmate, and he casually helps her with a recipe.

Simon tries home ec. Ruthie plays football. Annie and Lucy march for women's rights. Eric watches the babies and tries to explain the roles of men and women to newlyweds-to-be.

After being pressured by Lucy, Mary tells Lucy about Ruthie's secret—that she's playing football. They decide Eric and Annie can't know about it, since Annie would likely pull Ruthie out of such a rough sport. They will surprise them at the first game.

Later, Eric calls Jessica and leaves the message he'd like to see her. Matt comes in and asks him if he could check up on the background of Shana's dad. Matt's suspicious of a man who would reappear in his daughter's life after a twenty-year absence. Eric reluctantly agrees to help.

Downstairs, Jessica arrives with Ryan and apologizes to Eric: she and Ryan don't want him to be their minister. "Good job, honey," Ryan tells her, "just like I told you." The two leave a troubled Eric at the doorstep.

Eric tells Annie what he's learned about Shana's dad—he's "a mogul. He's also completely legit, no parking tickets, no criminal offenses, no records of any kind." Annie reminds him that he abandoned Shana, her brother, and their mother.

The next day Jessica's mother, Betty, arrives at Eric's office. She confirms that Eric doesn't want to marry her daughter to Ryan, then calls Jessica and asks her to come over.

Betty explains Jessica's attraction to Ryan. Unlike Jessica's own father, from whom Betty is separated, Ryan seems like a steady worker who wants his wife to have the "luxury" of staying at home. But Betty considers it a kind of imprisonment and hopes to enlighten Jessica. Betty reveals that she has filed for divorce, and hopes that Jessica will reconsider entering a similar marriage.

At home, Annie shocks Ruthie by giving her a few pointers on how to carry the football. Ruthie learns Annie found a sheet from the playbook in her jeans. Annie's okay with it, but she doesn't want Ruthie to let on to Mary she knows.

Later Annie finds out from Simon's guidance counselor that he's a whiz at cooking, which explains his popularity in home ec. Still, she tells him, she understands why he wants to switch to woodshop, and confirms that it's okay, but his first project, she says with a grin, will be building a spice rack!

Annie heads for a demonstration march to benefit women in Afghanistan and recognizes Lucy in the crowd. Lucy tells Annie she has permission to use her free period at school this way, and Annie makes her pride for her daughter clear.

That evening Eric's at home watching the twins. Simon says he'll cook supper.

At the football field, Ruthie collides with another player and gets a black eye. She couldn't be happier.

At Shana's apartment, her dad shows up with his decision. He tells her he'd like to help her with school, but he feels it might contribute to her losing her drive. Shana should work herself through college, as he did. Shana says his decision is fine with her, she just wanted to know if he was any kind of dad, which he isn't. She reminds him at the door that it was her mom who worked him through college.

At home, Simon gives his dad a few cooking tips. Then Ryan shows up, trying to salvage his wedding. He says that his own parents are going through a divorce. Eric senses a change in Ryan and is hopeful. He throws an arm around Ryan and leads him toward the kitchen.

"Do you know anything about sauces?" he asks.

Come Drive with Me

written by Ron Darian;
directed by Anson Williams

Eric keeps his fingers crossed for a pay raise while the cars break down all around him. Matt befriends a young patient at the hospital and finds a career path. Annie and Lucy bond over building a bathroom, and Mary feels left out.

Matt dutifully mops the floor at the hospital. It's hard work, especially compared to the job he finds out John just landed—he's been put in charge of music for the building.

At the house, Eric worries about the family finances. Their own cars are out of commission, and then the church's meals-on-wheels van they've been using breaks down. Annie says Eric and Ruthie should go out car shopping, but Eric hesitates. He's worried that his annual pay raise may not come.

Upstairs, Mary and Lucy are feeling good about having the attic room now that Matt's gone. Mary says all they need now is to be closer to the bathroom. Lucy suggests they install another one themselves.

In Simon's room, friend Jim has arrived to show Simon a spiral notebook that someone left on the bus. It's Beth Bagley's, and inside the pages are full of doodled hearts. Inside the hearts, Simon's name has been written, over and over.

Simon is mortified.

Downstairs, Eric and Annie hear out Mary and Lucy's plan to add a bathroom in the attic. Eric is worried about the money, but Annie says they can handle the expense, especially if they do it themselves. Annie and Lucy are excited to do the labor, although Mary is somewhat uncertain about it.

Back at the hospital, a tired and exasperated Matt gripes aloud about his job. A young patient named Adam overhears and gives Matt some advice. With unusual aplomb, he tells Matt to try climbing a tree. "It'll give you a new perspective," he says.

At school, Simon returns Beth's notebook. He tells her he didn't peek, but she can tell that he did. She asks why he

thinks he's the Simon she was writing about. She conde-scendingly says that she won't tell anyone about his arrogant misunderstanding.

Next day at the Glenoak hospital, Matt gets a little career counseling from Adam, who rattles off a list of potential career choices, then explains that it's time Matt sets some goals for himself. Matt jokes that it feels as if he's visiting a Zen master.

At the church, Eric hears some positive news from Lou about Eric's scheduled pay raise. He doesn't think there'll be a problem. Relieved, he and Ruthie venture out to look at cars.

At home, Deena assures Simon that Beth was thinking of him when she wrote "Simon" in her notebook. She adds that now Simon should invite her over to defuse an uncomfortable situation. Simon acknowledges he doesn't understand women sometimes.

In the kitchen, Annie, Lucy, and Mary rummage through a tool box, taking inventory of their tools, then head upstairs to work on the attic room.

At the hospital, Matt meets with a personnel officer, Cynthia, about applying for a new position. She surprises him with a letter she received from a patient, urging the hospital to find him a new job. It's signed "Tree Boy." She adds that while Matt may be overqualified for his present job, complaining to patients won't get him a better one.

Meanwhile, Eric and Ruthie get talked into test-driving a small convertible.

Back at the house, Mary is feeling left out as Annie and Lucy dive into the remodeling project. She leaves them totally absorbed in their work—they don't even notice she's gone. Simon calls Beth on the phone and invites her over after school the next day.

At the church, the deacons are reviewing the budget and considering Eric's pay raise. Suddenly, one of them spots Eric zipping by in the sports car from the dealership. They think it must be his new car, which doesn't substantiate Eric's claims about needing a raise.

Meanwhile, Mary makes a tray of tea and cookies and has carried it almost all the way upstairs when she overhears Annie tell Lucy they don't need Mary to go ahead with the project. Mary misunderstands and leaves again, hurt.

Next day at the hospital, Matt tells John what happened in the personnel office. Overhearing the whole thing is Adam, "Tree Boy," whose letter got Matt in trouble.

At the house, Simon's afternoon with Beth doesn't go well. She won't open up and talk, until Simon finally says he likes her. Ecstatic, she gives Simon a big hug and rushes off to tell her mother the news. Deena arrives just in time to see the hug, and then Simon's in big trouble.

That night Annie prepares a list of the family's expenses for the deacons, who have asked for it in consideration of Eric's pay raise.

The next day at school, Simon stops Beth at her locker for a talk about "friends who are girls, and girls who are girl-friends." It's a confusing issue, they agree. Beth says she hopes she can find a guy who will "like me and only me." Just then, a bunch of notebooks fall out of Beth's locker. Simon looks down and sees the names of many other guys scribbled across the various pages. He realizes her crush on him wasn't as severe as he thought!

At the hospital, Matt learns that Adam has patched things up with the personnel office—before going into surgery.

At the house, Annie realizes that Mary's feelings are hurt and apologizes for leaving her out of the project upstairs. Mary feels better, but there's bad news from Eric. The church board vetoed his raise.

Then Ruthie appears with Lou. They've come from the church. Eric and Annie find out that Ruthie went there and defended her dad before the board. She told them all about the sports car, how it wasn't theirs.

At the hospital, little Adam wakes up to find Matt outside his window, sitting in a tree.

Later, back at the house, Eric and Ruthie arrive in the family's new electric van. They'll apply the fuel savings, Annie figures, to Matt's college expenses, which they discover will be enormous: he's decided he wants to become a doctor.

With Honors

written by Sue Tenney;
directed by Harvey Laidman

Mary learns that her friend Corey is a teen mother and defends her when a local association strips her of an award. Matt's classmate James tries to buy a grade in American history class, but learns he has to earn it. Simon's friend Lee confronts his troubled father.

Season 4: Episode 70

At the Camdens', Eric and Annie are changing the twins. Ruthie's looking forward to a teacher workday vacation the next day, and Mary's preparing an acceptance speech for a local business "All Sports Award." She's sharing the award with teammate Corey.

Simon appears with a new friend, Lee, who stays for dinner. The Camdens' learn from him that he lives with his dad and grandmother.

That night at the library, Matt puzzles over an honor code pledge his American history professor has required of everyone in his class. Shana says it's simple: don't cheat, and if someone else does, turn them in. Classmate James arrives and pleads for Matt's tutelage before the big test the next day. Shana doesn't like him. "He cheats," she whispers to Matt.

The next day, Ruthie watches TV while the other kids go to school. Simon runs into Lee at his locker and invites him over. Lee tells Simon his dad is a private investigator, who's working with the FBI. He used to work for NASA, too. Simon's impressed.

At the high school, Mary meets a transfer student from Lincoln High who thinks she recognizes Corey. Corey says she never went to Lincoln. Meanwhile, Matt finds out more about James from Shana—his family is wealthy and prominent in town.

At home, Eric tells Ruthie he thinks she deserves the walkie-talkies she's seen advertised on TV, but only if she earns the money. Ruthie's not too happy about that.

Across town, Lucy is working at the high school attendance office when a handsome student, Tyler, enters and requests a pass. Lucy helps him figure out a good excuse.

Meanwhile, Mary's teammate Elaine shares a rumor that Corey dropped out of Lincoln at age fourteen to have a baby. Corey overhears.

At the library, Matt tries unsuccessfully to prepare James for the history test. But James admits he has a hard time focusing on work. James tries to bribe Matt into taking the test for him.

Back at the house, Eric gets some disturbing news about Lee's dad, Jeff Patterson. According to Sergeant Michaels, the only Jeff Patterson he knows who is involved with the police is someone who was recently arrested.

Upstairs at the house, Ruthie tries to get Simon to loan her money for the walkie-talkies, but to no avail. She has a reputation for not paying back.

In American history class, Matt finds himself seated right next to James. He assures James he won't cheat, but James has already made other plans. As soon as the professor leaves, he copies furiously from another student he's paid off.

Meanwhile, Mary visits Corey's house and meets Bernadette, Corey's young daughter. When Corey tells Mary she can leave now that she's confirmed the rumor, Mary refuses and says the two need to talk. Corey then shares how difficult it has been to be a teen mother, and how much she has sacrificed.

Lucy answers the door at home and it's Tyler, who asks her to the Spring Fling dance. Lucy says, "I thought you were dating Courtney Webber?" Tyler says they broke up, and Lucy happily melts.

At the college, Matt's history professor calls him in after class. Other students thought they saw something "going on between him and James," he says. The professor thinks they were cheating.

At the house, Lee spills his backpack and a plastic bag of marijuana falls out, right in front of Eric. Eric calls Sergeant Michaels to go with him when he returns Lee to his dad, Jeff. What he doesn't know, Lee tells Simon upstairs, is that the pot belongs to his dad.

Ruthie finds out Lucy needs a sweater and offers to get a special one from Mary, if Lucy will mow the lawn for Simon. It's all part of a complicated plan she has come up with to get the walkie-talkies.

Matt shares his problem with Annie and Eric. Then Mary tells Annie about Corey. Finally Sergeant Michaels arrives and tells Eric that Lee's dad is indeed the same Jeff Patterson who was arrested for drug possession.

Upstairs, Lucy gets a call from Tyler. He asks her to help him access the school's computer so he can improve his attendance record. Lucy is stunned. Later, Mary tells Lucy she's sure Tyler lied to Lucy about breaking up with his girlfriend. He was just using Lucy.

Later, at the pool hall, Matt and Shana run into James, who is happy and confident. His dad is having a meeting with the history prof, and he expects all to be well. He even taunts Matt.

Meanwhile, Eric and Sergeant Michaels take Lee home where they are challenged by Jeff, who quickly denies that the drugs in Lee's pack belong to him. Later Lee shows up and confesses to Eric that the marijuana belongs to his father. Eric calls Sergeant Michaels and together they decide to have a talk with Jeff.

In Annie's bedroom, Ruthie charms Annie into loaning her valuable earrings to Mary, another part of her secret plan. Mary barely says thank you to Ruthie, though, because she has something else on her mind—Corey. Her friend's share in the All Sports Award has been revoked because the sponsoring organization found out that Corey is a teen mother.

Meanwhile James's dad, Ray, has called a meeting with his son and Matt. He's going to talk to their history prof, but on Matt's behalf. He surprises both young men by saying that it's time for James to "learn to get through life on his own two feet." James decides to go to his professor and face the music himself.

Back at the house, Ruthie sees her secret plan dissolve. Mary's changed her outfit and doesn't need the earrings. Lucy's not going to the dance with Tyler, so she doesn't need the sweater. Simon will do his own mowing. Ruthie will have to earn the walkie-talkie money after all.

The next day the family attends the All Sports Award ceremony. Mary surprises everyone with her speech. It's not an acceptance speech after all. It's to explain that she's handing over her award to Corey, for completing high school with honors, for being a mother, and for being a role model to her, Mary. She and Corey hug onstage, and the whole crowd applauds.

Later, Eric and Sergeant Michaels visit Lee's family. To get Jeff to change his ways takes pressure from everyone, but most of all from Lee. "I lost my mother to drugs, and I don't want to lose you, too," he tells his dad. It's the kind of turn-around that makes Eric feel as if it's all worthwhile.

Sin . . .

written by Catherine LePard; directed by Tony Mordente

Coach Cleary suspends the basketball team, and
the players strike back. Simon tries to do "guy things" and gets
in trouble for making obscene gestures. Mary gets arrested.

Season 4: Episode 71

Coach Cleary stuns Mary and the rest of the basketball team when he cancels the season until the players bring up their grades.

At the apartment, Matt and Shana search the kitchen for food and come up with nothing. John feverishly crams for an English lit test. He stops long enough to share his pack of gum with his hungry friends. Bachelorhood isn't all it's cracked up to be.

At the house, Annie rebukes Simon for something she saw him do on the playground—a crude gesture with his middle finger. Then she tells Eric the principal saw "his son" gesture, too; they have a meeting with the principal the next day.

At the high school, Mary picks up Lucy at student court. Lucy wonders why practice was short, but Mary doesn't want to talk about it.

At the apartment, Matt gets his hospital uniform out of a dirty laundry pile and gives it a touch up with lemon air freshener. Loud music blares through the wall from the next apartment. Exasperated with his new lifestyle, he shoves all his dirty clothes into a bag.

At the house, Eric has a talk with Simon about making obscene gestures. Even though Eric sympathizes with Simon's desire to be "one of the guys," he wants Simon to know that guys often do stupid things when they get together. He doesn't want Simon to lose his ability to think for himself. Simon agrees he won't see his friends for the weekend, but he's still upset with his mom.

Matt comes over to say hi—and grabs a free meal and uses the washing machine. Then Mary and Lucy arrive, just in time to see a local news story on TV about Coach Cleary's lockout on the basketball team's season. Mary explains the decision to the whole family. It's a big deal because it could put Mary's basketball scholarship in jeopardy.

Upstairs, Ruthie offers to hang out with Simon, but he says she doesn't know anything about guy stuff. He demonstrates a "honk"—an obscene sound made under his arm with a cupped hand. Ruthie says she doesn't have to fake the sound, and Simon's eyes widen.

Meanwhile, Matt gives Mary a lecture on keeping up with her schoolwork. She gives him a shove and slams the door.

Downstairs, Eric and Lucy commiserate on their similar job challenges, his as a minister and hers as a student court judge. Eric quotes Gandhi, "You have to be the change you want to see in the world."

Big brother Matt turns his attention on Simon, chiding him for "fingering" and allowing himself to be led by his crowd. Then he invites both Simon and Eric to hang with him and the guys at the apartment. Simon plays it cool, until Matt shoots him a honk.

Meanwhile, Annie takes a call from the high school principal, Ms. Russell, who has called a meeting about Coach Cleary's lockout. Eric and she plan to attend, right after their meeting with Simon's principal, Ms. Gordon.

The next day, Ms. Gordon has bad news. Simon's action is considered gang behavior, which calls for a mandatory three-day suspension. That hits Simon hard, but there's more to his unhappiness. What really hurts is the thought he has that Annie "doesn't want him anymore." That's his interpretation of what Annie said when she told Eric about his bad behavior—she called him "your son." Annie explains it was only a figure of speech, reassuring him.

At the high school, a couple of varsity men's basketball players sympathize with Mary and her teammate Corey over the lockout. Lucy hears some of the crazy rumors that are going around—that the women's team failed drug tests, bought exam answers, even that some are Russian players, smuggled in to make a winning team.

At the apartment, the loud music from next door begins to get to Matt, along with everything that's happening at home. He tells Shana he's thinking about moving back, which ticks off John, who depends on Matt for half of the rent.

At the house, Eric and Annie leave the twins in Simon and Ruthie's care while they head for the meeting about the women's basketball team. It's packed with parents and players. Coach Cleary explains the reason for the unpopular lockout: grades. As parents shout out in disagreement, Eric stands up for the decision, stunning Mary and her teammates.

When they get home, Simon bugs Happy with the baby monitor transmitter to listen in on Mary, who gets a phone call from Corey. Simon and Ruthie hear their angry sister say someone might do something "extreme," and they're worried. But before they can react, Matt tells Simon it's time to go hang with the guys.

Then Ruthie talks her way into going along on Simon and Matt's "guys' night out." Meanwhile Mary meets her teammates for pizza, and they rant about the lockout and the Camdens' support for it. They decide to show the school just how they feel.

A little while later, under cover of darkness, they break into the gym, then toilet paper and spray graffiti on everything. Until the police arrive . . .

. . . And Expiation

written by
Catherine LePard;
directed by
Tony Mordente

Mary suffers the consequences for vandalizing the gym, including the loss of her scholarship. Simon and Ruthie seek enlightenment in a Christian church, a Jewish synagogue, and a Buddhist temple.

Matt, Lucy, Simon, and Ruthie wait at the house with the twins while Eric and Annie go to the police station to get Mary. She and her teammate Corey have been arrested for vandalizing the gym.

When Eric and Annie return later with Mary, everyone except Matt pretends to have fallen asleep in the living room so they can "get up" and learn what happened. Eric tells them all they'll talk about it in the morning.

Upstairs, Mary tells Lucy that Sergeant Michaels said she'll need a lawyer. Simon and Ruthie are in their room bemoaning the fact that they didn't report the conversation they overheard between Mary and a teammate. Simon's sure they should have done something as soon as they heard the words "take extreme action."

After school the next day Simon and Ruthie pray for the same good outcome God gave them when the twins came, and when Dad got well after his heart attack.

That night lawyer and family friend Bill Mays arrives. He tells Mary and her parents that she faces possible expulsion from school and worse, if she's convicted in criminal court. Bill wants to pursue a Diversion Program, a community service alternative to criminal sentencing. If he is unable to get her in the program, Mary could go to jail.

Lucy worries about Mary's fate in student court as well. She tells Shelby and Rod that she's seen kids expelled for less than what Mary did. They don't have to remind her that as a student judge, she'll be party to whatever happens to her sister.

The next day Ruthie and Simon go to confession at a Catholic church. They tell Father Hartman about eavesdropping on Mary and not reporting what they heard. They feel guilty and don't know how to make the feeling go away. Even though they've never visited a priest before, they believe he can point them in the right direction and keep them from going to the "hot place." The priest suggests an act of contrition—telling their mom and dad, in other words.

At the high school, Lucy sees the vandalized gym and cries to think that Mary was involved. At the apartment, Matt tells John he's decided to move back home to help out his troubled family. Then the stress of everything that's happened incites him to quarrel with Shana.

Ruthie and Simon proceed to a synagogue, where they confess to Rabbi Cohen their negligence. He explains that they've just missed Yom Kippur, the annual Jewish day of atonement. But his advice is similar to the priest's: talk to their mom and dad.

Matt arrives at the house and tells Eric about his decision to move back. Eric is unsure of how to react, and says, "That's very . . . thoughtful." Matt unpacks in Simon's room, where there's an extra bed. He explains why he is back, to "keep an eye on things."

Mary gets a call and learns that due to her delinquent behavior, she's lost her sports scholarship.

Annie returns home with a pizza, worried about what's going to happen to Mary. Then she finds out about the scholarship and it's almost more than she can bear. The phone rings, and it's Bill with a little good news—Mary's going to be interviewed for the Diversion Program.

The next day at a correctional office, a rough and cynical Ms. Williams, head of probation, takes Mary in for her interview. She fires rough, accusatory questions at Mary, testing her for any signs of arrogance. But Mary, for once, is quiet. She admits that there was no valid reason for her to have done what she did.

Meanwhile, Simon and Ruthie have moved on to a Buddhist temple, where they get more wise advice about what to do with their feelings of guilt and remorse: tell their parents. They're beginning to feel better.

The next day Matt decides his influence around the house isn't going to make that much difference; it almost feels like he's in the way. He checks with John to see if he has found a replacement roommate. John says he has one very annoying prospect and it'll be no problem dumping him. To celebrate Matt's return, he breaks out a bottle of laundry detergent.

At the house, Annie and Eric tell Simon and Ruthie that Mary got in the Diversion Program. Simon and Ruthie tell Eric and Annie they are just sorry they didn't say something before Mary took the "extreme action." They quickly find out that Matt and even Eric are feeling the same way about what happened, too. Mary, who's overheard the whole conversation, steps in and tells them the fault was hers alone. Eric reassures everyone that he is going to help Mary get through this. As her day in student court draws near, Mary's anxiety increases. On the last night before her court date, she crawls into her parents' bed for comfort.

The next day, the house is packed for student court. Ms. Russell presents the police report and damages and Mary and her teammates confirm their guilt. But before they are sentenced, Lucy has the floor. She acknowledges the seriousness of the players' actions, and how angry it has made everyone to lose a gym, lose a team, and lose the feeling that they're safe at school. "It would be easy to make you guys write a check and then kick you out," she says, "but this is your school, too. And I want you to make up for what you did." She finishes by saying that if anyone can change the situation for the better, it is her sister.

The players cross the opened door of the gym where a janitor is sweeping. Mary takes the broom from him and they begin the long process of cleaning up the mess they made.

Just You Wait and See

written by Linda Ptolemy;
directed by Paul Snider

**Ruthie finds a pet. Lucy gets
her driver's license. Aunt
Julie threatens to leave her
husband—and has a baby.**

Ruthie comes home from school and discovers a tiny kitten on the porch. She shoves it in her school bag and smuggles it into the house. When Ruthie abruptly announces on her own that she needs to do her homework, Annie knows something's up.

In the kitchen, Annie inquires about Lucy's driving. Mary and Simon complain that she drives at a snail's pace. Annie is relieved, then announces that there's something special in the mail for Lucy— from the DMV! It's her license, but she's horrified by her photo. Simon, Annie, and Mary think it's funny.

Eric arrives from his checkup with a bouquet of roses for Annie. She congratulates him on his good exercise and eating habits after his heart attack. Eric announces he's proud of himself, too, and how he's really learning to deal with stress. The doorbell rings. Eric goes to answer it, insisting he is strong, calm, and can handle any challenge.

Julie is at the door, disheveled-looking, eight months pregnant, and carrying a suitcase. She's leaving her husband. Eric takes a deep breath as Julie drops her suitcase and goes inside.

Julie tells Annie and Eric she's not having a baby with "that man." Eric doesn't understand; Julie just ignores him. The marriage was a big mistake, she says, and it's all Eric's fault. Julie always does the opposite of what people tell her to, and if Eric hadn't disliked Hank, she never would have married him. Eric exits to make some tea. Annie smiles. She knows she's dealing with a crazy woman.

Eric is pacing in the kitchen when Simon enters with Happy. He asks if there's going to be dinner, and Eric says they'll order some pizza. Simon shakes his head and says, "Cholesterol." Eric says maybe he'll pick up something healthy at the hospital after he goes to chat with his brother-in-law, Hank. Simon warns Eric that he shouldn't snoop in Aunt Julie's life without asking her, but Eric grabs the car keys and leaves anyway.

Ruthie is upstairs making a bed for her kitten out of a few towels and a cardboard box, and crosses quietly to her room, just as Simon reaches the top of the stairs. Ruthie dashes into her room and slams the door. Simon shrugs. Happy crosses to Ruthie's door and sniffs inquisitively.

Meanwhile, in Mary and Lucy's room, Lucy complains that she doesn't smell dinner. Mary says it's because their parents are too busy with Aunt Julie. Lucy says maybe they'll let them go out for dinner, but Mary stops her short, saying there's no way she'll let Lucy drive. Lucy looks hurt. The phone rings.

Mary picks up the receiver and hands it over to Lucy, saying it's Andrew Nayloss. Lucy grabs the phone and accepts his invitation to a movie. Andrew says he'll see her at eight in her car, since he doesn't have his license yet. Mary, who plans to pick up pizza, insists *she's* taking the new car. Lucy will have to take the old minivan, she says.

In the living room, Julie rants about Hank's cleanliness—he cleans the kitchen after she's cleaned it already. Annie says that this is typical of a doctor. She waits to hear more rational reasons for Julie's desire for a divorce. "One of his patients is a supermodel!" Julie shouts.

Lucy enters and asks Annie for permission to take the new car, and Annie agrees. Mary frowns. She wants it for an all-kid dinner trip so Julie and Annie can have the house to themselves. Annie tells her to take Eric's minivan. The girls go to get the keys and realize that one set is missing. Simon explains that Eric took the minivan to visit Hank. Mary reluctantly goes back downstairs and reveals this to Annie and Julie. As expected, Julie is upset at Eric's meddling, but she offers Mary the keys to her own car.

Andrew Nayloss is a strange date; his father gives Lucy the

kind of third degree usually reserved for boys, and Andrew seems to expect her to open the door for him.

At the hospital, Eric and Matt sit down with Hank and find out at least one of Julie's problems—Hank has a supermodel patient. Hank explains that yes, even supermodels go through difficult pregnancies. He adds that Julie knew about his profession before she married him, and that he will always have female patients. In fact, he will have only female patients. The three of them go out to dinner.

Back at the house, Julie goes into labor.

At the pool hall, Mary and Simon are approached by a fifteen-year-old named Diane, who immediately hits on thirteen-year-old Simon. They shoot pool together until Deena and her dad arrive and catch them in an embarrassing pose over a cue stick. Mary answers a page for Eric and it's Annie, who tells her Julie's having her baby. Annie adds that they can't take her to the hospital because they don't have a car! And to make things worse, nobody can locate Hank and Eric.

Mary and Simon get home at the same time Matt does. Matt heads back immediately to get Hank.

Meanwhile, back at the house, the real owner of the kitten

Ruthie's been hiding in her room shows up, and Ruthie has to hand over "her baby."

Over at the Nayloss house, Lucy and Andrew share a goodnight kiss. He's a great kisser, Lucy thinks as she turns to leave, but considering everything else about him, she assumes she'll never return.

Hank rushes to the Camdens' just in time to help Julie with her delivery. It's a scary and tender moment for both of them when he arrives. She admits that she's afraid he doesn't love her, and that he'll leave her. He counters that he loves her more than life itself. The baby arrives in Eric and Annie's bed.

It's a girl, and they name her Erica. Eric and Annie decide that Hank and Julie get to keep the bed.

Dirty Laundry

written by Elaine Arata; directed by Burt Brinckerhoff

The church gets a big check from congregation member Ms. Ishida. Eric learns about Japanese-American internment camps. Dark literature depresses Simon. Shana is haunted by her past. Eventually, hope shines through for all.

Season 4: Episode 74

Eric finds an envelope under his office door containing a check made out to the church for $20,000.

The next morning, Eric finds Simon at the breakfast table, depressed about newspaper stories of famine and war. The thought of eating makes him feel guilty. Part of his angst is from reading *The Outsiders*, a dark novel about a hero who dies. What's the point of trying to do good in a world with so much pain, Simon wonders.

Annie comes out of the bathroom in a towel turban and finds the twins on the loose. Ruthie says she has a big enough job looking out for herself; she's discovered you can't be nice to everybody, and even if you are, you'll get hurt trying. She wishes God would keep an eye on the twins so she wouldn't have to; she has enough problems and Simon's depression is rubbing off on her, too.

Annie finds Simon reading *The Outsiders* and suggests he steer Ruthie toward *Little House on the Prairie*. Simon finds even that book depressing, as well as the others he's reading: *Les Misérables*, *The Red Pony*, and *Crime and Punishment*. In history he's studying the invention of the atomic bomb. In Earth sciences, it's global warming. At least in math class it's just cold, hard numbers. At last, it's time for the school bus.

Eric tells Annie he's expecting Sachiko Ishida, the parishioner who wrote the $20,000 check, at his office. Eric is feeling guilty about the contribution, and Annie wonders if it's just another effect of Simon, the emotional "black hole."

At the apartment, Shana returns a shirt of Matt's that got mixed up in her laundry. Matt exclaims that ever since they did laundry together, Shana seems uncertain about their relationship. She tells him she thinks they should see other people, which makes Matt angry. When she walks away, Matt throws the shirt aside, calling after her "it's not mine!"

On the elementary school playground, Ruthie, Chloe, and Nina share a "girl power" handshake. Excluded from the group is Sarah, whom Chloe and Nina tease. "You're not a girl, you're a bird," they taunt. When Sarah runs away in tears, Ruthie gets elected to talk to her and get her not to tell.

At the high school, Lucy defends Mary's reputation against two girls who invite Lucy to a party from which the girls' basketball team has been blackballed.

At the church, Eric finds out Ms. Ishida's donation was the amount of a reparation check from the U.S. government. The check was given to her parents for their internment during World War II. To Ms. Ishida, no amount of money can make up for the humiliation and feelings of betrayal her family suffered on account of being imprisoned just for being Japanese—so the money means nothing to her. That's why she's given it away.

At home, Eric does some reading about internment camps and explains them to Ruthie. During World War II, when the United States was at war with Japan, the U.S. government feared that Japanese Americans might disclose secrets to their family or friends living in Japan, possibly giving the Japanese an advantage. To prevent this, Japanese Americans were taken from their homes and held in oppressive camps until the war was over.

Annie comes in with news that Ruthie's school called about what her group did to Sarah. Annie insists that Ruthie apologize, regardless of what it means to her reputation with her "cool" friends.

Lucy finds Simon in his room collecting his possessions so he can give them all away, especially the toys.

Matt comes in and raids the fridge for leftovers. He tells Annie about his fight with Shana, and Lucy volunteers to leave the room, since the details might be "intimate." Matt blows up and orders Lucy to stay out of his private life. When Lucy runs upstairs in tears, Annie suggests he talk to her again, after he's cooled down.

Upstairs, Mary tells Lucy it's no big deal. Lucy says it was Matt's fault, for leaving her out of the conversation. Mary says Lucy has no idea what it's like to be left out, compared to the way she's being treated at school after getting arrested.

Downstairs, Matt cleans up while eating from a bag of cookies. Simon rejects his offer to share because the cookies are full of "additives, preservatives, chemicals . . . All because of money." Eric takes one. Go ahead, Simon says, "we're all just pawns being manipulated by the corruption of politics and big business anyway."

The phone rings, and Lucy answers it. It's Chloe, calling to scold Ruthie. One, for not making Sarah keep quiet about the teasing. Two, for not telling Sarah she couldn't play with them. Three, for not signing up her family's home phone for three-way calling.

At his apartment, Matt hears a message on his answering machine from Shana. She doesn't really want to see other people, but she does want a break from Matt, the message says.

The next morning before school, Annie puts down her laundry basket to have a talk with Simon. "Bad moods are contagious," she says, "but so are good moods. So we're going to put on a smile and pretend to be in a good mood." Then she wants him to do some good for someone else, and "smile, baby, smile."

At the high school, Mary feels hurt and shunned when she finds out that Lucy's been invited to the party that's not allowing girls' basketball players.

At the elementary school, Ruthie apologizes to Sarah, but misses the opportunity to strike up a friendship. She doesn't want to go back to Chloe and Nina either, so she's alone.

At home, Annie finds out from Matt that he and Shana are having trouble talking about whatever it is that's bothering them. She says she'll try to talk to Shana.

Eric meets with Henry Muranaka, a friend of his dad, the Colonel. Henry has come to meet Sachiko Ishida, whose brother fought beside Henry in World War II. As a Japanese American, he fought while his family was in an internment camp, too. Eric hopes hearing his thoughts on the reparation program, which are positive, will help Sachiko reconcile her feelings about the sincerity of the government's offer.

At home, Simon knocks on Mary and Lucy's attic room door. "Go away!" Mary says. Simon tells her he's there to help her get in a better mood, then breaks into a song-and-dance routine. Mary can't help laughing. Lucy's outlook gets a lift when Simon suggests she help him get some things together for a Kosovo relief clothing drive. Then he suggests to Ruthie that she call that "mousy bird girl" she insulted and make friends; mousy bird girls are preferable to loudmouthed frog girls, anyway.

In the laundry room, Shana tells Annie that her problems with Matt are really problems with how they handle problems. She says that first, Matt talked to John instead of her about a private issue. Then Matt suggested seeing a counselor on campus. Shana knows about therapy, having gone through it, and doesn't want to air "dirty laundry" again, especially in front of Matt—at least not so soon in their relationship. Annie gives her a comforting hug.

Meanwhile, Eric takes Henry to visit Sachiko. As soon as she hears that he is involved with the Japanese-American veterans, and that he fought alongside her brother, she slams the door in their faces.

At home, Matt and Lucy apologize and hug. Lucy explains that her "intimacy" comment came from Matt and Shana doing laundry together—"yuck." Matt suddenly realizes that's what he has to talk to Shana about: their dirty laundry. They get together at the apartment to clear the air. Shana just needs time before she can feel comfortable being that close—close enough to mix laundry with Matt, silly as that sounds. And Matt understands.

When Ruthie calls Sarah, she finds out about an even more advanced telecommunications technology than Nina and Chloe have: conference calling. They get Chloe and Nina on, but they scoff at them for "showing off." Ruthie and Sarah don't mind the rejection. They're looking forward to seeing each other at school, without Chloe and Nina.

Mary and Lucy make up, too. And ultimately Sachiko invites Henry back to her house. Eric understands her feelings: good Americans who knew that it was wrong to imprison her people did nothing to stop it. Now those feelings she keeps bottled up inside are what imprison her heart. Eric is sure that talking with Henry and learning about her brother will free Ms. Ishida in the end.

Who Nose

written by
Suzanne Fitzpatrick;
directed by Harvey Laidman

Simon's mural project teammate goes to the hospital for getting high on art materials. Ruthie discovers a talent for sculpture. Shana gets accepted at NYU, 3,000 miles away from Matt. Mary meets Robbie.

Simon proudly delivers a written assignment to Mrs. Jasper, a junior high school teacher. Since it's turned in early, he wonders if he can get extra credit. Not for that, she says. But he can for extracurricular work after school with the "visual arts guys." Later he discovers they're not very friendly. They give Simon a job cleaning brushes and buckets. One of them, Steven, promises some "real fun" later. As soon as Simon's out of earshot, Mitch says, "What do you want to bet Camden's a spy sent in to bust our whole operation."

At the elementary school, Ruthie turns in her art project. "What is it?" Ms. Mason asks. It's a modeling-clay form of her nose, "but I stepped on it," Ruthie replies.

At the high school, Mary tells Lucy she needs to tell her something important. Lucy doesn't want to know.

At Crawford University, Matt brings Shana a sandwich from the hospital cafeteria. "It was meat at one time," Matt admits about the filling. Shana knows it's the thought that counts.

Later that day Eric is on the phone with Carl Doker, an admissions officer at NYU. The call is about Shana; Eric gives her a glowing recommendation. Doker tells Eric that they'll be offering Shana a scholarship for a midyear transfer, starting in January.

Up in his room, a paint-spattered Simon is reading *How to Win Friends and Influence People* when Ruthie asks if she can make a modeling-clay impression of his nose. Simon says okay.

Downstairs, Matt takes Eric aside and asks what a change in Shana's kisses might mean—they feel different, like they're guilty or sad. Eric shrugs and disturbs Matt by saying "there's lots of life ahead and things can happen." Annie overhears, and knows Eric's hiding something.

In the attic bedroom, Mary tells Lucy her secret: She met a fellow parolee at her community service project. He's gorgeous, he goes to school across town, and his name is Robbie Palmer. Lucy covers her ears because Mary is on restriction from dating. Mom and Dad don't have to know about him, Mary adds.

The next morning Simon rushes downstairs and grabs a muffin on the way to school. He tells Annie his plan to get into the visual arts guys' group by faking interest in their work. He wants that extra credit for extracurricular activities.

Eric stops Mary on her way downstairs and warns her about seeing someone while she's on probation; she's not supposed to enjoy her punishment.

At school, Ruthie turns in her art project, an impression of Simon's nose, which she calls "Simon Nose," because when someone knows something, they're usually sticking their nose in someone else's business. Ms. Mason is impressed, but she tells her to keep working on the project.

At the high school, Mary accuses Lucy of telling their father about Robbie Palmer. When Lucy says she didn't, Mary worries that they were seen together. Lucy promises to keep Mary's confidences, but not to go to bat for her love interest with their mom and dad.

At Crawford University, Shana has tears in her eyes as she hides a folder with NYU information from Matt.

After hours at the junior high, Simon asks Pete, one of the visual arts guys, about his can of spray paint. He just laughs, but then Simon discovers the whole mural crew has been huffing—getting high on the aerosol paint. Pete swears him to secrecy, even though Pete's nose is bleeding from it.

On the community service road crew, Robbie Palmer and Mary can hardly take their eyes off each other. Something is definitely happening between them.

At home, Eric confides in Annie about his dilemma: he was Shana's reference for NYU, but Shana has made him promise not to tell Matt. Later, Shana tells Eric she's been accepted and is truly excited. He tells Shana to tell Matt, too, "the sooner the better."

Simon gets home and dumps his paint clothes in the trash. He tells Annie he's quitting because he doesn't like the visual arts guys. Annie, who doesn't know the whole story, convinces him to give them another chance.

That evening, Robbie Palmer shows up to speak with Eric and Annie. He explains how he got in trouble and asks their permission to call Mary on the phone. Eric and Annie are moved but still unsure.

At the apartment, Matt tells Shana he saw her talking with Eric, and she gives him the news: she is going to NYU. Matt doesn't take it well. New York seems so far away. When he finds out that Eric knew all along about her application to the school, he is hurt and humiliated.

Eric takes Simon to school where Mrs. Jasper tells him Pete collapsed on the way in. He's in the hospital. Eric takes him aside, and they talk about the huffing; then they're confronted by Pete's mom. She accuses Simon of being responsible for her son's condition: Pete told her it was Simon's paint. Later, Simon confronts Pete at the hospital, and Pete reconsiders. He decides to tell the truth, that Simon wasn't involved. It'll mean turning in his friends, but as Simon points out, it's for their own good.

Later Matt and Eric talk about Matt's feelings about Shana's decision to go to NYU. If he really loves her, Eric says, Matt will support her decision.

Upstairs, Mary tells Lucy she just found out their mom and dad had Robbie transferred to another job to keep them apart. Then she confronts Eric and Annie, who explain their reasons. They want Mary's community service to be a punishment, because that's what it is. But they want to allow Robbie to call her, and, once her probation's over, to visit. Mary accepts their decision.

At the apartment, Matt tells Shana he's had a change of heart, and that he wants her to go. Even though they know that love isn't always easy, they decide they'll try to make a long-distance relationship work.

Forget Me Not

written by Sue Tenney; directed by David Plenn

Season 4: Episode 76

Ginger, Annie's new stepmother, arrives with shocking news—Annie's dad has been diagnosed with Alzheimer's, and she doesn't know where he is.

At the high school, Lucy asks her friends Carol, Susan, and Lisa to cover for her at Habitat because she has a schedule conflict, but she doesn't say what the conflict is. Robbie, who attends another high school, shows up unexpectedly to say hi to Mary. At the junior high school, Simon's friends envy his plans to stay overnight at his big brother's.

Later, at home, Mary tells Ruthie to quit worrying about Y2K; everything will be okay. At the pool hall, Lucy is spotted with a date, Brad, by Carol, who gets mad. "You blew off the Habitat project to have burgers with some guy?" she scolds.

In Eric's study, Mary asks if she and Robbie can go on a date and gets a definite no. She's still on restriction. Annie's dad calls to tell her he stopped on the way to their house to spend the night at the Sagebrush Hotel, where he and Annie's mom used to stay when they went fishing. At least they know where he is, he seems okay, and he's on the way. When he arrives, he surprises Annie with his own shocking news: it's Ginger who has Alzheimer's. Now Annie is totally confused. Who can she believe?

At Matt's apartment, John leaves, turned off by Matt's melancholy over Shana's plans to go to school in New York. The fact that Simon is there cheers him up, though. Then Shana calls from New York—and Matt learns that her three new roommates are all guys.

Simon plans a sleepover at Matt and John's. Matt mopes because Shana's leaving. Grandpa Charles arrives with a diagnosis of Alzheimer's. Ruthie prepares for Y2K. Mary gets closer to Robbie.

Back at the house, Ginger helps Ruthie pack a coffee can with "essentials" for Y2K. Annie comes up and gently tells her she knows about Ginger's Alzheimer's. Ginger balks. She insists it's Charles!

Lucy calls her friends to apologize about missing the work date and vows to be there the next day. Annie turns to Eric to discuss her dad and Ginger. Neither one of them feels confident about which one is really ill; most of the time, people in the early stages of Alzheimer's don't seem abnormal. Yet if they think about it, both Eric and Annie can think of instances when both Charles and Ginger have behaved suspiciously.

Outside, Ruthie gets her grandfather to make a fire in the barbeque pit as part of her Y2K-readiness program, and it flares up while he's distracted. Annie rushes to the rescue and decides from this accident that it really is he who has Alzheimer's.

Eric talks to Ruthie about the fire and her concerns about Y2K. He compares the millennium hysteria to the panic caused by Orson Welles's famous *War of the Worlds* broadcast, when people listened to a radio show about Earth being invaded by Martians and thought it was the real thing.

Robbie turns down Mary's invitation to visit her at the house because they can't go out on a date, suggesting to Mary that he is not as genuinely interested in her as he claims to be. Simon calls for a ride home from Matt's; it's no fun hanging around with a lovesick older brother. Meanwhile, Lucy apologizes to her Habitat friends and promises to be more committed to the organization. Later, when she takes Brad's phone call, she reluctantly says she can't see him anymore.

On the way to get Simon, Eric stops at the grocery store and runs into Robbie, who has a job there. Robbie explains that he's a good kid who has made the honor roll and may be released early from the Diversion Program. Eric realizes he feels judged and convinces him to drop by the house so they can get to know each other better.

Matt arrives at the Camdens' and apologizes to Simon for being so self-absorbed in his love life when they were supposed to be hanging out together. Then Brad appears with a plan to be with Lucy—by working alongside her at Habitat—followed by Robbie, who's had a change of heart about visiting Mary at the house after a talk with Eric.

Grandpa faces up to his illness at last and goes with Annie, Eric, and Ginger to visit a doctor. The doctor is encouraging, and he reminds them that Alzheimer's typically progresses very slowly. The most important thing Grandpa has to keep in mind is something he has known all along: that his family is there for him, and always will be, no matter what.

All by Myself

written by Brenda Hampton & Sue Tenney; directed by Kevin Inch

Annie takes a break at the beach. Lucy compares the kisses of Brad and Andrew Nayloss. Eric tries to keep things under control while Annie's away. Matt and Shana say good-bye.

Annie has a bad morning: David dumps cereal on his head, Ruthie can't find her book bag, Simon's lost his shirt, Mary and Lucy are fretting about their boyfriends and Matt wants her to help him find Shana. Annie explodes unexpectedly, then goes upstairs to pack a suitcase.

"I just need to get away for forty-eight hours," she tells Eric, "to recharge my batteries."

Across town, Matt goes to Shana's to help her pack for college. Simon goes to junior high school and has a tiff with Deena, who's mad he didn't wear his blue shirt, which matches her own. When he explains that his mother didn't wash it for him, Deena snaps that he should be old enough to do his own laundry. She storms off, leaving Simon to ponder the priorities of girls. And Ruthie gets in trouble at school, hoping to be sent home; she wants to join Annie on her trip.

At the house, Annie gives Eric some final parenting instructions before she goes. Then Ruthie's principal calls to tell Eric she's in trouble for pulling a boy's hair, which he hides from Annie.

That night Lucy and Mary complain about their boyfriends, who haven't called. The phone rings and it's Andrew Nayloss, who asks Lucy out. She turns him down, hoping for a date with Brad. The phone rings again, and the teenagers all reach for it, but it's just Annie. Ruthie races up, asking if it's Mom. Mary tells Ruthie she arrived safely at the beach and Ruthie passes this on to Eric. Simon adds again that he wishes they'd stay off the phone in case Deena calls; she's still mad about the shirt he was supposed to wear that day and didn't.

Annie calls again, gets Eric, and asks for a report on the family. She reminds him to call Matt, which he does, getting the answering machine. When the twins finish eating, he gives them to Lucy to "hose down" upstairs.

Brad calls at last and asks an ecstatic Lucy out. Simon wishes again that everyone would stay off the phone. Ruthie, who's already in a bad mood, gets madder when she finds out Annie called—Eric forgot to tell her. The phone rings again.

This time it's Matt, calling to check in. He makes a lame attempt to cover the fact that he slept over at Shana's. Eric is suspicious but doesn't press the matter because he has too many things to do already. Meanwhile the twins spill baby powder all over their room.

Out on the beach, Annie cries from exhaustion. A stranger named Hattie walks up to deliver a message—Eric called

because Ruthie wanted to say hi. When Hattie asks if everything's okay, it's like opening floodgates: Annie lets all her problems spill out. She has seven children, a husband who just had a heart attack, and a father who's been diagnosed with Alzheimer's. Hattie is sympathetic.

At the house, Mary, Simon, and Ruthie try to watch TV together with Eric, but the kids just wind up bickering. Eric decides to serve lunch: ice cream, potato chips, peanut butter. His "cooking" may not be nutritious, but at least the kids sound happy when Annie calls back.

Deena shows up at the door and chides Simon for not calling. She says she's been calling him all day, but the phone's been busy. Lucy leaves with Brad for the movies, where they run into Andrew Nayloss, who's jealous. Andrew buys a ticket to the same movie and follows them inside.

Matt and Shana share warm good-bye kisses. When Matt says that if she's not packed she won't have to leave for New York, she gets upset. She tells him to leave and come back with a better attitude. Later he returns with burgers, and the two share a quick but painful good-bye kiss. She's leaving for New York the next day.

At the beach, Annie and Hattie talk over dinner. Hattie is older and wiser about life; for Annie, it's good therapy. At home, Matt and Mary comfort each other, too, about their girlfriend-boyfriend problems.

At the movie, while Brad's in the rest room, Andrew "proves" he's better for Lucy with a surprise, passionate kiss. When Brad gets back, Lucy asks him to kiss her, secretly comparing. She thinks Andrew may be right.

At the house, Simon makes up with Deena on the phone, while downstairs, Eric and Ruthie watch a movie. Lucy comes in and doesn't mind at all when Eric asks how it went with "Chad." Annie calls, and everybody's glad to get to tell her "good night."

The next morning, when Annie checks out and the manager says he's never heard of her friend "Hattie," she wonders if she spent the previous evening with something supernatural. Then Hattie appears and explains to Annie that the manager simply doesn't know her by her nickname. "And I thought you were an angel—you must think I'm nuts," Annie tells her.

"No, I don't," Hattie replies. "Because when you think about it, what's the difference? Angels, friends, family, they're all the same thing, aren't they?"

Who Do You Trust?

written by **Brenda Hampton
& Ron Darian;**
directed by
Joel J. Feigenbaum

**Simon and Nigel try cigarettes.
Mary and Robbie try a double
date with Lucy and Rick. Eric
tries to hold his temper.**

Season 4: Episode 78

At the drugstore, Nigel and Simon buy candy bars—and a pack of cigarettes. The cashier doesn't bat an eye, except to remind them to take matches.

At the house, Lucy and Mary are being overly nice to Matt in light of the fact that Shana's moved to New York. But he is full of self-pity. "Oh, put a sock in it," he tells them. Shana forgot to call the day before, when it was her turn.

Robbie calls Mary and asks if she's gotten permission for them to date outside the Camden house yet. He says dating her under such strict rules is "boring" and he has an idea—they double with Lucy and his younger brother, Rick, whom he volunteers.

Mary goes to ask Eric and Annie if it's okay and gets intercepted by Ruthie, who collects a dollar from her. That's the fee to know what her science project is. It's hidden in a paper bag in the refrigerator. When Ruthie divulges the secret, Mary's actually impressed.

Eric and Annie say okay to the date, but Lucy is perturbed that she didn't volunteer to go on the double date. She's never even met Rick.

At Matt and John's apartment, John has set up a date with two new girls in the building. He's counting on Matt to cohost dinner at their place. Matt resists because he's still pouting about Shana's absence. Annoyed, John tells him he had better be pleasant and charming when the attractive women arrive.

Shana finally calls and apologizes for not calling the day before—she's really loaded with homework, and she spent the night celebrating her aced test with friends. "Aren't we more important than 'friends'?" Matt exclaims, and Shana accuses him of being jealous.

At home, Annie asks Eric to check on Simon and Nigel, and he does, just in time to see Simon dropping his cigarette pack in his dresser drawer. Eric assumes the boys are smoking.

Meanwhile, Rick and Lucy get acquainted on the phone, and it goes just fine. They end up looking forward to their blind date.

Downstairs, Annie complains that Eric should have "busted" them with the cigarettes right away. Eric wants to make his point in a more dramatic way. He plans to have dinner with them. Before he can do this, Robbie and Rick arrive. Despite Mary's efforts to whisk the boys outside, Eric sits them down in the living room for a talk.

Upstairs, Simon and Nigel talk about the cigarettes. They

were only buying them for a school project, to show how easily underage customers can get them. But now that they think Eric's on to them, they figure they might as well try a puff. They know it's wrong, but they justify the idea by making it part of the project: it will give them firsthand knowledge of the thrill that smoking holds for teens.

In the kitchen, Eric gives Ruthie a dollar to know what's in her science project bag. He likes what he hears so much he gives her another dollar to tell Annie. Then Eric goes out for a walk, and to spy on the double date.

In the movie theater, while Mary and Robbie make out, Lucy and Rick hit it off. Rick says they should leave the theater so they can talk. They talk for a while outside the theater, then at Lucy's initiative, they kiss—passionately. Just in time for Eric to see.

Back at the house, Simon and Nigel light up in the garage. Eric returns, livid over what he saw at the theater.

Meanwhile, at Matt and John's, the dinner is spoiled for John by Matt's moping. Instead of having fun, Barbara and Angela spend the evening consoling poor Matt while John does a slow burn. Then Shana calls, and Barbara picks up the line, which gets Matt in trouble!

At the house, Robbie and Rick say good night outside. They all smell cigarette smoke and expect trouble. When Mary and Lucy get inside, Eric has it out with them.

Then the cigarette smoke drifts in.

Eric turns his attention on Nigel and Simon, who defend themselves by explaining their project. Eric lets them know that selling to minors isn't the only thing that's illegal. Buying is, too. And smoking should never have been part of the project. He and Annie and Nigel's parents will have to decide on an appropriate punishment.

Meanwhile everyone has learned about Ruthie's science project in the refrigerator. It's a bag of straw. By charging others admission to see it, she's "turned it into gold."

Upstairs, Lucy and Mary argue about whose fault it is that they're in trouble. Then, as quickly as it began, the fight is over and they're laughing. Mary quietly says that for some reason, she doesn't trust Robbie. Little does Mary know: when Robbie gets home it's to meet his other girlfriend, Cheryl.

Meanwhile, the phone at Shana's apartment rings and rings. Matt waits in vain for someone to answer.

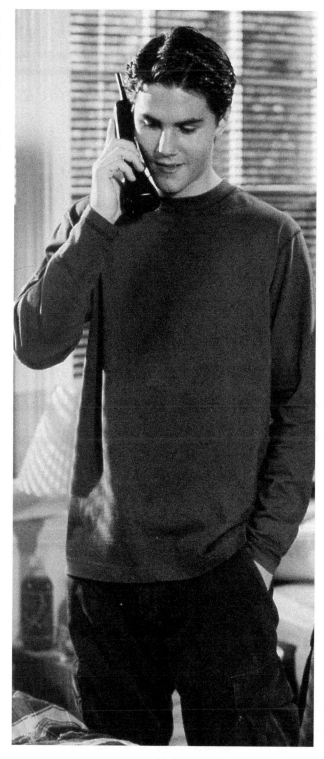

Season 4: Episode 79

Right before Eric's sermon, Ruthie asks Annie if she can be excused to hang out with the twins in the nursery, like Simon. Annie says no, Simon's there on volunteer duty. Mary, meanwhile, tells Lucy she's mad at Simon but won't say why.

Eric begins his sermon by introducing a new family in the church, the Carvers. Then, suddenly and without explanation, the Carvers' young son begins to loudly mimic Eric. Hastily, his father ushers him out of the church.

After church, Sheila Carver explains their son has ADD—Attention Deficit Disorder. But privately, Eric suspects it's something more serious.

Back at the house, Annie sees Matt feeling gloomy about Shana. The phone rings, and it's her. "Say I'm not here," Matt tells her. Annie puts Shana on hold and asks Matt to explain. Instead, he runs out the door; Annie tells Shana the only thing she can—that she just missed him.

Upstairs, Ruthie confides in Lucy about a substitute teacher who's been calling her "stupid." She says she wants Lucy to do something about it: "teach me to not let words hurt me." Lucy says they should tell Mom, but Ruthie makes her promise not to.

In his study, Eric asks Simon to tell him about Bobby Carver, the boy who yelled in church. Simon says he's known as "Spazman" at school, then adds that he himself does not participate in the ridiculing. Eric reminds Simon that "evil triumphs when good people do nothing."

Upstairs, Mary lets Lucy know why she's mad at Simon. While they were playing basketball she fell, and Simon called her "big butt." Lucy wonders what makes that such a big deal, and Mary reacts: maybe everyone thinks she has a big butt; maybe that's why Robbie hasn't called. Her big butt!

Lucy changes the subject to Ruthie's substitute teacher calling Ruthie "stupid." Mary's shocked out of thinking about her own problems for a minute. She tells Lucy she can't keep it a secret—she has to tell Annie.

At his apartment, Matt hears Shana talking to him through the answering machine. It's been three days, she knows he can hear her, and if he doesn't pick up, she may not be there when he's ready to talk.

Back at the house, Eric gets a visitor, a parishioner with Tourette's syndrome. The man is concerned about the Carvers' son, who he's sure has the same condition. Eric sets up a meeting with the Carvers.

Meanwhile at school, a popular kid named Brian picks on Bobby. Simon surprises Bobby by standing up for him.

Words

written by Sue Tenney; directed by Burt Brinckerhoff

Simon's words on the basketball court hurt Mary's feelings. A teacher's words in the classroom hurt Ruthie's feelings. Words fly out of control for Bobby, who suffers from Tourette's syndrome. Bobby's father learns to talk about his son's problem and to deal with his own.

Annie visits Ruthie's teacher, who says she didn't call Ruthie stupid, she called her answers stupid. Annie flares up, saying that an eight-year-old might not recognize the distinction. The teacher angers Annie further by saying "the apple doesn't fall far from the tree."

At the high school, Mary listens disapprovingly as Laurel, a popular girl, heckles "fashion-challenged" classmates in the hall.

Eric's meeting with Bobby Carver's parents doesn't go well. Bill Carver is especially affronted by the assertion that Bobby has Tourette's. He regards Eric's interest as an intrusion and walks out of the meeting.

At the junior high school, Brian promises Simon a beating in the morning, when teachers are not around. Later, Simon learns that Bobby plays video games better than anyone he's ever seen. Suddenly Bobby has an attack. After it's over, Bobby talks about his problem and comments that Simon is the nicest person he's ever met.

At the house, Annie tells Eric about Ruthie's substitute. The principal, she says, even backed up the teacher. Sheila Carver shows up and asks for help. She's made an appointment with a pediatric neurologist and wants Eric to persuade her husband to go.

At the high school, Mary tries to befriend Denise, one of Laura's "fashion-challenged" targets. Denise is suspicious, then defensive. "They insult me and hurt my feelings, but they're not aware of it because they're shallow and self-centered," she tells Mary. "You don't join in because you know it's wrong . . . yet you do nothing to stop it." Then she leaves.

At Matt's apartment, Shana calls. He tells Shana he thinks they need a break from each other.

At home, Annie finds Ruthie in the twins' room. They have a talk about her substitute teacher, and when it's over, Ruthie doesn't feel so bad. She then shocks Annie by revealing that the teacher treats the other kids the same way. "Maybe if the other kids' moms yelled, too," she says, "maybe she wouldn't call them names." It gives Annie an idea.

Meanwhile, Simon tries to find out why Mary is mad at

him. Lucy's afraid to say—she's already in trouble with Ruthie over repeating information. She does give him a clue, however. It's "because of something you said while you guys were playing basketball." Simon still doesn't get it.

In the kitchen, Annie tells Matt that breaking up with Shana, just because a long-distance relationship is difficult, may mean that he loses an amazing woman. She asks him to consider his decision very carefully.

In Eric's office at the church, a group led by Louis, the parishioner with Tourette's, meets Bill. It's a support group for parents of children with the disease. Bill is surprised Louis seems so normal, and Louis tells him why—the symptoms tend to lessen with age. Louis, in fact, became a neuropsychiatrist to help others with Tourette's. But Bill is upset that the reverend has interfered in such a private matter. He storms out, but Eric is on his heels.

Outside, Eric discovers the reason for Bill's defensive attitude. As a child, Bill teased a cousin with Tourette's. Now his own son reminds him of his cruelty. He is certain Bobby got the gene from him, and he feels guilty.

At home, Mary finally tells Simon why she's upset, and he apologizes. Mary warns that words can really hurt people. Meanwhile, Ruthie makes up with Lucy, and Annie organizes other parents against the insensitive teacher.

Shana calls Matt and apologizes for taking their relationship for granted. Matt says her apology is accepted, then hangs up . . . because Heather's there.

At the high school, Mary apologizes to Denise. Then, when Laurel won't quit making fun of her, Mary suggests to Laurel's friends they might be targets, too, when they're not around. Realizing the verity of Mary's words, the girls walk away, leaving Laurel all alone.

At the junior high school, Simon suggests to Brian an alternative to fist fighting. What about a duel, he says. Brian vs. Bobby on a Game Boy. Later a victorious Bobby and his mother get a surprise visitor at the pediatric neurologist's office—Bill. Eric's words worked after all.

Loves Me, Loves Me Not

written by Brenda Hampton; directed by Bradley Gross

Valentine's Day plans and the twins' first birthday party collide. Simon and Deena exchange hickeys and avoid their parents. Ruthie learns to stop being jealous of the twins. Mary finds out Robbie can't be trusted.

Season 4: Episode 80

While Annie looks forward to the twins' first birthday, Ruthie wishes it could be moved to another day besides Valentine's Day. Annie frowns and orders her to start thinking about a couple of presents. Soon Lucy runs through, apologizing for sneaking off to the garage again. She explains that she's working on a secret present.

Robbie calls to ask Annie if she'll let Mary go with him to a Valentine's Day dinner that's a tradition with his family. He explains that he respects the rules she and Eric have established for Mary, but adds that he would love to surprise her with this outing. Annie promises to ask Eric.

In the living room, Deena pulls down her turtleneck and shows Simon the hickey he gave her. He laughs, but she isn't amused. To be fair, she thinks she ought to give him one, too.

Meanwhile, Heather has arrived back in town and surprises Matt at the hospital. When the two arrive at the apartment, John mentions that Shana called—seven times. Then he finds out Heather has transferred to Crawford. "Have you told Shana the good news?" John asks Matt.

"Not yet," Matt says with a smile.

Eric suggests a Valentine's dinner out with Annie, who tells him no on account of the twins' birthday. No one, she says, is allowed out of the house that day. Not until after the birthday party, anyway. She tells Eric about Robbie's plan to take Mary out. Eric is skeptical, but Annie wants to let her go. Meanwhile, Robbie calls Mary and invites himself to the twins' birthday party.

Lucy tells Annie how her love life's going this Valentine's Day—not so hot. But she adds with an unexpected air of maturity that she would prefer to spend the evening with her family than with a random guy. Annie nods sympathetically until Lucy leaves, then she dances a happy jig.

In the garage, Lucy finds Simon and Deena under her covered-up project. No sooner has she chased them out than Ruthie is at the window, spying in.

Upstairs, Eric and Annie talk about trusting Robbie, trusting Mary, and trust in general—when Matt shows up with Heather.

While Heather helps Annie in the kitchen, Eric and Matt talk about her, and Matt, and Shana. Matt doesn't see a problem, since Shana doesn't know Heather's in town. Eric throws up his hands. Matt and Heather head out for a cappuccino.

Minutes later Simon comes downstairs wearing one of Lucy's turtlenecks. Ruthie kids him about it, and Eric and Annie are suspicious that something is up. But they don't ask.

The phone rings, and Mary answers; it's Shana, who's worried that Matt hasn't called. Shana asks if he's seeing somebody. Mary says not to worry, he's just hanging out with a friend, Heather, and she'll get *them* to call. Then Mary calls Robbie and lets the phone ring and ring, just making sure he's at work like he said he'd be.

While they're out, Heather and Matt run into Robbie with another girl. Robbie tells Matt she's his brother's girlfriend, but Matt doesn't believe it. When he gets back to his apartment, although John suggests he call Shana right away, Matt calls Mary first, to tell her that Robbie's cheating on her.

Mary counters that Robbie's already called and explained that the girl is his brother's girlfriend. Matt's still skeptical.

The next day, Valentine's Day, the Camden house has a good crowd for the twins' birthday. All the Camden kids are there, as well as Deena and Robbie.

In the foyer, Simon and Deena worry about the hickeys they've given each other; Deena's parents are upset and have forced Deena to come to the party with her neck exposed. She's embarrassed to face Eric and Annie, and Simon is terrified. Meanwhile Robbie can't wait to get *away* from the party—he tells Mary about the surprise date he has planned for later.

The twins plunge right into their cakes, and then it's time for gifts. Mary and Lucy present the babies with cowboy hats. Simon and Deena offer to baby-sit—if Eric and Annie will let them after they see their necks. Matt's had the babies' hospital ID bracelets laminated. Ruthie gives each boy a raw egg, which Eric confiscates. He's recorded the whole party on an audiotape as his gift to them. Annie snatches the recorder, frustrated by the turn of events. Simon knows he'll be punished later.

Lucy then reveals that the gift she's been making was not for the twins. Lucy takes Ruthie out to the garage to show her what she's been making—for her. It's a clubhouse. "I thought if I showed you how much I love you," Lucy tells Ruthie, "you could show Sam and David how much you love them."

Matt heads home to call Shana, armed with cake and a gallon of milk from Annie, who's sure he'll need it when Shana breaks up with him.

Meanwhile, Robbie and Mary pull up in front of a small motel, not the Tick Tock Cafe, where Robbie promised his parents would be waiting. Confused, Mary gets out of the car and asks where the restaurant is. When Robbie says there is no restaurant, Mary punches him!

Matt and Shana have it out on the phone. When they say good-bye, it sounds like good-bye forever. Then Heather's at the door, to say good-bye to Matt, too. When she leaves, and Matt calls Shana, no one's home; she's out with one of her roommates, Brett.

Back at the house, Mary returns, angry and tearful. She tells Eric and Annie about Robbie's lie, how they were right not to trust him. What Eric and Annie know from this is how right they were to trust Mary.

Meanwhile, Ruthie has come up with a real gift for the twins. She has taken "Blinkie," her treasured old blanket, down from its safe hiding place and has cut it in half so each boy can have his own.

Love shines through after all.

Say a Little Prayer for Me

written by Brenda Hampton; directed by Harry Harris

Eric tracks down the source of a touching, anonymous child's letter. Ruthie prays for a pony. Simon prays to get back with Deena. Mary prays that Robbie will be forgiven by the family. The truest prayer of all is in Eric's sermon.

Season 4: Episode 81

Annie makes dinner with Mary, Lucy, Simon, and Ruthie helping, but mostly talking about Robbie, the ex-boyfriend who tried to take Mary to a motel for Valentine's Day. Eric arrives from work with a letter he wants to share, but the kids are uninterested. He explains that the author of the letter has asked for his prayer. That night Eric reads the letter to Annie.

"Dear Man Who Works for God," it begins. "Two years ago my brother was shot by a boy who brought a gun to school. After that, my father started drinking again. . . ."

Eric hopes he can find the boy and help him.

In Simon's room, Simon and Mary commiserate over losing their respective girlfriend and boyfriend. Even though Simon will be able to see Deena after a two-week hiatus, it feels like forever. Lucy stops in and tries to cheer them up, but she sees it's no use.

"Pray Robbie gets back in with our family," Mary says.

"Pray I get back in with Deena's family," Simon says.

"I wouldn't tie up the God lines for either of those things," Lucy tells them.

In her room, Ruthie prays for a pony.

At their apartment, Matt and John pray, too. John prays for a woman with whom to share dinner. Matt prays for something he won't talk about.

In his study, Eric phones Sergeant Michaels to see if there's a way to find the boy who wrote the letter. He adds that the letter asked for Eric to pray by the coming Sunday, and Eric thinks it is important to find him before that time. The policeman is doubtful about being able to find the letter-writer, but he agrees to help. Ruthie enters wearing pajamas and tells him she's getting a pony, thanks to the power of prayer.

The next day Matt runs into John on the street. They talk about the night before, and Matt admits he was praying to meet a girl, too. Suddenly an attractive girl comes up and asks something—it doesn't matter what—and both boys answer before she can finish, "Yes!"

At the house, Eric gets a call from Sergeant Michaels, who has a list of children under eighteen who died violent deaths in the previous two years. Eric feels as if he has a twenty-four-hour deadline to trace the letter he received; he leaves to pick up the list.

Upstairs, Lucy tries to shake Mary out of the misery she's feeling over Robbie. She invites her to take Sam and David for a walk, but Mary won't go. Simon, who's brooding over the fact that Deena hasn't called, won't go either.

Meanwhile Eric's going door-to-door down Sergeant Michaels's list with the letter he received, trying to find the author.

At their apartment, Matt and John go over the details of their afternoon with Raven, the pretty girl they met on the street. John is sure *he* is the one she was interested in, not Matt. Matt has the exact opposite opinion. At least they gave her their phone number. They both go to bed praying for the phone to ring.

At the house, Mary and Simon get into a quarrel when Robbie is compared to Deena. To Simon, Robbie seems like such a scoundrel. They snap at each other. Then Annie comes in and tries to be understanding, but when it comes to Robbie, she just can't be.

At the park with the twins, Lucy gets some disapproving looks from people who think she's a teen mother. One woman even scolds her. Tired of all the dirty looks, she finally yells an announcement to everyone within earshot, "Brothers! They're my baby brothers!"

By the time Eric gets home from his search for the letter-writer, Annie has everybody in time-out. She explains: "Mary and Simon are mad at each other, Simon's mad at Deena's par-

ents, Mary's mad at me, Lucy's mad at the general public, and Ruthie's mad at God." She adds that it's Eric's fault for introducing the idea that prayers can make miracles.

The phone rings, and Sergeant Michaels reports that he's found the kid Eric's been looking for.

Annie talks with Ruthie about why she wants a pony. She needs it, she says, to get "that feeling of being carried from earth back to heaven, or by angels" when she came to earth. Annie suggests she write or draw about that feeling.

Mary and Simon talk out their feelings with each other while they set the table. Lucy helps and talks out her feelings by talking to herself.

Matt and John go to Raven's, and she introduces them as "her friend John, and John's roommate, Matt." At least Matt knows where he stands. "Thank you," whispers John, looking upward.

Eric meets the letter writer, Jonathan, in a rough neighborhood. The boy asks him not to get involved, just to pray. "The man upstairs will take care of all of us," he says. "Have a little faith."

Back at the house, Simon practices an apology to Deena's parents in the mirror. When he thinks he's ready, he picks up the phone and calls. Mr. Stewart answers, Simon goes into his routine, and it works. Deena is called to the phone. "Thank you," Simon whispers upward.

In the attic, Mary asks for, and receives, a promise from Lucy, Eric, and Annie. She wants them to pray for Robbie to go from being bad to being good. Lucy wants them to pray for all the young mothers who have to endure ridicule and criticism.

The next day, Sunday, Matt does something for Ruthie. He takes her to a riding school where she can be on a horse. In church, after the Lord's Prayer, Eric gives a sermon about prayer.

"My family has been talking a lot about prayer this week," he begins. "The discussions began when I shared my feelings about a letter I received in the mail, sent anonymously. . . . I will now pass the author's request on to you.

"Say a prayer today for the millions of children in the world who have become victims of violence . . .

"Ask God to help those children who are trying to recover from the death of a playmate or friend or family member . . .

"Pray for the children, that they might have peace . . .

"Because if we won't stop the violence in our children's lives by taking the right actions and behaving responsibly, then the very least we owe them might be the most powerful thing we can give them, our prayers."

Twelve Angry People

written by Carol Tenney; directed by Tony Mordente

Eric does jury duty. Ruthie gets in trouble over a haircut. Matt gets caught playing the church organ after hours. Mary and Lucy play phone tricks on each other.

Season 4: Episode 82

In the kitchen, Annie gets a phone call from an angry mother. Ruthie confesses to giving her friend a haircut at school; Annie grounds her.

Meanwhile, in a criminal courtroom, Eric serves on the jury in a murder case. When they vote on a verdict, they get eleven "not guiltys" and one "guilty." Eric is the one.

After supper that night Matt borrows the keys to Eric's office so he be alone to study—there's a basketball game on at his apartment.

Mary and Lucy ask permission to go out for cappuccino and Annie says no—they've gone overbudget on their allowance already. What about just going out, no cappuccino, Lucy wonders. After all, the real reason was just to check up on their ex-boyfriends. Mary takes a swing at Lucy's shoulder and misses. Lucy gets a black eye.

Simon comes downstairs reeking of shaving lotion; Annie figures out right away that he's got a date with Deena. But she doesn't feel like chaperoning. Simon begs, and Annie relents, as long as Simon finds the missing Ruthie.

In the jury room, the others complain about Eric's lone guilty vote. He's just as baffled by their votes not to convict.

Mary is the one who finds Ruthie, though, coming in the back door from a visit with Mrs. Hinkle, despite being grounded. Annie's angry. Ruthie explains she just went in order to tell Mrs. Hinkle she was grounded—since she didn't have Mrs. Hinkle's phone number (oops).

At the church, Matt sits down at the computer and promptly spills hot cappuccino in his lap. Then his pencil point breaks. He finds a couple more in a desk drawer and gets distracted by his own pencil drum solo on the desktop. Bored by the lack of stimulation in the office, he exchanges his wet clothes for Eric's freshly dry-cleaned robe.

In the jury room, Eric tries to persuade the other jurors with the evidence, but he gets nowhere. The defendant is charged with shooting a police officer. In light of a recent scandal in the police department, the other jurors are voting against the police. Later, during the dinner break, a black juror, Caleb, tells Eric about another case. His black nephew was sentenced to fifteen years in prison by a judge who released four white defendants in a deal on the same day. Eric sees that they have been influenced by racial politics and are blind to reason.

At the house, Annie takes a call from Matt, who's looking for something to listen to in Eric's office besides Nitty Gritty Dirt Band tapes. Annie wonders if the quiet is getting to him. Then the doorbell rings, and it's Deena. Both of them have been warned against making out, so Simon suggests they try just talking, maybe while playing a board game. Deena thinks that's a good idea.

Upstairs, Lucy examines her black eye in the mirror. Mary offers to compensate by calling Andrew Nayloss to set up a date for her, but Lucy doesn't want that. She would like a glass of tea from the kitchen, though.

Ruthie wonders why she's being punished for cutting her friend's hair, when her friend asked her to in the first place. She tells Mary they're just alike. "We've gotten ourselves in trouble a few times this year, and now everything we do looks bad and we get punished for nothing." They've been labeled the "bad girls," in other words.

Mary gets Lucy a drink and tells her a mischievous lie: she called Andrew Nayloss. But since Andrew wasn't home she talked to his dad, who said Andrew has another, nicer girlfriend who doesn't want to make out all the time, which leads to sex, which Andrew isn't ready for.

Lucy believes her, too.

In the jury room, Eric asks the other jurors to set aside their feelings about the racism they all know is in the judicial system.

"I'm asking you to rise above that," he says. "The evidence shows that the defendant is the murderer here."

When they take another vote, Caleb has changed his to guilty. Then Anthony, a young black man, changes to "guilty" as well.

At the church, Matt heads for the sanctuary. "Welcome everyone!" he says from the pulpit. "Welcome to the church of Matt!" And then he mimics the sound of a crowd going wild.

At home, Lucy dials the number for the Naylosses. Mr. Nayloss answers and Lucy tells him she's not ready for sex either. "We're not interested in changing our long-distance service," he replies, not understanding who's calling or what it's about at first. Then he does, and Lucy realizes she's made a fool of herself. Mary didn't really call at all!

In the kitchen, the board game between Simon and Deena has become competitive and argumentative. The tension doesn't break until the game's almost over, and the real thing that's bothering Deena comes out. She's mad at Simon for the trouble they got in, making out and exchanging hickeys. "Or maybe I'm mad at myself," she says, and suddenly it's all better.

Mary runs from Lucy into Ruthie's room. Ruthie's wearing a hat, and it scares Mary, then Lucy and Annie, too, that Ruthie has cut off her own hair. When she lifts the hat it spills out, still attached, fortunately. But the look on Annie's face when she thought it wasn't has told Ruthie what it must have been like for Sarah and her mom. "Maybe I should ask Sarah if she wants to cut my bangs," Ruthie says. "Then we can have bad hair together." Annie shakes her head but agrees to call Sarah's mom.

At the church, Lou discovers Matt playing chopsticks on the organ in Eric's robe. Matt tries to explain; Lou tries to understand.

In the jury room, Eric's arguments about being fair in the trial, regardless of how unfair the system has been, are having a powerful effect. Everyone changes their vote to "guilty," except for one juror named Bill.

At the house, Mary gets Lucy to laugh about what happened with Andrew's dad; Lucy says she just hopes Mary doesn't mind the call she made to Robbie. Actually, Mary does. Very much. She doesn't want anything to do with Robbie, or the kind of trouble he represents, anymore. Then Lucy breaks into a smile; she was only kidding.

At the church, Lou ends up helping Matt with his homework, while at the courthouse, the jury delivers its verdict: "guilty."

Hoop Dreams

written by Jon Bastian; directed by David J. Plenn

Mary dreams of a career in the WNBA. Ruthie dreams of a career as the Queen of England. Matt dreams up a way to move to New York. In the end, everybody has to deal with reality.

Mary gets a call from Coach Cleary: "Bring your sweats and be ready to work out this afternoon." She just knows he's invited some pro players to see her game—she had a dream just the night before that she was in the pros!

Ruthie would like to have a prophetic dream, too. One that makes her the Queen of England when she grows up.

Upstairs, Annie finds Lucy fixing a dresser drawer in the twins' room. Annie, who likes fixing things, too, smiles. Lucy's a chip off the old block. She shoos her off to school.

At their apartment, Matt tells John he knows what he has to do to patch things up with Shana. He has to move to New York. John thinks he's being a little hasty, considering his financial situation.

At school, Mary has trouble convincing her friend Corey and her sister Lucy that Coach Cleary's call means she's going to play in the Women's National Basketball League. After school, Mary goes to the gym and finds out what Coach Cleary has in mind. "It's a great opportunity," he tells her, but it's not exactly the pros. He wants her to coach a Special Olympics team.

Meanwhile, Eric has overheard Simon saying that he would never want to be a minister. Hurt, and worried that they haven't spent enough time together lately, Eric arrives at Simon's classroom door and invites him to the movies. Simon is a little surprised to learn he's already cleared it with the school.

Matt goes to the house to see what he can find to sell, to finance his move to New York. With the kind of money Annie expects him to make, she thinks a move to Kansas would be more likely.

Eric and Simon arrive at the theater in time to see half of a movie they've already seen.

At home, Lucy and Ruthie wonder about the possibility of Mary playing pro ball. Lucy would miss her as a roommate.

At the flea market, Matt lays out a pitiful selection. The vendor next door, Joyce, offers him $10 for everything. She really just wants his booth space.

Eric and Simon stop at the flea market and discover Matt's table, and Matt. Eric starts to buy something, just to help out, but Matt's prices are way too high. Joyce lets Matt know her offer is still open, but he decides to stick it out.

At home, Mary tells Annie and Lucy about the Special Olympics team. She's a little disappointed, but she's going to coach. Annie's proud of her. But it doesn't do anything for Mary's sense of loss about what she wants to do with her life.

"If it makes you feel any better, neither do I," says Lucy.

"Even though I have a lot in common with Mom, I don't want to be 'just' Mom."

Annie overhears everything, unfortunately.

Over supper at Pete's Pizza, Eric tells Simon how he enrolled in the seminary. When he wasn't drafted during the Vietnam War, he took it as a sign from God that he should be a minister. Or, Simon suggests, maybe he was just avoiding the draft.

At the apartment, Matt shows John his earnings for the day: twenty bucks. It's not enough to move to New York. "It's not even enough to buy a book about New York," John points out.

Across the country in Shana's apartment, the phone rings. Roommate Bobby answers and tells Matt she's at the library. Matt leaves a message—he's coming to town.

At the house, Ruthie comes downstairs and finds Annie and Eric in the kitchen. Simon's been telling her a story, she tells Annie. "Did you know Dad was a draft dodger?"

Mary gets a call from a Special Olympics player named Molly, who wants to know if Mary can play the next day. Mary says yes, and then Molly tells her something that goes like an arrow through her heart.

"You're my hero," Molly says.

"No," Mary says. She doesn't feel as if she deserves that.

That night Ruthie has a dream. She's the Queen of England. She wears a cape and crown. Loyal subjects bow in the streets. . . .

"Ruthie! Hey!" Simon shakes her out of it. Time for pancakes.

Downstairs, Lucy tries unsuccessfully to patch things up with Annie over her "just Mom" comment. Annie tries to get Simon to understand that he's hurt Eric by suggesting he became a minister to dodge the draft.

In the backyard, Molly's dad drops her off to shoot hoops with Mary. He's very appreciative and seems to agree with his daughter that Mary's a hero.

At the hospital, Matt meets a fellow worker who narrowly missed becoming a doctor. Instead, it's his thirty-ninth year at the hospital, doing menial tasks because he dropped out of med school on account of family responsibilities.

At home, Eric and Simon have a meeting in Ruthie's playhouse. Simon apologizes to his father, who says he was hurt by the tone of voice Simon used when he said he didn't want to be a minister. In the kitchen, Lucy and Annie make up, too.

Out at the basketball goal, Mary finds out about Molly's dad's job. He's a scout for the WNBA. Suddenly, she's in the clouds again, certain he wants to draft her for the pros.

The next day Ruthie watches a tape about the British monarchy and is disturbed to learn the queen has work to do.

Lots of it. It makes her wonder about changing her dream. . . .

Lucy tells Simon what she wants to be, and it's Mom. "If I turn out to be half the woman she is, that'll be fine with me," she says.

Matt decides what he wants to do. He calls Shana's apartment and talks to Bobby again, and leaves a message that he's not coming after all. Matt's decided it's time to get serious about school and not end up like Bobby, who is there to answer the phone all the time because he dropped out of med school. Or like that coworker at the hospital, even though he knows that was fake . . . John set that up.

Eventually Mary finds out what Molly's dad really wants her to do—and it's not play in the WNBA. It's to coach Molly's Special Olympics team. Although there is a part of her that is disappointed, she is also honored, and realizes that to make her dream a reality, she must work at it.

Talk to Me

**teleplay by Elaine Arata;
story by Brenda Hampton;
directed by Tony Mordente**

Season 4: Episode 84

A young woman shows up at Eric's office dressed in many layers of clothing. He invites her in to talk, but she says she'll be back, tomorrow. Then she slips away.

That afternoon at the house, Annie wakes the twins from their nap. Eric arrives. He tells Annie about the girl. Adding to her mystery is Eric's sense that he's seen her before.

Downstairs, Mary, Simon, Ruthie, and Lucy arrive home from school. Annie and Eric go down to talk, but the kids make excuses and disappear. It's like they're hiding something. But what?

Upstairs, Lucy demands a confession from whoever did whatever, because obviously Eric and Annie suspect something. Everybody passionately proclaims their innocence.

At the hospital cafeteria, Hank runs into Matt, and they talk. Through the hospital grapevine, Hank has learned that Matt is going to New York. Everybody knows. Matt tells him he changed his plans. As his beeper goes off, Hank tells Matt that he needs to talk to him later. Matt stops by the office to talk to Hank, but Hank has just left to deliver a baby. Julie comes by looking for her husband. She knows something's been bothering him, but she leaves, miffed when she learns that Hank has asked Matt, rather than her, over to talk.

Eric happens to see Sergeant Michaels in front of the house and stops to describe his mystery visitor, who he thinks might be a runaway. Ruthie and Simon spot their dad and the policeman from Ruthie's window and decide to tell Mary and Lucy. One of them must be in trouble, for sure!

Mary and Lucy insist they're not. Mary says they should just ask Eric and Annie what's going on. When she does, Eric and Annie deny anyone's in trouble. Eric tells them about the young woman who came to his office and how that made him realize they need to communicate more. Mary feels she's communicated more than enough over the past year, but the others are more than happy to comply. They decide to talk that evening.

After supper Ruthie tells Eric about her friend Maryanne and the way she smells. Simon tells Annie about a prank his friends pulled in class that led to the substitute locking herself out. Annie doesn't think it's funny.

"Maybe I told it wrong," Simon says. "I'll start over." And he does.

Lucy makes a list for her turn to talk to her parents. She asks Mary what she's going to say. Mary says she's exempt from the night's chatfest because there's nothing about her left to tell. Lucy says, "Nothing about you, but maybe something about someone else?" Mary says she can't tell anyone about that. Not even Lucy.

At Matt and John's apartment, Hank arrives with a small suitcase. Julie's kicked him out for going to Matt to talk instead of to her.

At the house, Annie asks Lucy about Simon's friend Luke, the head prankster. Lucy says she's not sure he's real. "Mary and I have discussed the possibility that there is no Luke, that Simon is just telling stories about himself." Annie says she'll invite Luke over for dinner to find out. Then they talk about Lisa Lunby, one of Lucy's coworkers at Habitat for Humanity. Lisa, who Lucy says "is getting weirder and weirder," used to be outgoing, but now she's a real loner.

"Are you talking about me?" Mary says, coming around the corner. They assure her they're not. And Lucy assures Annie that they have not neglected any of the other kids while they focused on Mary's problems this year.

On the Glenoak Promenade, Sergeant Michaels spots a girl who fits the description of Eric's mystery visitor. A young man tries to make conversation, and she reacts violently, screaming "Get away." When Sergeant Michaels goes down to check it out, he gets her name. It's Lisa Lunby.

Sergeant Michaels phones Eric with the information, and Mary overhears on an extension. She tells Eric she's the one who sent Lisa to his office. And she can't tell him why. Eric

understands her position. They all hope that Lisa will turn to Eric again.

Matt and John wake up at their apartment determined to get rid of Hank, who's in the bathroom getting ready for work. Matt nominates himself to speak to him later in the day.

At the house, Annie serves breakfast to Simon and Ruthie. Simon says he isn't sure Luke can visit because he's so popular. Ruthie wants to have Maryanne over so she can tell her she stinks. Annie tells her that's not very nice, and questions if Maryanne really "stinks" or if it's just something the kids made up to be mean.

Eric leaves early to work on a sermon. The phone rings, and it's Julie, checking on Hank's whereabouts. Simon tells her he wasn't there the night before. Julie hangs up and calls Matt's, finds out she just missed Hank, and wheedles a favor. Matt agrees to try to find out what Hank isn't telling her.

At the house, Annie confronts Simon about Luke, letting on what Mary and Lucy said, that he might be imaginary. Then Maryanne arrives at the front door, and she *does* smell. Upstairs, Ruthie figures out the answer to the mysterious odor. Maryanne lives with her grandma, and the funny smells are mothballs mixed with "other grandma stuff." Plus they live across from the meat store.

At the hospital, Matt rushes in and finds Hank at last, already in conversation with Julie. He's spilled his secret to her. He's Jewish. He just never mentioned it to Julie. They laugh because it's not some deep, dark, serious problem. And it won't become one, either, when his parents come to town and learn that Julie isn't Jewish.

Lisa shows up at Eric's office to talk. Her emotional problems, it turns out, stem from having been raped by her mother's boyfriend. The man has disappeared, and her mother doesn't want to discuss it and won't let Lisa tell her brothers. She's frightened.

There really is a Luke. He visits the Camdens, and like Simon said, he's funny. Matt comes by. He tells Annie the big secret: Hank's Jewish. Annie says she's known that for a long time—starting with the time he called to check on the date of Christmas Eve.

At Eric's office, Lisa and her mother have a tearful talk about what happened, and about whose fault it's not: Lisa's or her mom's. With Eric's help, Lisa's mother understands that it needs to be talked about and acknowledged. It's the only way they eventually will be able to make things better. Lisa and her mother decide to go to therapy together, realizing that anything can be resolved if people will just talk to one another.

187

Liar, Liar

written by Brenda Hampton;
directed by Paul Snider

The Camdens let it all hang out for the newspaper. Chrissy steals Ruthie's story and wins a contest. Eric points out the advantage to being less than perfect.

Season 4: Episode 85

Ruthie's school librarian announces a story contest—the student who tells the best original story will win a $5 prize. Ruthie figures it'll be easy. Her friend Chrissy's not so sure.

At the church, Eric gets a call from the newspaper. They want to do a family story on the Camdens. Eric figures it'll be great publicity for the church.

When Matt hears about it on the phone, he's not so sure. "Reporters have a way of digging up the family dirt," he says. Then he gets some advice from Annie on how to remove a bloodstain for a patient at the hospital.

The patient happens to be the wife of a hospital board member. And Elizabeth, the orderly who helps her to her car, happens to mention that Matt is known to be a little unstable. "You never know when he's going to snap," she says. "People are a little afraid of him."

Matt has no idea.

As the kids arrive home from school, Eric tells them about the newspaper interview. They're all wary about it. They agree with Matt that the press isn't always friendly. Look what it did for the White House.

At the apartment, John gets annoyed as he hears a politician on TV misquote Harriet Tubman to pander to a crowd of African Americans.

That night, Annie rearranges and dusts everything in the house, preparing for the reporter's visit. Eric says she rearranges only when she's anxious. He doesn't want any of them to be anxious, and why are the kids all running back and forth? Annie says she told the kids to be thinking of nice things to say about him in the interview.

In fact, they've been naming things to each other that they *don't* want said about themselves. Off limits: boyfriends, arrests, trouble at school, embarrassing anecdotes of any kind.

The next day at the hospital, Matt helps Elizabeth with a wheelchair brake. He warns her to switch it before moving a patient, and says he'll get her a new one. While he's away, Elizabeth tells a nurse that she's the one who gave the warning—to Matt. The nurse thinks she may need to speak to Matt about his attitude. Elizabeth cautions her. "He has a really nasty temper."

At school, Ruthie tells Chrissy her story for the contest. It's a short biography of her Aunt Julie. Chrissy says she hasn't come up with her story yet.

Annie gets a call from the personnel officer at the hospital. Elizabeth's stories about Matt's short temper have made their way to her office. If she has to talk to Matt about it, it will become an "official" conversation that will have to go on Matt's record. She asks if Annie might mention the situation to Matt before he does something he'll regret. Annie agrees to talk to her son.

In the elementary school library, Chrissy tells her story, or rather, *Ruthie's* story. Ruthie steams, but there's nothing she can do about it. Mrs. Beasley thinks it's a great story and that Chrissy may be a contender for the cash prize.

Annie drops by the hospital to have lunch with Matt, who tells her he's already set up an appointment with the newspaper reporter for after work. Annie tries to tell him diplomatically to take it easy, but she succeeds only in leaving Matt clueless and mystified.

Elizabeth comes in just as Annie leaves. She takes advantage of Matt's temporary confusion and comments to another orderly, "He's a zombie. Which I prefer, by the way, to his other personality."

Sam Robbins, the newspaper reporter, meets with Eric and assures him the story is not an exposé. "You'll have full approval of the copy and pictures," he promises. Eric feels good about that. "With seven kids, five of whom talk, the odds are pretty good that someone will say something that might not look good in print."

Sam says he can't wait to meet them. Eric is a little less relieved.

First Sam gets Mary to talk about her arrest, the work program, and the boyfriend she met there who couldn't be trusted. Mary unconsciously puts the basketball she'd been holding under her shirt and rests her arms on it. The photographer takes the picture. . . .

Then Lucy talks about her boyfriends; the photographer snaps her picture while she's bending over to retrieve Sam's dropped pencil, showing a little too much cleavage. . . .

Simon talks about the hickey he gave Deena and the time he tried cigarettes, and demonstrates for the camera by puffing a pencil. . . .

Ruthie gets her picture taken in a playful pose, showing a little leg and winking. Then she talks about her drunk aunt Julie. . . .

Finally it's off to Matt's, where Sam and the photographer have arrived. The photographer finds the place a wreck. The picture is snapped of Matt and the disaster area. . . .

At home, Eric and Annie are disturbed by how little time Sam spent with them. Annie talks about her conversation with the personnel officer about Matt. Before they can discuss it further, Ruthie comes in. She tells them about her problem with "this rat fink Chrissy," who stole her story and won the $5 cash prize. Annie asks what the story was about. Ruthie says it was "about Aunt Julie being a drunk. . . ."

They find out Ruthie told Sam Robbins about the story, too.

It's just the beginning; by the end of the day Eric and Annie have found out that all kinds of skeletons have been let out of the closet.

John has gone back to the hospital to do some work. He sees the politician on TV again and gets so angry that he throws a videotape at the screen. A security guard sees this, and John gets fired. But it seems the real reason is someone has accused him and Matt of doing drugs.

The next day Matt and John manage to clear up the misunderstandings with Sharon Peacock in the personnel office. Matt knows who's sabotaging him, but he doesn't know why and doesn't care. His focus is on doing his job.

John finally meets the politician only to find his absurd and incorrect speeches are being written by a black college woman, a fact of which the politician was unaware until that moment. He's so unaware that he doesn't realize he's being sabotaged by his own speechwriter. John just laughs and leaves.

At school, Ruthie speaks with Chrissy, who won the story contest. "If you ever decide to apologize," she says, "we'll do it in the library, in front of Mrs. Beasley."

In Eric's office, Sam Robbins hands over his story and the photographs, with the advice that the Camdens are not ready to go public. Neither of them wants the story to run.

But the paper's editor decides otherwise, and it does run, in full embarrassing color. Eric has about a minute after seeing it to address the congregation.

"We are far from being the perfect family," he says. "But being the imperfect family that we are, we have the opportunity to practice unconditional love. How easy it would be to love perfection, but to love imperfection is the challenge, and the reward is that we learn to love and accept ourselves as well as the many imperfect people we come across from day to day."

"Wow," Ruthie says. "That's the best sermon I ever heard. And the shortest."

Love Stinks, Part One

written by Sue Tenney; directed by Burt Brinckerhoff

Complicated affairs entangle the Camden kids. Shana returns as Matt again falls for Heather. Mary and Robbie get back together. Lucy dumps Andrew Nayloss again. Simon and Deena break up. And Ruthie strikes a boyfriend-girlfriend deal with an admirer named Burt.

Season 4: Episode 86

Outside the church, Matt and Heather exchange amorous glances. Annie notices and asks Matt about his girlfriend Shana. He tells her she's moving back to town for the summer, and that she'll be working at the hospital.

Simon looks around expectantly for Deena, who hasn't arrived yet. Ruthie appears with powdered sugar on her mouth and admits to Annie she's been eating doughnuts in the church kitchen, but it's not her fault. "The devil made me do it," she explains. Burt, a young boy with an obvious crush on Ruthie, stops by to say hello.

In the church garden, Mary finds Lucy hiding from Andrew Nayloss and "his creepy parents." As they enter the church together, Lucy tells Mary that Shelby's older brother is back from college and suggests that Mary go out with him. Mary says she is not ready to date; she's still getting over her breakup with Robbie. They join the other family members in a pew, when suddenly Robbie himself appears at the door, along with his drop-dead gorgeous step-brother Ronald. The family is shocked to see Robbie; he and Ronald even wink at Mary and Lucy.

After the service Eric expresses his concern to Annie about the reappearance of Robbie, who lied and tried to take Mary to a motel on a date. Annie warns Eric that Mary may take him back anyway.

In the church garden, Robbie apologizes to Mary. He thanks her, saying her rejection made him decide to mend his ways, adding that he's even started going to church regularly. Then he walks off.

Inside, Matt and Heather say hello, and both find it very hard to break apart. Lucy, meanwhile, is trying to get rid of Andrew Nayloss when Ronald approaches and introduces himself. Lucy is obviously flattered, and Andrew tries to send Ronald away. Meanwhile, Simon's friend Wade tells him he saw Deena with another guy.

Later Matt visits Shana at her new apartment and discovers she's changed her ways: she no longer drinks coffee, and she's a hockey fan; both on account of the influence of her college roommate, Brett. "Who are you?" Matt says, only half jokingly.

Burt shows up at the Camden house. Annie offers him a snack and finds out he's a vegan, is juice intolerant, and even has some "trouble" with carbonated water. Ruthie enters, and he practically swoons.

Upstairs, Simon talks to Happy about Wade's information that Deena was with another guy. He can't imagine who it could be.

Matt and Shana go to the pool hall, where Shana continues to surprise Matt with new habits she's learned from Brett, like eating French fries with vinegar. Suddenly Brett actually appears and announces to Shana that he has moved to town and has a job at the hospital. He and Matt size each other up.

Meanwhile, Mary goes to Robbie's house and before long they're back together. "Don't break my heart, and I'll have no reason to break your jaw," Mary jokes, referring to the punch she gave him when he tried to take her to the motel.

Eric gets a call in his office from Mr. Simms, Mary's guidance counselor. He has disturbing news: he sent a letter with a list of junior colleges home with Mary because she missed the fall semester application deadline at Crawford. He's worried about Mary, who told him she's not planning to go to any college in the fall.

When Mary gets home later, she shocks Eric and Annie with the news that she's back with Robbie, and then confirms that she is not planning to go to college in the fall.

Meanwhile, upstairs, Burt and Ruthie work on the end-of-the-school-year collage, on which their teacher has made them partners. Burt spends most of his time staring at Ruthie. Finally, he gives her a clumsily wrapped Steuben crystal cat and asks if she'll be his girlfriend.

Across town, Shana finds Brett waiting for her at her apartment. He makes fun of Matt and tells Shana he loves her. Even

when she tells him she loves Matt, Brett remains steadfast and determined to win her over.

Lucy finds Andrew Nayloss waiting for her in the Camden backyard, and just like at church, she puts him off.

Deena arrives at the front door. Simon is momentarily relieved when he finds out that the guy with whom Wade saw her was a cousin. Then she shocks him by saying she thinks they should see other people.

At the apartment, Matt tells John how Shana has changed under the influence of Brett, who is here, he is sure, "not because there are no medical jobs in New York." John advises Matt to break if off with Shana—he knows Matt is really in love with Heather.

Back at the house, Ruthie strikes a deal with Burt—he can be her boyfriend if he'll do anything she says and will continue to bring her presents.

Downstairs, Lucy asks Annie if it's okay to invite Ronald over for dinner. Annie reluctantly agrees. Then Eric enters, and he and Annie decide it's time to have a talk with Mary.

Mary explains to her parents how everything changed for her after she got arrested and lost her college basketball scholarship, then didn't get to play professional basketball in the WNBA. She doesn't know what to do with her life, and doesn't want to waste money on college while trying to figure it out. Her mind's made up.

At the apartment, Heather arrives and talks to Matt. She asks about Shana and then tells Matt she's in love with him. John exits with a smile.

At the house, Simon calls Cynthia, a thirteen-year-old friend of Deena's, hoping to get information about why Deena wants to break up. Eric is on his way outside with the trash when he finds Robbie in the backyard. Angered at seeing the boy, Eric is worried to learn that Annie has given Mary permission to go out for

ice cream with Robbie. On their way out, Mary tells Robbie she is not going to college because she wants to spend as much time as possible with him, and they kiss.

Annie advises Ruthie that relationships are "not all about one person," and that Burt should be getting something in return from her.

In the living room, Ronald and Lucy talk. They are practically kissing when Eric comes in. "I don't like your family," Eric tells him when they meet each other, and Ronald nods appreciatively. "I would never take Lucy to a motel," he says, referring to what Robbie did with Mary.

Eric goes into the kitchen and makes a deal with Annie. If she gives him some pie, he'll tell her his plan to get Mary into college in the fall.

Matt and Shana go to the movies, where Shana tells him why she came back: it was to try to make their relationship work. Shana senses Matt is distracted; what she doesn't know is that his mind is on Heather.

Cynthia calls Simon back with the details on Deena: she does have another boyfriend, she says. What she doesn't say is that Deena is with Cynthia and the whole thing is made up. Deena is trying to get Simon to forget about her so he won't be hurt when he learns her family is moving away.

Meanwhile, on the street, Robbie and Mary are spotted by Robbie's ex-girlfriend, who plans revenge.

Later, at the house, Lucy and Mary are stunned to hear about Ruthie's boyfriend deal with Burt. Then Eric gives Mary another surprise by handing her a bill, her first monthly room-and-board charge for as long as she is living there and not going to school. It's really Eric's ploy to persuade her to enroll somewhere.

Heather shows up at the house and tells Matt it is deadline-time with Shana. She insists on a real breakup before she will see him again.

At school, Ruthie gets teased for being "in love" with Burt. Ruthie defends herself by announcing the real reason she let him be her boyfriend—so he'd do things for her. Burt runs off with tears in his eyes. Meanwhile, Simon gives Deena a promise ring he'd been saving for her birthday, to show he cares for her even though they're breaking up, and Deena runs away crying. Later, Andrew tells Lucy he's giving her another chance to make up with him, and she turns him down.

Robbie arrives at home and finds his ex-girlfriend Cheryl waiting. She lets him know she's going to tell Mary all about him.

Meanwhile, at the Camden house, Mary delivers some news to her parents: she's figured out a solution to her room-and-board problem. Robbie is getting an apartment and has invited her to live there for free. . . .

Love Stinks, Part Two

written by Sue Tenney; directed by Burt Brinckerhoff

Mary accepts Robbie's marriage proposal, and Eric is outraged. Simon learns that Deena is moving away. Lucy realizes she likes Andrew after all. Matt breaks up with Shana and takes Heather to a wedding chapel.

Season 4: Episode 87

In the kitchen, Eric expresses his outrage at Mary's decision to share an apartment with Robbie. "He's a liar . . . and I don't even want you to share a fork with him," he says. Annie shocks Eric and Mary when she says she supports Mary's decision. Later, when speaking privately to Eric, she explains she's using reverse psychology to get Mary to change her mind.

Lucy comes in and complains to Annie that Andrew Nayloss has told her he likes her, just when she was starting to develop a relationship with Ronald. Annie is skeptical about her relationship with Ronald—Lucy only just met him.

Simon tells Eric about Deena's confusing reaction to the promise ring he gave her. She told him she's not seeing someone else after all, but still won't see Simon. Eric can't figure that one out, either.

Upstairs, Annie and Ruthie talk about the way Ruthie hurt Burt's feelings. He said he was going to "tell" on Ruthie, and Annie wonders if that's why Ruthie's upset, that she might get in trouble. Ruthie says the real reason she's upset is because she thinks she may like Burt after all.

That night, at the apartment, Matt paces the floor, wondering aloud what to do about Shana, who's trying to hold on to

their relationship. In his heart Matt is sure he's in love with Heather. John finally shoves him out the door and says, "Break up with Shana, and don't come back until you do."

The next day Cynthia shows up at the Camdens to tell Simon the real reason Deena wants to break up with him. Her family plans to move back east, and they're leaving at the end of the week.

Shana arrives at her apartment and finds Brett waiting for her. "I love Matt," she protests weakly, but the chemistry between them is undeniable, and they kiss.

At the house, Lucy asks Annie for permission to meet Ronald at the pool hall for a soda. "Ronald, huh?" Annie says skeptically. Lucy knows what she's thinking: "I don't like Andrew!" she protests and exits.

There's a knock at the door, and it's Jill, Burt's mom. She's not upset with Ruthie—Burt has been "falling in love" with girls since preschool, wooing them with presents he steals from home. Annie hands over the Steuben cat that Burt gave Ruthie.

On the phone, Mary tells Robbie that a girl named Cheryl tried to get in touch with her. He explains she's an old girl-friend, and lies that they haven't dated for a year. "She's a little nuts," he confides. So Mary decides not to call her back, to Robbie's relief. "Tell your parents about us," he urges her. Mary hangs up the phone and looks at her hand. She is wearing a small diamond ring! "Mrs. Robbie Palmer," she says, trying out the name she will have when they are married.

When Mary tells Eric and Annie she's engaged, Eric practically goes into shock. "Over my dead body," he says about the wedding plans, and he's not kidding.

Annie, on the other hand, says "Congratulations." Mary recoils, thinking Annie's trying to confuse her into calling the whole thing off. But Annie stays firm. "I'll make you a beautiful dress," she promises. Mary storms out, and Annie reassures Eric that their daughter won't go through with it. "She'll crack, and we'll find out the real reason she doesn't want to go to college this fall."

Outside the door to Shana's apartment, Matt rehearses for the breakup. "Shana—we're breaking up," he says, oblivious to a neighbor walking by. "Don't cry . . . please don't cry," he goes on. Then Matt spots the neighbor and tries to cover up. "School play," he says, and he leaves without ever knocking on Shana's door.

Meanwhile, Simon's at Deena's house, where they're making up. Simon promises to think up a plan that will prevent Deena from moving, even though her mom has already arranged for the transfer at her job.

At the pool hall, Ronald tells Lucy all about his brother and

Mary's wedding plans. Lucy is flabbergasted and tries to leave for home immediately. Then she spots Andrew Nayloss coming in with a beautiful girl on his arm.

At home, Ruthie and Burt have an on-again, off-again phone conversation—calling, hanging up on each other, and then redialing all over again.

Simon rushes into Eric's study and asks him to help keep Deena in town. "Find her mom another job," he says. "You have until the end of the week." Although Eric can't promise anything, he says he'll talk to the family.

At the apartment, John refuses to let Matt in until he has broken up with Shana; he simply can't take any more of Matt's whining about the situation.

At the house, Mary helps Annie fold laundry. "Have you thought about what kind of wedding you want to have?" Annie asks. Mary says she wants to hear Annie's honest opinion about the whole idea. Annie says she thinks it's a mistake, but it's not her life. Then the phone rings—it's Cheryl again.

"Mary, don't hang up," Cheryl says. "Robbie and I broke up last week. When did you and Robbie start dating?"

"Seven months ago," Mary says, shocked.

All Cheryl needs to say is, "Do the math."

Eric visits Deena's dad and finds out Deena's parents are getting a divorce. The dad plans to follow Deena's mom back east to be near Deena, although neither of the parents wants to be married anymore. Deena enters, and her dad decides then and there it's time for her to know the truth.

Lucy arrives from her date with Ronald and complains to Annie that he met another girl at the pool hall and the two of them just dropped her off. Then Annie learns it happened while Lucy was spying on Andrew Nayloss and his date. Annie suggests to Lucy that she call Andrew at home.

Lucy goes upstairs and pounds Mary with a pillow, once for making wedding plans with Robbie, once for deciding not to go to college in the fall, and once more for generally messing up her life. Mary flees, but she manages to get in a comment about Lucy's own mess with Andrew Nayloss, and Lucy reacts by smacking herself with the pillow.

Later that night Simon is in his room, brooding about Deena, when Ruthie enters and asks for some advice on how to get a guy to like her. Simon figures out she's thinking about Burt. "Tell him how you feel," he says. Ruthie flinches and tells him she was expecting better advice!

Matt arrives at Shana's determined to break up their relationship and is shocked to find her with Brett.

Eric visits Robbie and tells him all the reasons he and Mary should not get married. Robbie says he is a changed man, but

Eric doubts it. "Have you prayed about this?" Eric says angrily, doubting it even occurred to Robbie.

Lucy calls and speaks with Andrew's dad, who says his son is not there. But when he hangs up, Andrew is beside him, smiling because she actually called!

Outside, Annie and Mary talk about the real reason Mary decided she didn't want to go to college. After all that's gone wrong since her arrest, she's grown afraid that she will only fail. She doesn't know what to do with her life, and maybe she'd rather give her life to somebody else than figure it out herself. Later, she gives the ring back to Robbie and says, "I have to figure out me before I can figure out us."

At Shana's apartment, Brett, Shana, and Matt talk. It's really over—Matt and Shana have broken up, finally. Meanwhile, Eric and Annie spy on Burt and Ruthie making up. The two kids even try to kiss, but with their eyes closed, and they both miss. Simon and Deena reaffirm their feelings for each other, and Simon says they will always stay together in their hearts, even while they're apart in different cities. Lucy and Andrew decide that if they're not exactly in love, they can be "in like." And Matt and John are on good terms again when John learns that Matt has broken up with Shana. But John's in for a surprise when Matt tells him to get dressed, as Matt needs his help with something. . . .

Moments later, in Matt's car, Heather wonders if they should have told their families about their big plan. Then John pulls them out of the car, and the three walk into a wedding chapel.

Cast Interviews

Catherine Hicks (Annie)

Catherine Hicks took time in between scenes and during her lunch break to talk about 7th Heaven. She even asked the crew to wait an extra moment so she could finish a question! Her love for the show, and for acting, really shows.

Q: *7th Heaven* has been on for four years, and Annie's gone through a lot, especially the death of her mother. Has the character changed?

C: Well, when I look at old shows—ha, ha! Old, that's four years ago.

Q: That's old for a television show!

C: I know. It's so weird. I know my acting has changed. I'm more calm and centered, so therefore Annie seemed more excitable early on, but more deep and steady now. Solid.

Q: Do you think they're writing her that way for you or you're bringing that to the character?

C: I don't know. Both, I think.

Q: Are there things you admire about Annie? Things you think she should be working on?

C: Well, in real life I have one little girl, and I can barely do that right. I don't know how Annie does it right for each child, so I admire that she's not selfish. There's no time to get a manicure or a pedicure or get her massages or facials. She's there for the kids and yet she's funny; she has a sense of humor. She's not just a hausfrau.

Q: How are you and Annie alike?

C: I'm pretty much a lot like Annie. My mom was a very good mom from the Midwest, and I'm like that. I cook dinner every night. Mashed potatoes, meatloaf, gravy. But then I'm also not like her. My husband says, "Oh, if you were only one eighth, one tenth what Annie is I'd be happy." I can't even run the VCR. Annie's changing plumbing and pipes, everything in the house.

Q: Do you ever find yourself taking things out of the role of Annie and applying them to your own life?

C: Yes. From Annie I learned how to be authoritative. My husband used to get so frustrated because I'm not strict, so I'd say to my little girl, Catie, "It's 9:30 at night, don't you think you ought to go to bed?" She'd say, "No, Mommy," and I'd say, "Okay!" And now, because I bark these orders all day, I'm much stronger.

Q: In the press and on the web site, the Camdens are described as a functional family. What does that mean to you?

C: Well, in the 1960s it became very acceptable and

fashionable actually to get divorced. Women wanted to get out of the kitchen, and men wanted to find themselves. Well, that was fine for them, but there was a generation created called latchkey kids. They came home from school, and no one was there. So I'm hoping that the "functional" word for the Camdens means that short of really big problems, you try to stay together, especially if you have children. You create a solid, secure home for them from which they will then have the confidence and courage to go out into the scary world.

Q: Favorite episode?

C: I liked giving birth. I wanted to do that believably, and thank God, a lot of mothers said, "Finally, we saw it portrayed believably." I think that's the greatest compliment I've ever received. I'd never seen a believably acted birth, and I knew it was coming up and I thought, Don't you fail there. It's quite hard to do. My husband said I had veins popping out of my forehead. I won't give away the secret, but it worked.

Q: Anything about the role that grabbed your interest at the beginning?

C: The humor. I didn't want to play a TV mom. But I got the script and I couldn't resist it; she was so funny.

Q: Any life experiences or acting experiences that helped you with this role?

C: Motherhood. I couldn't play this role without being a real mom. I know automatically what to do because I've been through it.

Q: How did you realize you were interested in acting?

C: It was a real out-of-the-blue calling. I was an English lit major at Notre Dame, and I didn't make cheerleading by one vote. That was my obsession. My grades dropped, and I was depressed all sophomore year. Two things saved me. I had to keep reading, so I read James Joyce's *Portrait of the Artist as a Young Man*. It awakened something inside. And my room was across from the arts buildings, and I could see them unload sets for traveling productions. I just thought, What goes on in that building? I'd never even thought of going in. It became this holy place I dared not enter, but I wanted to. I got up enough nerve to take an acting class. Of course, in college the drama majors get everything, so I was one of twelve squid tentacles. But I was happy because I was onstage. Then I'd run to the back and read *Paradise Lost* for my English classes. The last day of school my senior year my acting teacher asked, "What are you going to do?" I said I'd go to grad school and be a teacher. He said, "You should be in acting." That was enough. The heavens parted. I went back to Phoenix and waitressed. I didn't know how to prepare an audition. They were nice enough to nominate me for the URTAs because they knew I needed training. Because I was such a late bloomer I worked so hard. I think some of the drama majors didn't work as hard. They had been fulfilled, or they were cocky or whatever. I ended up getting a scholarship to Cornell, and then I went to New York quite confident.

Q: The show's really popular. Any comments on why you think it's popular?

C: I think it came at a time when my generation, as parents, don't know what we're doing. We read a lot of books but we don't want to be as strict as our parents were, so as a result we're very lenient. I think Annie and Eric are role models. I think parents look to us, the kids look to the show. Everyone can see themselves represented in one or another character.

Beverley Mitchell (Lucy)

Beverley was exhausted from shooting scenes and had actually gone to her trailer to nap between shots. But she was still kind enough to do this interview. A real trouper!

Q: The show's been on the air for four years, and your character's gone through a lot of different experiences. Do you think Lucy's grown?

B: Definitely. She's grown up a lot. She was a very naïve, self-centered little girl when she started because most teenagers only care about themselves and what's happening in their lives— and she's definitely grown up this year. She's gotten involved in community service, which I think is very important and very good to portray to kids out there today. It's so important to get involved in the community and give back. We're lucky for what we have, and it's good to give to those who aren't as lucky as us. And she realizes what her life's about. It's not about boys, although she's boy crazy still. And she realizes it's not so important to be popular—just to enjoy school for what it's worth and life for what it's worth.

Q: Well, I think you already answered my next question, which is what do you like about Lucy. But the second part of that question is what's her biggest flaw now?

B: I think she's still finding herself, and she thinks being accepted by boys is a big part of that. But I think it's important for teenage girls to realize that whether or not guys like you doesn't have anything to do with how special you are as a human being. I definitely found out because I'm single and have been for a really long time. I just think it's important to know who you are, and if you need to step away from everyone and just find that through yourself, it's important. You need to not have people judge you and just realize what you like about yourself.

Q: It's very cool. You're answering the next question, which is, how are you and Lucy alike? So let me ask, what's your real family like?

B: I'm an only child, so I don't have brothers and sisters. My parents are my best friends. I can talk to them about anything and everything. I'm very open with them and I trust them. They're the greatest, and I don't think I'd have made it this far without them. Actually, I know I wouldn't have.

Q: I know a lot of times actors take parts of themselves to put into their roles. But do you ever find yourself taking things from Lucy and applying them to your life?

B: Well, Lucy's younger. Most of the things she's going through I've already been through. I told Brenda and Sue Tenney because I wanted them to write my love life during the hiatus because Lucy's got a great one and I don't. I told them they had to write some great guys into my life and I want it to really happen. They said they were working on it.

Q: On the web site people often call the Camdens a "functional" family. Any comments on what you think of that?

B: I really don't like those words *functional* and *dysfunctional* in regard to families. Every family has problems. In ways they work and in ways they don't, and to classify them into categories—I just don't agree with that. We're a family that get along, but we do have our problems. It does get chaotic and hectic like real families do.

Q: What's Lucy's part in holding the family together?

B: I think she's a big part of it. She's very interested in what's going on with the family. She's very close with all her siblings. At first she wasn't, but now she's growing up and realizing how important it is to watch out for her little sister because she's an example now. And I think she's done a really good job of showing how excited she is to do these community service projects, because she's conveying to the younger sibling that when she's old enough it'd be great to give back. She adores her family and would do anything at the drop of a hat for any of them.

Q: Favorite episode?

B: That's everybody's favorite question. That one episode where my friend died because it was such a special tie to my own life. I lost my best friend three years ago. Still to this day I get all that fan mail down there. [*She points to a pile of fan mail that must have put the mailman in traction.*] The majority of them basically refer back to that episode and how it touched them. The letters I've gotten from people who realize how important life is, and learn to deal with grief because of it, make that episode my favorite.

Q: Was there anything about the role of Lucy that made you really want it?

B: When I read the role, she was a kooky character. The first episode, she thought that by standing on her head she would get her period. She was that naïve, young, excited-for-life person. It reminded me a little bit of myself when I was so excited for everything. I also liked the fact that it was a family that people could relate to. There's something within the Camden family that any person could relate to if they looked hard enough, and there aren't enough shows like that on television. I knew this would have the power to go somewhere. I didn't exactly know it was going to go this far. I thank my lucky stars every day to be here.

Q: Did you always want to be an actor?

B: Since I was four years old when I learned what it was. I started when I was five and I loved every minute of it. But I had an agreement with my parents that if I decided I didn't want to do it, that I'd be yanked. As soon as I said, "I don't want to go," I'd be done. I'd never go back to the business. The other thing was that if my mom noticed that I thought I was better than other kids, I'd be gone. And I thank them for that. I never lost any of my elementary school years. I went to elementary school with normal kids, I went to junior high school with normal kids, I went to high school with normal kids, and I'm going to college with normal kids. My life is pretty much the same as other kids' except that I have a lot more responsibilities and my job takes up a lot of time.

Q: Do you get recognized on campus a lot?

B: Not so much on campus. Whenever I go to a Ralph's [a supermarket chain], it's ridiculous. But I thank my parents because I've been very grounded. Granted I grew up a lot faster because I've always been around adults, but I've always wanted to act. I'd do it and not get paid for it.

Q: We won't tell the producers that.

B: [*laughs*] But it's a passion of mine.

Q: Any funny outtakes or funny accidents?

B: Well, I fell down the stairs.

Q: That seems to happen to everybody!

B: Once we were in the kitchen, and I was supposed to run out the back door. I caught the rug and totally flipped over and I had keys in my hand and totally stabbed my leg, and they're trying to go with the scene. There I am spread-eagle in my skirt trying to hang on 'til the end of the scene, and [the crew] is starting to laugh. I pulled down chairs with me and stuff from the kitchen, anything I could grab on my way down. It kinda hurt afterward, but I was okay.

Mackenzie Rosman (Ruthie)

This interview took place with the interviewer, Mackenzie, and Mackenzie's mom in Mackenzie's school next to the studio. She had some time between shooting scenes and was wonderful to talk with.

Q: *7th Heaven* has been on the air for four years now, and I know Ruthie's gone through a lot of stuff, like going to school. Do you feel like the character's changed a lot?

M: Yeah. When she was littler she used to be like the baby of the family, and now she's not the littlest kid anymore. She's acting more like an older kid.

Q: Yes, you just shot a scene where she surprised her sisters with the fact that Ruthie has a boyfriend.

M: Yeah [*smiles and laughs*].

Q: Are there things you really like about Ruthie?

M: I think she's really honest.

Q: Anything you don't like? Anything you think she should work on?

M: Um, I think—

At this point, Mackenzie's mom jumps in and says: Ruthie gets away with more than Mackenzie.

All: [*laughter*]

Q: That leads us to another question. Are you kind of like Ruthie or not?

M: In some ways yes and some ways no. I'm older than her. I'm ten and she's eight. She's in third grade and I'm in fifth.

Mackenzie's mom adds: And Mackenzie has the same sense of humor as Ruthie and [the producers] pick up on that.

Q: Someone else was telling me that when the character first started she wasn't as funny, but when they found out how funny you were they put more of that into the character.

M: Yeah [*with a smile*].

Q: What's your real family like? Is it anything like the Camdens?

M: I have one brother, and my mom and my dad.

Q: And do you have animals?

M: Yeah [*brightens up*]. Oh, yeah! Want to hear all of them?

Q: Please.

M: We have three dogs. We have a Lab, a Yorkshire Terrier, and Shih Tzu mix. The Shih Tzu mix is Gizmo; he's old. And then there's Milly, she's the Yorkshire terrier. Zach is the Lab, the big dog. Then we have two birds—they're both parakeets—and horses.

Q: Do you ride a lot?

M: Every day. My mom's [horse] is a chocolate brown Thoroughbred. Her name is Mocha. My horse is a chestnut Thoroughbred. Her name is Xena. And then we have two cats. Eddie, he's a silver tabby, and then Cassie, she's my cat. She's a calico. Do you know what a calico is?

Q: That means lots of different colors, right?

M: Yeah, she's a big mix of all the colors.

Q: Does she sleep with you?

Mom laughs and adds: On her head!

M: Or she sleeps right on my legs.

Q: So when you stop acting, do you find yourself acting the way Ruthie would act, or is it difficult to tell the difference?

M: I pretty much know.

Q: Do you have a favorite episode?

M: My favorite one was the one where I got to ride the horse.

Q: Of course! So, was there anything when you first got a chance to do the role of Ruthie that made you want to do it? Was there anything that made you say, "I really want to do this?"

M: Well, to audition they gave me part of a scene, kind of like a sample from the pilot. And it was really good.

Q: Did you always want to be an actor?

M: When I was little, I thought people were inside the screen.

Q: In the TV itself?

M: Yeah. I started when I was like five. People kept telling me, "You should be an actress, you should be an actress." So I tried and I got this show!

Q: What's a typical week like? Is it tiring, is it fun, is it exciting?

M: I have two or three scenes a week. If I have a really long, long scene, it can get kind of boring; but if I have quick scenes, it's exciting. When I'm not on the set, I go to school, and I ride my horse, and then I do my homework, and get up early the next morning.

Mom adds: Tell them how often you go to real school.

M: I go to real school maybe once or twice a week.

Q: Did you ever have anything funny happen on the set? Any outtakes?

M: *[laughing]* Oh, yeah! About five times every day. A lot of times when you're going up the stairs—you know, the stairs to the kitchen—we're supposed to run up them and we always fall, and they hear "Boom!" and the next thing you hear is "Cut!"

Q: This show's really popular. Why do you think it's so popular?

M: I guess it has a lot of things that real families would have.

Shawna Suffredini (Happy's trainer)

Shawna Suffredini, of Boone's Animals for Hollywood, is the trainer of 7th Heaven's Happy.

Q: On TV, Happy really seems like part of the Camden family. But as her trainer, you and Boone's Animals for Hollywood are her family, too, right?

S: Happy is definitely part of the Camden family, but yes, she belongs to Boone's Animals for Hollywood. She plays at a five-acre ranch with the dogs from *Mad About You* and other shows, and she comes home with me a lot.

Q: Isn't she kind of a rags to riches story?

S: Happy was a stray dog that was found and rescued. She was about six months old. Brenda Hampton, who created the show, discovered her on another set and wrote her into the show. Happy did the pilot for *7th Heaven* when she was just seven months old.

Q: Does Happy have a favorite Camden?

S: She's most comfortable being around all the kids on the set. She really likes women, too.

Q: Do you work with any other animals?

S: Boone's has lots of other animals—cats, birds, mice, camels, and chimps, to name a few. I worked with cats for *Stuart Little*. And I worked with mice for *Mouse Hunt*. I also train our chimp, and I work with the other animals when *7th Heaven* takes a break.

Happy

A Heavenly Photo Gallery

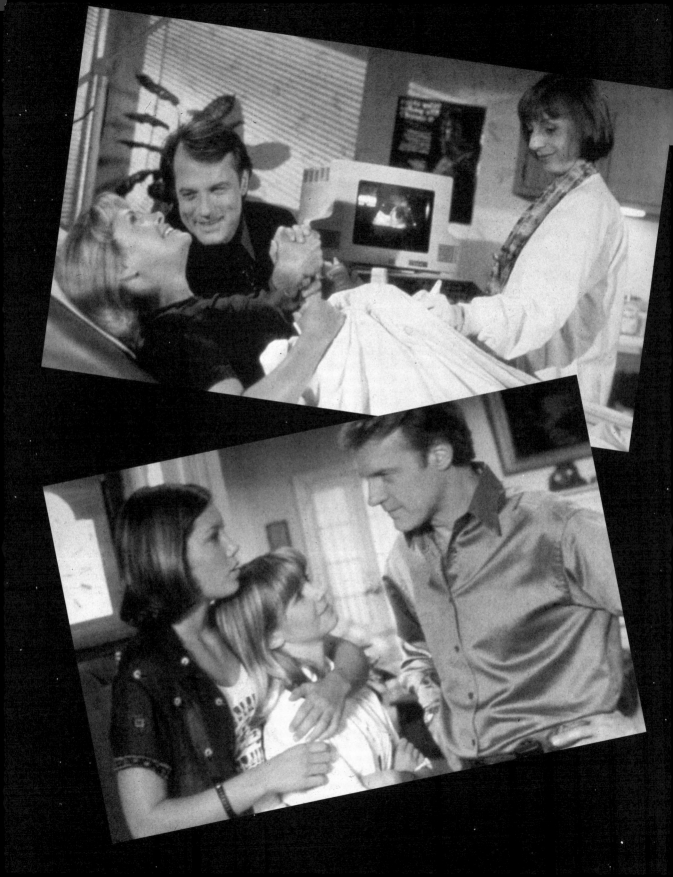

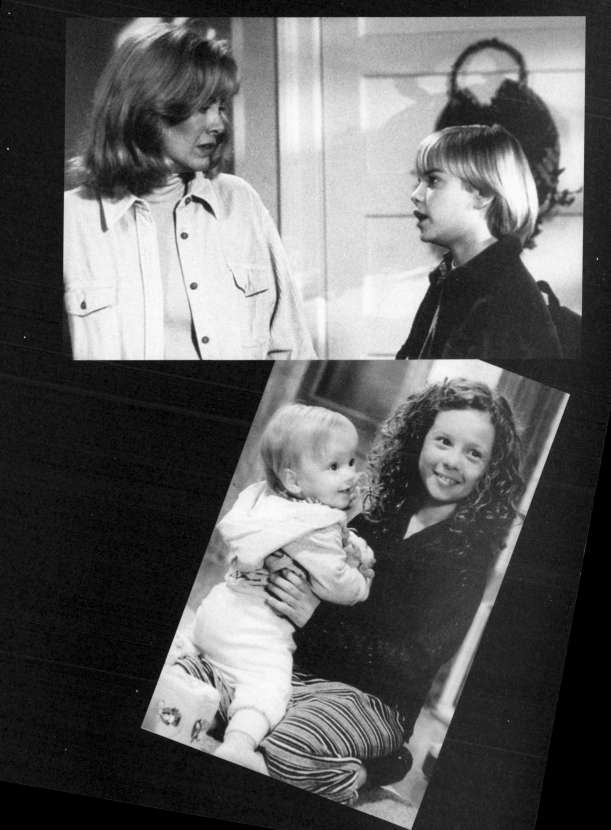

A Special Thanks to...

Aaron Spelling
Brenda Hampton
Renate Kamer
Nan Sumski
Theo Sofianides